The Business of Writing

Professional Advice on Proposals, Publishers,
Contracts, and More for the Aspiring Writer

The Business of Writing

Professional Advice on Proposals, Publishers,
Contracts, and More for the Aspiring Writer

Edited by Jennifer Lyons

With a Foreword by Oscar Hijuelos

ALLWORTH PRESS
NEW YORK

This book is dedicated to my father,
author, editor, and publisher Nick Lyons.

Contents

Foreword
by Oscar Hijuelos

E very writing life begins at a certain moment of falling in love with prose, of entering inside literature, as one might a forest clearing at dusk. In my case, this happened while reading a few lines from Walt Whitman's *Leaves of Grass* in high school. I don't remember just which lines they were, but I do recall thinking that some kind of magic had been involved, for it had amazed me that so much of one's universe could be captured in words. I may have then aspired to write poetry like Whitman, for a few weeks at least, scribbling down my own New York City teenage verses, but, for the most part, that first enchantment simply made me a more careful—and discerning—reader. Later, at City College, that same attentiveness blossomed into an all-consuming interest in literature by authors of every kind—from Rabelais, Cervantes, Shakespeare, and onwards. One day, while reading an especially wonderful passage by Jorge Luis Borges, I felt so uplifted by the grace and cunning of his prose, that, wishing to imitate him, I began my first attempts at writing fiction. They were, of course, awful, awkward, and crude. But, while doing so, to reconjure my earlier image of the forest, I began, perhaps naively, to see the act of writing as something akin to the lighting of a lamp in the window of a house somewhere deep within a woods, toward which one is always striving.

Or at least that's what I once told an interviewer, years hence, during the prepublication phase of one of my novels. He'd actually concluded that I was going through a depression of some kind. "That's what really comes into your head when you think about why you write?" he'd asked me incredulously. Well, yes, indeed it did. But I'd only intended that image to sum up my feelings about literature and writing and, to go a step further, to explain the wildly romantic, somewhat nutty dream that the writing life represents to blossoming authors—something that I still stand by now, especially given what experience has taught me: that writing—in whatever form it takes—is about as difficult a profession as any, and especially so if your dream, aside from the romance of the endeavor, includes making a reasonable livelihood from it.

And what an uphill struggle that is, particularly given this day and age when so much freelance and freebie writing of varying quality is floating about on the Internet. But even during my formative years as a writer, in the 1970s and '80s, when the turnaround time from a final manuscript to publication date took at least a year, if not longer (in a way, a wonderful thing), learning how the business end of that profession worked remained a daunting, learn-as-you-go thing. Take one element from my own story: I published my first novel with a small New York press in 1983 without an agent, while working full-time for a transit advertising company. I had managed to negotiate an advertising campaign of poster ads for my book in some quite primo New York City routes, like the Fifth Avenue lines. Now, I do not know how many passengers were persuaded to seek out my book after seeing those ads, but I will tell you that one of the first lessons I learned is that to make a sale the book had to be stocked in the stores, which was not always the case. Though I often look back on that time now with amusement, I sometimes simply wish I had known far more about the selling, publishing, and marketing of books than I did.

Which brings me to this book: filled with the practical ins and outs of the publishing trade from about every perspective, with contributions from agents, editors, and publishers, as well as marketing and publicity experts, it's the kind of book I wish had been around during my formative years as a writer. For it's one thing to have a burning passion to write a novel or a book of essays or children's tales, but it's quite another to get it out into the world in the best way possible. And that is what this book seeks to help the young writer accomplish. With over thirty articles written by some of the most savvy folks in the business, this anthology of insights and helpful hints about the business of writing is the brainchild of agent extraordinaire Jennifer Lyons, who conceived of it as a response to the kinds of questions that aspiring young writers have often asked her at publishing conferences around the country. As an agent of unquestionable taste—one of her young authors, Jesmyn Ward, won last year's National Book Award in fiction—and twenty-two years of experience, she has put between these covers the accrued knowledge and insights of some of the very best folks working in the publishing world today, and she has done so with the tender loving care of one whose own passion for literature has illuminated the way.

—*Oscar Hijuelos*

The author of eight novels, Oscar Hijuelos won the Pulitzer Prize in Fiction for The Mambo Kings Play Songs of Love. *He has also written a memoir,* Thoughts Without Cigarettes. *He lives in New York City.*

Introduction
by Jennifer Lyons

Over the years I've visited many MFA (Masters of Fine Arts) programs, including those at Iowa and Michigan universities, and Sarah Lawrence College. I've spoken to undergraduates who are majoring in writing and to writers from a variety of backgrounds at symposiums such as the James River Writers Conference in Richmond, Virginia; the Philadelphia Writers' Conference; and the Pikes Peak Writers Conference in Colorado. I have also taught a Business of Writing course at Sarah Lawrence College, in addition to creating and leading hundreds of informational conferences for potential clients. My conclusion—after speaking to all these writers and to some of my published clients—is that the industry is still shrouded in a lot of mystery, including what those of us "in the business" do all day, and what changes are occuring and how it will affect them. Writers rightfully feel as though they do a lot of waiting around, and they are not always sure what's going on while they wait. Most of all, however, they want to know how to get their works successfully published.

In an effort to help demystify the publishing industry as much as possible, I started teaching a Business of Writing course. I invited a wide spectrum of industry professionals into the classroom to walk writers through the entire process—from how to get an agent to how to keep one. I invited a specialist in contracts, a publicist, fiction and nonfiction editors for both children and adults, and guests from *The New Yorker* and *The New York Times,* and smaller literary journals such as *The Paris Review* and *Fiction.* In addition, we always included published authors who, with their own testimonials, could shed more light on how to get published; what better source than writers who have been through the process and landed a publisher? True, we picked success stories, but not all had instant happy endings. On the road to getting published, there are often ups and downs, setbacks and roadblocks. You have to be prepared for the challenges that might come your way.

After twenty-two years in the business, I can say that the industry is clearly getting more complex. Recent changes in the economy, the emergence of the Kindle and e-books, and the shrinking advances and venues (given the consolidation of smaller houses into larger ones), all mean that there is an even greater need to help writers understand this process, and what the role of larger and smaller houses is today, including that of e-book publishers and outlets that help authors self-publish. Trade publishing has changed and the stakes and requirements for large houses to take on works are very high, so it is essential that emerging writers, especially, be open to being published in an e-book first, or small press, university press, or paperback. There are many new roads to publishing success that writers should be open to travel. And sometimes smaller places can "grow" a book and give you and it more attention.

Undergraduates in their final year of college and MFA candidates would greatly benefit from such a minicourse. It could be a four- to six-week course, taught just before the students graduate, with experts from different fields in the industry offering advice that would better prepare hopeful writers to face the realities of the business of writing. So many promising writers do not know how to find an agent, write a pitch letter (first off, do *not* write on colored or scented paper. Photos are also an annoyance!), or craft a proposal. Such a course could be of great use to anyone trying to publish.

These experiences all led me to the idea of organizing a book publishing workshop in book and Kindle form. This workshop consists of over thirty industry professionals generously sharing their perspectives on the nuts and bolts of publishing. As you will see, in spite of publishing's changing landscape and the fear of the very extinction of the book, there is still a vibrant industry with many passionate people who got into publishing because they love to read and publish new voices. In fact, just working on the book with all of these dedicated professionals and seeing what they have written has reminded me that, in spite of a much-altered industry, there is still a strong publishing business. Every one of these individuals got into what they do because they want to work with words or authors.

I'm going to be the "moderator" as you meet each of these industry professionals, including an e-books editor, experts on books in translation, a magazine editor, an expert on self-publishing, and a poet, among many others. We all hope that by the time you finish reading this book, we will have given you some real tools to function in this business.

We put our thoughts down to help you develop better strategies for becoming a successful writer by introducing you to the people and the fields that are integral to the publishing industry. It is important for budding writers to remember that those of us in the publishing business live and breathe our work—a lifestyle that can be very full and like you writer, we need to have a lot of grit and patience. Regardless of our title or role, each one of us works long, long, *long* hours. While it is becoming more and more difficult to sell books, it's still a wonderful profession and, at the end of the day, we all want you to succeed!

At the beginning of my career, I walked into a large agency and there was a telex machine in the mailroom! The agent I worked for still had a dictaphone, but that was rare, even then. In those days, I spent my time at the office fielding calls from clients and prospective clients, and reading queries, proposals, and whole manuscripts. Gradually, I was invited to sit in on the "grown-up" agent meetings in which the industry was discussed. Then came the next step in my own education: a chance to have lunch with editors and personally pitch the work clients had entrusted to me. After that, I began taking multiple trips to domestic and international book fairs and "managing" writers' lives, with the chance to help develop work and build up my client base. My passion for representing talented writers led me to eventually found my own agency. Two thousand eleven was especially exciting when my client Jesmyn Ward won the National Book Award. I met her at the University of Michigan MFA program. I read queries and proposals and edit them to varying degrees. Time is spent negotiating with publishers, dining with publishers, and pitching authors to publishers. I also read whole novels and work on submission letters, oversee foreign film rights, etc. Then there are the details of running a small business. There are tons of emails and packages and FedExes. It's not all "doing lunch." Every day is a long day for a literary agent. I'm sharing this so you know what many of us do all day, and often into the night.

Perhaps the most important part of attracting an agent is writing a great cover letter. Agents see hundreds of submission letters every week, so keep the letter brief (not more than a page) and focused. You might open by letting the agent know why you are writing to them in particular. Did you hear about them through a fellow author, writing teacher, mentor, someone at a conference? Or maybe you read the acknowledgment section of a book you liked, which mentioned the agent you are approaching, or you read the *Jeff Hermann's Guide to Book Publishers, Editors, and Literary Agents.* Whatever the sources, know whom you are writing to and what they represent. Then pitch the book. In the last paragraph, you can add your credentials—where did you get your MFA (if you have one)? What have you published before? Were you in any journals? How are you uniquely qualified to write this?

Here is a query letter we received by email recently. (By the way, be sure to check an agent's submission requirements.) It hits the points I mention. First, the author establishes a connection to me, then the pitch and the platform. I recommend being as specific as possible about any places your work has been published.

Dear Jennifer

I worked at Seven Stories from 2008–2011 in the editorial department, so I knew of you then. More recently, a friend from grad school, _____ , suggested that I send you my manuscript. I hope you don't mind that I'm contacting you via email.

_____ is an effort to confront a series of questions I have about my relationship to Israel, where I was born, where I hold dual citizenship, and where my grandmothers still live. One thinks she is a sinner for having come there from South Africa in 1948. The other was a determined Zionist who arrived in 1967 from Argentina. The narrative is fragmented, split, and driven by personal and politically charged questions about identity, tradition, family, piety. I think the manuscript is timely and, inasmuch as it's not polemical and is written by someone who knows parts of the U.S. as well as Israel from the inside, I think it offers an original and hopefully useful perspective.

Right now I teach expository writing to freshmen at Columbia, where I'm set to graduate from the MFA program in nonfiction writing this fall. I'm also under contract with Seven Stories to carry out the first English translation of Argentine author Rodolfo Walsh's classic work *Operación Massacre* (1957), to be published in 2013.

Please let me know if you'd like me to send along the manuscript; it's just over 41,000 words long. I sincerely appreciate any time that you can give to my work.

Be prepared to go with an agent if they offer you representation. Try to figure out who you want to work with, and, if you are submitting to multiple agents, it is good to let them know, so they, too, can decide if they want to compete for a book. Some agents may ask for an exclusive look, so be ready to answer if that is okay with you. Hopefully, you will find a great match.

Agents are often the "constant" in an author's life these days. Your relationship with an agent is very important, so be sure to cultivate a good one that can grow into something long-lasting.

Now, a veteran agent and book packager walks you through a cover letter and the concept of a platform. He also includes a pitch he used to interest publishers. Agents may ask you to write a synopsis so they have one on hand to work into their cover or to give to the publisher. Go to any event featuring agents, such as panels, lectures, etc., so that you can learn more about how to submit your work.

Queries and Cover Letters: A Cosmic Approach

by Bob Silverstein, QuickSilver Books Literary Agency

Nowadays, agents and writers alike know that it is harder than ever to get a book published by a mainstream house, especially if you're a new or unknown author. Look around: There are fewer bookstores, thanks in large part to Amazon, and most of the books that get attention are written by authors with proven track records and media clout.

Given the choice, I think it's fair to say that most authors would want their books published by a commercial house rather than going the self-publishing route, although there is a clear trend towards authors publishing with smaller houses or putting out their own e-book editions. So, assuming you are among the noncelebrity authors, what then can you do to get the attention of agents, editors, and publishers? After all, they receive hundreds of query letters each week pitching every kind of project imaginable, and so what then is the best way to get an invitation to submit your proposal or manuscript for review?

For most unconnected authors, essential tool number one is the query letter: the door opener to make your dreams come true!

A quick search of Google using keywords "How to write a query letter" will turn up dozens of websites and blogs. The advice given is usually very valuable, and I heartily recommend that you utilize this vital resource.

But this is primarily a practical approach, whereas I would suggest that you go even deeper and search your own soul for answers. Therein resides hope and vision and a unique voice that, with a bit of fine-tuning, can stand out and be heard above the crowd.

Why go through the normal motions when within you is a powerful creative force?

So, to begin with, think with your heart as much as your head. We know you're clever, but are you sincere? Can you convince us that what you have to say is authentic, original, and distinctive enough to make an impact in a world with a great many competitive options?

If you believe in something strongly enough, the first rule of writing an attention-getting cover letter is simple: Tell the truth. Let the words you use to describe your work—be it fiction or non-fiction—flow from your heart, the center of your being. The more centered you are on expressing the deep conviction you feel for what you have created, the more your words will resonate in the minds of those you wish to engage as allies in your quest for publication.

To state it another way: "Write what you know; write from the heart." This holds true at every stage of the creative process. If you believe it and embody it as truth at a cellular level, your words will ring true, and I firmly believe that in time, and with perseverance, you will achieve your goals.

—————

Okay, that's the inspirational part of my message. Now for some nuts and bolts.

Here are things to avoid like the proverbial plague in query letters. They are common mistakes of writers who rarely receive positive responses.

Don't handwrite or use a typewriter for a query letter. It denotes a dated, faded mind-set and serves as an immediate turnoff.

Use a computer and choose a lively font, usually Arial or Times New Roman. As the saying goes, you don't get a second chance to make a first impression.

Don't list multiple projects that cross over from one genre to another, e.g., novel number one is a suspense thriller; number two a Western; number three, sci-fi, etc. Unless you have sequels in mind, as in a fantasy/adventure trilogy, pitch only one project at a time. Otherwise you'll come off as a complete amateur and will not be taken seriously.

Don't be shy or vague. It's imperative that you establish your credentials for writing about the subject. Storyline is important when pitching a novel, but be sure to also provide sufficient biographical information to show that you are credible, qualified, and prepared to market your book. Platform is especially crucial if you're writing nonfiction. If you can't stand up for your work via lectures, workshops, and media appearances, why should a publisher invest in you? It all comes down to this simple adage: "Publishers print. Authors sell."

Never start your letter with "Dear Agent" or "To Whom It May Concern." Instead, always write to a specific agent or editor. Make sure you know his or her name and spell it correctly. Do your homework and learn as much as possible about an agent's areas of interest and preferred categories, otherwise your efforts are bound to backfire.

Please, no three-page query letters. One succinct page will do fine, thank you! More than that is asking an awful lot from harried agents and editors already up to their eyeballs in reading material. You can always include supplementary material, but don't bury us in paper. Of course, many queries today arrive via email, so a few attachments are permissible, but kindly keep them relevant.

The key thing is to accentuate the positive, as if you were job hunting. I very much like it when authors tell me they belong to Pen International or the National Writers Union; or were previously published by Little, Brown or another mainstream publisher; or were referred by one of our clients or a well-known author. That always grabs my attention.

So, too, do reviews, news clips, flyers, copies of covers (preferably in color—it's like a wake-up call), endorsements from peers, celebrities, etc.—in short, bells and whistles!

The bottom line is that publishing is a business and its objective is to make money, so in addition to being a writer, you also have to think of yourself as a super-salesperson. Authors today wear many hats. In this media age, that's the new normal in publishing. Novelists don't necessarily need the kind of platforms that nonfiction writers require, but let's just say it helps to have some kind of professional or educational status, as well as a public persona, in addition to, of course, the raw talent you possess.

Now on to a query letter from an author to an agent.

Here's a query letter that eventually landed me a client, a best-selling author, and a friend all at the same time:

Dear Mr. Silverstein:

As an author, psychologist, and executive coach, I've spent the past twenty-five years helping people get—and keep—the jobs they want. My last book, _____, was named "the best unsung business book of the year" by *Fast Company* magazine. I'm writing to ask that Quicksilver Books consider representing my next book,

_____.

From there, the letter goes on to describe the book in two engaging paragraphs. The all-important marketing information came next:

In addition to my several well-received books related to women's issues, I've also had numerous articles published in professional journals and have been interviewed for television, magazines, and newspapers. I am committed to being a full participant in the process required to ensure the success of _____. It would be a pleasure to send you the complete proposal, sample chapters, and press kit. I look forward to hearing from you and thank you in advance for your time and consideration.

Sincerely,

_____

PITCH NUMBER TWO:
SUBMISSION LETTER TO A PUBLISHER

By way of example, this is what I would call a pretty decent submission letter. Most of its content was derived from the proposal and/or the author's original query letter. (Happily, we sold this book to a very good publisher.)

Dear _____ :

Once in a blue moon an idea comes along that, once heard, seems so obvious that you wonder why somebody hasn't written about it before. _____ presents a new paradigm for the twenty-first century—a philosophy that values receiving as much as giving and demonstrates that giving is enhanced when receiving is embraced. With the formula: Believe + Receive = Achieve, _____ presents a wholly original yet easily accessible road map for people to follow, showing readers how to restore balance to their overextended lives and attract the life they desire and deserve.

_____ begins where *The Secret* left off. As many readers of the law of attraction literature have discovered, just because you know how to attract something, that doesn't mean you know how to receive it. And while _____ delivers huge benefits to these readers, this book was not written for only one audience. Countless individuals desperately want more reciprocity in their relationships and to experience a life where people give to them as much as they give to others. This is especially true of "women who give too much" and receive little in return.

_____ is a highly regarded consultant/coach in the areas of spirituality, empowerment, and self-improvement; has a loyal worldwide fan base; and has earned accolades from her peers. Best-selling author _____ calls _____ *"brilliant, elegant, profound,* and *enormously practical."* The author's "_____" seminars have transformed the lives of thousands.

_____ has written numerous articles, columns, and website content for the self-help/new age markets. Her first book, _____ (Three Rivers Press, 2001), was written to help teenagers and young adults develop confidence and self-knowledge through the lens of their Sun sign.

We believe _____ has broad mainstream appeal and look forward to your timely, enthusiastic response.

Here's yet another example of a dynamic submission letter to a publisher, once again largely drawn from the author's initial query letter. (It's good to work with smart authors. They make us look so intelligent.)

Dear _____:

I'm pleased to enclose for your consideration _____ by _____. This is a compelling new proposal

from the highly regarded author of _____
and _____, both solid performers for
_____.

Hamilton and Madison were among the invited guests at Jefferson's table, an occasion the author looks upon as the most important dinner party in American history, a single great evening that achieved the compromises that put the young nation on the path to power and respect and led to America's mighty expansion. Excellent source material for the project has already been identified.

_____, the remarkable story about the men behind the Louisiana Purchase, with five printings so far and an appearance at #26 on *The New York Times* extended best-seller list, has been especially praised because its cast of characters were brought to life without sacrificing historical accuracy. (See starred *Publishers Weekly* and *Library Journal* reviews enclosed.) Likewise, _____ has had contemporary relevance and success because the author dramatically recreated the events and key players at the Constitutional Convention, with references to thoughts and arguments among those men that insightfully showed how they would have felt about issues featured on today's front pages and TV news.

_____ is a master storyteller whose appearances on radio and C-Span have stirred great interest.

_____ is the kind of dramatic narrative nonfiction—focusing on a single significant event—that has widespread appeal nowadays. We feel that it will further Mr. _____ reputation as a popular historian/raconteur. FYI, _____ made a decent offer for this book, but for reasons other than money, we have decided to seek out a new publisher. Thanks for giving this outstanding proposal priority attention and for your timely response.

And finally this submission letter, elicited an immediate substantial offer without our agency having to submit a proposal. This is something that rarely happens in our business, and it exemplifies the power of a dynamic cover letter:

Dear _____:

The best-selling book of all time is the Bible, and one of the best-known parts of the Bible is the story of Exodus. But what if there were more to Exodus than the ancient Hebrews' escape from bondage in Egypt? What if, viewed through a new and different interpretive lens, Exodus revealed itself as a powerful road map for the spiritual journey—a timeless teaching tale with direct relevance to all our lives, right here, right now?

Written by psychiatrist _____, _____ reveals the deep, hidden structure of Exodus that comes to light when we recognize Moses, Pharaoh, and the Hebrews not just as historical figures, but as archetypal aspects of the human mind. Pharaoh represents the ego-mind: stubborn, arrogant, convinced of its own rightness, and resisting freedom to the point of death. Moses represents the deep, intuitive part of the mind that remains connected to the Spirit and its infallible guidance as it seeks to free us from the ego's bondage; while the Hebrews, quite simply, are the rest of us in our confused striving as we journey through life. Although the Hebrews of Exodus never did make it to the Promised Land, _____ will help the reader to achieve what they could not, or at least to get started down the right path toward freedom, abiding happiness, and inner peace.

_____ is a psychiatrist and psychotherapist in private practice in the _____. He has served on the board of the Foundation for Inner Peace, publisher of *A Course in Miracles*, since 1992. He is a former Assistant Clinical Professor of Psychiatry at _____ in Philadelphia and at the _____ School of Medicine. He is also a novelist and screenwriter. _____ is his first work of nonfiction. Please see attached endorsements from other writers and spiritual figures familiar with Dr. _____ and his work.

We hope that you'll see broad appeal in this groundbreaking new book and look forward to your timely, enthusiastic response.

I hope what I've offered here has been helpful. It's a privilege to share this information with you and, to sum it all up, I'd like to leave you with one guiding principle in keeping with my cosmic approach. It's an old Sufi saying: "Trust in God and tie your camel."

Bob Silverstein is president of Quicksilver Books Literary Agency, a former book packaging and publishing firm responsible for the creation of many national and international bestsellers, among them Last Tango in Paris, Chariots of Fire, The Dogs, Nice Girls Don't Get the Corner Office, *and* Children Learn What They Live. *Prior to opening his agency, Mr. Silverstein served as managing editor of Dell Books, senior editor of Delacorte Press, and senior editor for Bantam Books, where he worked with such authors as Rod Serling, Irwin Shaw, Melvin Van Peebles, Dick Gregory, et al. Earlier in his career, he worked as story editor for Anthony Quinn Productions and as a senior unit publicist for United Artists, MGM, Carlo Ponti, Harry Belafonte, and David Wolper on major motion pictures throughout Europe and the United States. For more information, visit www.quicksilverbooks.com.*

If you are offered representation by multiple agents, be prepared to decide quickly and don't take up everyone's time or hold "agent auctions." Try to cultivate good relationships from the start.

Once you have landed an agent, you will usually be offered an agency agreement, which will lay out the basic terms. This is an important document and worth having a lawyer look at or to ask questions about. Do not attempt to rewrite it, because no agent has the time or desire to rewrite his or her agreement. The publishing agreement is mighty important and you should be familiar with the basics of it. Now, a contract expert walks you through an agency agreement and publishing contract.

God Forbid . . .
The Legal Stuff

by Paula M. Breen, Publishing Consultant

Every writer's main goal in his or her career is to become a published author. Writing and publishing a full-length book—whether it be fiction or nonfiction—is the pinnacle of a writer's career. Unfortunately, many writers enter into publishing contracts without fully understanding the terms of these agreements and the meaning of the terminology used in these documents and later on experience the pitfalls and long-lasting effects of doing so.

Though the publishing process is a collaborative one involving the writer/author and the editor and publisher, writers need to protect their interests during the process. The editor and publisher are not your friends. As harsh as it may sound, these people are involved in a business transaction with you, the writer/author. Though writing and having a book published is a creative endeavor and a rewarding personal achievement for an author, the process remains primarily a business transaction for the publisher. While friendships may form as a result of working closely together, the publisher's interests, concerns, and opinions about the book are often not the same as the writer's and the business side will most likely prevail in decision making.

Okay, so you've written a book; now let's get this book published! What are the next steps that a writer needs to take to accomplish that? First, find a literary agent to represent your interests. An author needs an advocate during the publishing process. Many publishers will decline to peek at your proposal, outline, or sample writing materials if you have no representation. Sure, you can submit your manuscript to an editor or a publisher for consideration. At most houses, these unsolicited materials are put in the "slush pile," which are toiled through by the editorial assistants who then meet for lunch monthly (sometimes weekly) to discuss any interesting manuscripts they found. The odds of having your book actually published via this process are slim to none. A good literary agent will have contacts at publishing houses and know which editor at which house would not only be interested in your book, but also be a good match for you to work with on the book. A literary agent is an author's first line of offense (and defense for that matter) in an author's attempt to be published. In order to find a literary agent to represent you, you need to do some homework.

Check out the invaluable resource book *Literary Marketplace* (LMP), which you can likely find at your local library. There are both domestic and international editions published each year, and you can find most agents listed together with some information about the agency. The number of agency employees, email addresses, website information, types of books represented by the agency, and contact information can all be found in this terrific resource guide. And it's free! Take some time to peruse the various sections of the *LMP*. Reading through it is informative and a good education for the uninitiated. Then make some phone calls and send some emails. Send some snail mail for that matter! Some agents may provide information about submissions on their websites. Agents and authors cannot survive in the publishing world without each other, but taking the time to find the right match is critical to a successful ongoing relationship.

Once an author and an agent decide to work together, an author should never proceed without signing an Agency Representation agreement with a literary agent. Each literary agency will have a slightly different form, but each agreement should incorporate similar provisions. A basic Agency Representation Agreement should be signed for each book/project on which you and your agent work together. Some agents prefer an agreement that covers multiple books on one agreement. If you have not worked with this particular agent before, I would advise that an Agency Representation Agreement should be signed between you and your agent each time around. Of course, if you are writing and hope to publish multiple books in a series, all of the books that will be on the eventual publishing agreement need to be included in the single Agency Representation Agreement.

An Agency Representation Agreement will cover the following basic details:

1. A clearly stated list of the rights the agent will represent (i.e. try to sell) for you when submitting your book to publishers. The most important rights are the publishing rights in any and all formats—print and digital (e-book), book club, anthology, omnibus, large print, and so on. Also, a literary agent will represent the audio publication rights to your book. Traditionally, a literary agent will also represent the Performance Rights (movie, TV, stage play, video), Commercial and Merchandising, and Interactive Multimedia rights to your book. As the publishing world continues to change and evolve before our eyes these days, some of these rights may be retained by an author and not granted to a literary agent to control on behalf of the author. An author may hire a talent agent to represent these rights instead. In your Agency Representation Agreement, there may be a provision permitting the literary agent to engage the services of a talent agent who will work collaboratively with the literary

agent. This is often the more desirable approach for an author since the literary agent and the talent agent will share a smaller commission percentage than if you had two agents working separately. Remember that if you allow your literary agent to find a talent agent, you should have approval over the selection of the talent agent.

2. The geographic areas and languages in which the literary agent may sell these rights. Often, an agent will represent the book to be sold throughout the world and in all languages. Depending on what rights the U.S. publisher negotiates with your literary agent to acquire, these sales could involve multiple deals and contracts for each, which the literary agent will represent on your behalf. The literary agent's commission is usually 15 percent for domestic rights, 20 percent for foreign rights (as two agents are involved), and 15 percent for performance (movie, TV, stage, video) rights. A writer might also need to hire the services of a lecture agent, and the fee for that agent will likely be 25 percent. The literary agent does not usually participate in this. A film agent is often hired by the literary agent to assist in selling film or other performance rights for the work. This is beneficial to the author as a film agent knows all the principals at the film and production companies in the same way that a literary agent knows all the book publishing professionals. Often, the total commission paid to your literary and film agents will be around 20 percent, with each agent taking a 10 percent commission on the monies payable for the disposition of such rights.

3. The literary agent will communicate with you about all offers on your book and shall not agree to any deal or enter into any agreement on your behalf without your prior approval.

4. The literary agent may incur any number of expenses in trying to sell your book. These expenses should be included in and paid by the agency commission percentage you pay to the literary agency from the proceeds you receive from any publishing contract. If the book is never sold, however, you may be responsible for reimbursing the agent, in part or in whole, for the agent's expenditures and efforts on your behalf, even if they were unsuccessful. Typical chargebacks include costs for copying, messengering, overseas mail, etc. It's advisable to discuss and agree upon a cap on these costs when finalizing your agreement with your literary agent.

5. The literary agency needs to be authorized by you, in the Agency Representation Agreement, to collect all sums due to you under the publishing agreement and to then pay you these monies, less whatever agency commission you decide is fair and equitable. The overwhelmingly consistent established agency commission is 15 percent. In some circumstances, 10 percent is agreed upon, but that is not so common these days. The agent receives 15 percent of all monies paid to you on the publishing agreement in the United States and on any other agreements that the agent may negotiate and finalize on your behalf. This 15 percent is their salary. Normally, the literary agent will continue to receive these monies until the publishing agreement(s) is terminated and the rights revert to you. If your relationship with your literary agent sours at some point and the publishing agreement is still in effect, the literary agent should continue to receive the 15 percent commission even if the agent no longer represents you on other projects. The commission is still paid since the initial work was done by the agent in marketing and selling the book on your behalf. Should the literary agency agreement be terminated (see next point), you or your agent may request that the publisher(s) send separate checks and accounting statements to you and your agent.

6.   A termination clause should be included in your Literary Agency Representation Agreement. Either party should have the right to terminate the agreement, subject to a notification period. This is usually sixty days. If the literary agent has already finalized a book publishing deal for you but final contracts have not yet been signed, the literary agent should still be paid for his/her efforts. Depending on the stage of the agreement at the time of termination, the literary agent may receive part or all of the agency commission. These terms need to be stated clearly in your agreement with your agent.

7.   There will be a warranty clause in the Literary Agency Representation Agreement, where you will need to warrant that you have the right to enter into the agreement with the agent and that you have not otherwise engaged anyone else to perform the same services as you are engaging your literary agent to do.

8.   There should be an arbitration clause that permits you and your literary agent to arbitrate disputes that may arise, which cannot be resolved by you and your agent alone. The clause in your Literary Agency Representation Agreement should require any arbitrator to be experienced in arbitrating book publishing matters.

9.   There should be a governing law clause. Likely the governing law will be New York State regardless of where you live. The book publishing world is centered in New York City, and there are more book publishing laws in New York State than any other state in the country.

Once your literary agent has found a publisher interested in publishing your book, the long process of waiting for the publishing agreement begins for you and for your literary agent. Please remember to be patient during this process. It can seem never end-ing (as it sometimes does to those of us negotiating on your behalf). You want to "get started" and you want to be paid. Both are valid points. But, in my experience on both sides of the negotiating table, I have found that the lengthy time spent negotiating the deal and the contract have benefited all parties in the long run. In larger publishing companies, there are contracts departments that prepare each contract based upon a contract request form generated by the editor. This request will reflect the deal points agreed upon with your literary agent. Your agent may send you a deal memo outlining these basic terms, but then the contract request can take a couple of weeks (or months) to travel through the editorial department to the publisher for all of the administrative approvals before the contracts department even receives the request to prepare the contract. The turnaround time to prepare the contract in the contracts department is also at least two or three more weeks. These departments are usually understaffed and overworked. Thereafter, your literary agent will receive the contract draft and the contract negotiations begin. The contract approval and drafting process can take more time at a smaller publishing company as they will likely not have staff dedicated to the contracts process. In this event, the editor may actually negotiate the fine points of the contract directly with your literary agent.

A literary agent will sometimes hire someone like me, a publishing consultant, to assist in this arduous and time-consuming process of negotiating the publishing agreement that is of the utmost importance to an author. I am a contract expert, having worked for twenty-two years in contracts departments on the book publishing side, starting as a contracts trainee and working my way to vice president and director of contracts for Bantam Doubleday Dell and then Random House for the last eight years of my corporate career. Since 2003, I have had my own consulting business that operates from the "other side," working closely with my clients to negotiate book publishing, motion picture, digital e-book publishing, merchandising, agency, and collaboration agreements. My fee is based on an hourly rate, but others may charge a flat fee per project/contract. I work predominantly with literary agents but have worked with authors who have no agency representation as well. Some agencies have prenegotiated boilerplate contracts with publishers that just need some tweaking or tailoring. Other contracts need to be fully and carefully vetted and negotiated with revisions requested in order to change the contract terms to benefit the author.

The Publishing Agreement specifies all aspects of the deal between an author and a publisher. Generally, the Publishing Agreement covers the Grant of Rights; Title and Book Description; Manuscript Delivery, Acceptability, Revision Process, and Unacceptability; the Editing Process; Publication Formats, Time Frames, Cover, Artwork, Book Design, and Failure to Publish provisions; Copyright; Subsidiary (or Ancillary) Rights Licensing; Competitive Works restrictions; the Option for the next book to be written by an author; Warranties, Representations, and Indemnifications provisions for both parties; Termination clauses; Royalties and Accounting; Auditing; Remaindering; Reversion of Rights; Out-of-Print; Bankruptcy; Assignment of Rights; Governing Law; and other special clauses and provisions about any other number of aspects of the publishing process and your specific deal.

If you include any material (text, photographs, illustrations, poems, song lyrics, quotations) from a third party that is not original to you, you will need to obtain the permission of the person who wrote (or illustrated) the material before including it in your book. Since the third party owns the copyright to the material, you cannot authorize the publisher to print it as part of your book without that permission. The publisher should be able to provide the writer with a sample form to use in obtaining these permissions.

We could devote an entire chapter to electronic publishing and e-books, but the technology is ever-changing and by the time this book is published, the information would likely be out of date. One exciting area of electronic publishing is the advent of print-on-demand (POD) technology. Essentially, the final manuscript is digitized into a format that allows copies of the book to be printed one at a time. If your book is available in a POD edition, a buyer can order a copy in a bookstore even if it's not on the bookshelf in the bookstore.

When I was at Random House, I taught contracts seminars to my own staff as well as for the editorial, royalty, and production departments. One point I would stress is that the publishing agreement was the most important document since it follows the life of a book from birth to death, i.e., from the granting of a book's rights to the termination and reversion of rights. The publishing agreement is a living and breathing document that you need to refer to at each step of the process of publishing your book—both to protect your interests and to make sure that you are fulfilling your obligations in a timely manner.

I also work with both authors and ghostwriters on collaboration agreements. These are contracts between two parties—often a writer and a celebrity—regarding the preparation of a book proposal and then a manuscript for a complete book if a publisher is interested in the proposal. A collaboration agreement is a "work made for hire," as that term is used in U.S. copyright law. Simplified, this means that the writer is an employee of the author, and the author owns all rights to anything written or researched by the writer. Why would a writer do such a thing? Often, because both the money and the experience of doing so are positive factors for the writer's career. Many writers are specialists at being ghostwriters. Sometimes a ghostwriter (or collaborator) is credited and sometimes not. Often the writer's name may not appear on the cover of the book and, if it does, it will be in a smaller type size than the name of the "author." Sometimes a writer will only receive a credit in the acknowledgments section of the book. This is an unfortunate aspect of the terms of this type of an agreement.

When entering into a collaboration agreement, you must protect your interests as you would in any employment situation. You want to be paid for your performance but also expect to be penalized for any lack of performance such as nondelivery or late delivery of materials and unacceptable materials. You must also be aware of termination provisions in such an agreement and make sure that there is an arbitration clause that will set out what happens if there is a dispute between you and the publisher.

Compensation for a writer in a collaboration agreement can take many forms. You can receive a flat fee, a flat fee with a percentage of royalties, a flat fee with a share of any additional advances or bonuses payable to the author under the publishing agreement, a share of subsidiary rights licensing income in addition to a flat fee, or any combination of these payouts. There are no hard and fast rules about what a proposal is "worth" or what a complete manuscript is worth, but there are many writers' groups that might be able to advise you on some general guidelines.

It may seem like common sense, but it bears saying anyway: Do not do any work without a signed agreement. This applies to a publishing agreement, literary agency representation, or collaboration agreement. If you decide to proceed with writing anyway, in good faith that any or all of these agreements will eventually be signed, remember not to turn in your materials until those documents actually are signed. If you do so, you have absolutely no leverage to try to negotiate the terms you want. These agreements are essential and need to be airtight. If there is ever a dispute, these documents serve as the last word on any number of issues.

Paula M. Breen has been a book publishing professional specializing in contracts since 1978. She has an encyclopedic knowledge of various types of book publishing contracts, including book contracts, subsidiary rights, licensing agreements, performance options, merchandising agreements, works made for hire, agency and marketing, and promotional agreements. Paula spent twenty-two years negotiating publishing contracts for major book publishers in New York City and almost a decade working for authors, illustrators, and literary agents. Known as a fair, but tough and tenacious negotiator, Paula maximizes a deal's potential and fine-tunes contract terms to give her clients the edge. Her interests include reading (of course), music, movies, tennis, and spending time at the beach. Paula lives on the North Fork of Long Island and is thrilled there's no commuting involved to get to her office!

Once you submit your work, the desired outcome is, of course, a contract and money in the form of an advance to go off and work on the book. The basic concept is that any monies paid up front are an advance against royalties. These days, the money is broken into many payments. The advance is only officially yours to keep once work is accepted, so set as much as possible aside until the work is accepted. Writing is a business, so you need to plan and set it up as such. There may be cause, for example, to incorporate. Certainly, all receipts should be kept for taxes. Ask your accountant what is best for you, and remember, you will be paying an agency commission and you will owe taxes to the government. You should fill out a W-9 for the agent and receive a 1099 from him or her if you earn money.

Next, the "Tax Doctor" will walk you through the things you need to do to be a viable business as an artist.

Writers: Tax Rules, Rituals—and Reminders!

by John Giacchetti, Tax Consultant

"There's only three things that's for sure—
Taxes, death and trouble."

—*Marvin Gaye,* Trouble Man
(title track and theme of the movie with the same name)

No one knew better than Marvin Gaye about taxes, death, and trouble. Sadly, death came at the hands of his father, who shot Marvin while he was trying to protect his mother during a domestic quarrel in 1984. Marvin died on April 1, 1984, one day short of his birthday.

Trouble was a staple Gaye had to contend with most of his life. But it was the nonpayment of millions of dollars in taxes that sidelined much of his work in 1978 and sent him into hiding in Hawaii to avoid tax fines and prosecution.

How do tax messes like this arise? It happens quite easily, when an artist overlooks the fact that the money being made is not all his or hers to keep. As a matter of fact, every artist who makes money in the United States is never without a partner named Uncle Sam. Marvin Gaye may have thought of himself as the "Trouble Man"; all artists would do well to remember themselves more as "Double Man." This means that the day you decide on a career as an artist, you must see yourself as a type of split personality.

There is the personal you and the writer you.

STEP 1: SEPARATION AND IDENTIFICATION OF THE WRITER YOU

As a writer, that dual existence is a reality. Why? For the most part, your expenditures reduce your income, but they can also reduce your income taxes when those cash or credit outlays are a result of necessary costs for you to carry on business as an artist. Still, these transactions will only marginally help you reduce your tax bill. The real tax reducers are the monies you spend to directly support the production of your work.

It starts mentally by asking yourself this specific question as you move through each day: Who am I now, the writer me or the personal me? For example, when you are hailing a cab, buying a computer, having a lunch or dinner, traveling to another city or state or country, are you laying out money for these things to further your career or for personal reasons? If the answer is "career," then the expense of that item can be used to offset any income you've generated from your art through the "tax year." The tax year, also called the calendar year, from January 1 to December 31, is the period of time the U.S. government requires taxpayers to total up their income and be prepared to be taxed on the net income. Net income is the income that remains *after* expenses are deducted from the total income brought in through the tax year. Since expenses involving you as an author figure so significantly in how much tax you must submit to the Internal Revenue Service, it's important that you clearly differentiate and document when you are involved in an endeavor that involves your writing in some way or was related to publishing. Keep and label all of your receipts. Please also note in the case of book deals that monies paid by a publishing house are advances which are not really yours until the manuscript is accepted, so do not spend much until you turn the work in and you have been told, preferably in writing, that your manuscript has been accepted. Also, the payments will be subject to an agency commission, and you will owe the taxes to the government. Keep in mind that advances are paid in installments, so calculate the minimum you need as you go along. You will not see royalties until the advance is earned back!

STEP 2: CONVINCING THE TAX AUTHORITIES THAT THE AUTHOR YOU EXISTS

Once you have recognized and differentiated the personal you from the writer you, the next vital hurdle is to convince the IRS that the writer you exists. Of course, having a book or other writing is key. *How* you think of yourself will not be convincing enough for the IRS.

In the eyes of the taxing authorities, writers are individuals who perform their art in *pursuit of making a profit.* In order for the IRS to allow a writer to deduct expenses against his or her income, one must be able to establish, to the IRS's satisfaction (not one's own), that the time, energy, and sweat equity that has been exerted in connection with one's involvement in an artistic project was *not* purely for pleasure or charity. In other words, you weren't involved in a hobby. The IRS has a hobby rule: if an individual does not generate an income in three of the past five years while involved in an artistic endeavor, this is a strong indicator—to the IRS—that the individual was not involved in this endeavor to make a profit. It was, therefore, a hobby. And even when individuals who have collections of music, art, stamps, butterflies, and coins exchange these things with other collectors and generate a profit, since their primary motivation for the activity is pleasure—not the pursuit of a profit—their outlays will not be recognized by the IRS. In other words, in order to be rewarded by the federal government with deductions to reduce income generated from an artistic activity, one must be involved in this activity in an effort to support oneself.

This presents a significant problem to individuals starting out in the business who find it hard to get their artistic endeavor on its feet. As a writer, it may take years to get published, and in this economy the advance may be small. And, although a lot of money is often spent to get things going, unless an individual can establish acceptable justification that his or her writing is a business (and not a hobby), the costs expended will *not* be recognized by the IRS as deductions against the monies made by the writer in conjunction with the projects. The reality is, if a writer is supporting himself as a waiter, office worker, or taxi driver, the IRS will consider this the individual's *primary* job and his or her writing as a hobby. (I know what you're thinking, "Who runs themselves ragged, spends all their money, and practically spills blood just for fun?") The taxing authorities have heard this many times and their answer is always the same: "We applaud hard work but can only reward efforts that generate money, and that money is rewarded with allowing deductions against it."

So how do writers convince the IRS that they are a business? First, the writer's clear pursuit must be to generate a profit—even though one has not, as yet, done so. This is accomplished by showing through degrees and resumes that the background of the individual is clearly in the same field as his or her artistic endeavor. For writers, a BA in literature or an MFA helps, along with selling works to newspapers, magazines, and journals. In this regard, rejection letters received from a publisher or magazine are good evidence that a person is trying to make money. Additional proof to support this would be the establishing of websites and the actual creation of work, with clips of your writing submitted to interested parties.

STEP 3: FOLLOW THESE TIPS TO ASSIST IN DOCUMENTING

Documentation and established procedures will go a long way in convincing the IRS that you mean *business*. Try to keep ATM machine withdrawals to a minimum. It will become more difficult to match your receipts and invoices to those withdrawals later. Better to write yourself a check made out to Petty Cash and cash that check. Use that money and remember to receipt and file it. Make the petty cash withdrawal amount and frequency of withdrawal constant. This is called an Imprest system and is recognized by the IRS as a valid cash record-keeping system. When you have a viable system, the IRS will test that system, on a sample basis, to see if it functions the way the taxpayer says it should. This cuts down on how much of your materials the IRS has to investigate. But more important, the taxpayer's verbal evidence becomes more creditable and reliable to the examiner. How much the petty cash amount should be set up for will be based on the taxpayer's monthly or weekly needs. Always remind yourself: "I need to keep a paper trail in order to justify my tax calculation and the tax I say I owe the government."

Keep a daily calendar book of your comings and goings. Get one with large date areas for written entries. Electronic devices also give a lot of flexibility for information storage. Document lunches, dinners, local travel, overnight travel, etc. Remember, a business deduction must be about business, so use some sort of shortcut legend system to mark where you went, with whom you ate, and the reason. (Remember, a deductible business expense has to do with furthering business, not personal pleasure.)

I've used scare tactics here, but I just want you to be prepared. Good luck with your writing careers.

John Giacchetti is a certified public accountant and a tax consultant who has specialized in writers and other performing artists for the past twenty-five years. His tax practice is called The Tax Doctor, Inc., and is located on the Upper West Side of Manhattan. He prepares taxes for several prominent authors.

Great publicists can really help promote and "position" a book. They come up with an overall strategy. If you are publishing with a traditional house, make sure to go and meet your publicist. You may be joined at the meeting by marketing people and by the publisher, your editor, and perhaps an assistant. You might want to bring a list of questions to ask (you will also eventually fill out an author questionnaire). Make sure to dress in a very presentable way and be prepared to mention any ideas you have. Also, be ready to verbally pitch and discuss your book. Bring a list of any contacts or leads you have that will aide in the promotion of your book. This is no time to hold back. Whether you meet the publicist right after the publisher has bought your book or while it is being sold or at a later point, you can always ask the publicist how he or she sees positioning your book.

There may be reasons to hire a publicist if you are with a small press, are self-publishing, or even working with a larger house.

Here is an interview with ROSE CARRANO, a seasoned publicist who has worked at many large houses and now owns her own publicity firm. Following that is a piece by FAUZIA BURKE, the founder of a publicity and social media firm specializing in on-line publishing.

An Interview with
Rose Carrano, Rose Carrano PR

JL: **Rose, tell us how you got into publishing and how many years you have worked in publicity.**

RC: I've worked in publishing for over thirty years and have had many different jobs. I've worked as an assistant to a publisher, as well as in editorial, marketing, sales, and publicity.

JL: **Where have you worked as a publicist?**

RC: I have worked for Macmillan, Franklin Watts, McGraw-Hill, and HarperCollins Adult Trade Division.

JL: **What did you do as an in-house publicist? Can you walk us through a typical day?**

RC: A typical day as a publicist involves pulling lists for a particular title and preparing press kits, which might include a Q&A with the author, the author's biography, and any other books the author has written. I also have to follow up with the contacts to which I sent the book and create a schedule for the book.

JL: **What does a PR campaign look like these days for a well-known author vs. a first-time author?**

RC: A well-known author is in some ways easy to book—depending on whether it's fiction or nonfiction. For a first-time author, it's a bit more difficult to get attention for a book. Internet contacts are a valuable resource for unknown authors. They are more open to first-time authors, who often have great personal stories that lead them to write their debut books.

JL: Now that you are an independent publicist, can you tell us what the difference is between an in-house publicist and a private publicist?
RC: They do pretty much the same job: pulling lists, creating press releases, and following up with the contacts.

JL: What can a private publicist contribute to the marketing of an author if there is already a publicist at the author's publishing house?
RC: When the publisher already has an in-house publicist, I can play more of a role in the bigger publicity picture, whether it's splitting contacts depending on which one of us has a good relationship with a particular reviewer or producer, or finding other ways to maximize our efforts for the benefit of the author. In some cases, the publishers do very little to support their author, which is a sad thing.

JL: What do you like about being an independent publicist?
RC: Business is up and down. One minute I think I'll never work again, and then the phone rings and I am being offered terrific projects. I handle nonfiction titles only as director of Rose Carrano Public Relations, but I also work on children's books as well—both fiction and nonfiction. It's a challenge, but the rewards are there.

JL: When do you think authors should consider having a private publicist, and how do they find one?
RC: They should work through an agent if possible. If they don't have an agent, then they can go to the *Literary Market Place* online and search for a publicist who might be a good fit for their book.

They are ready for a publicist once the book is under contract with a publisher.

JL: **How has publicity changed over the years given the economic atmosphere and the explosion of social media?**
RC: It's changed dramatically. Publishers are printing fewer books, and self-published authors are publishing at a very fast rate. Social media is a great way for self-published authors to attract attention to their books.

JL: **What are the best things an author can do to help a publicist with his/her work?**
RC: *Know who their audience is.* That is key. If it's a parenting book, then the publicist reaches out to parenting publications. If it's a children's book, the publicist reaches out to children's book review editors. If it's a military book, the publicist reaches out to military publications, etc.

JL: **What kind of fees do you charge? Are there industry norms for the cost of a private publicist?**
RC: It's hard to say. Some authors don't have a lot of money to pay a freelance publicist; others have lots of money to pay a freelancer. It all depends on the project. Sometimes I take on a project even though the fee the client is paying me is low. I do it because I believe in the book.

JL: **Who would be an ideal client for you be?**
RC: Ideally someone who is established, but that is a rare occurrence these days. A publicist has to pull contacts, write press releases, and send them out to his or her network, and let the chips fall where they may.

JL: **Are you sometimes hired by a publishing house to be the outside publicist in place of its own? How does this work? Does the author have to pay for this?**

RC: Yes, I've been hired by numerous publishers either when they are short on staff or if they have a really big book to which they need special attention paid. We negotiate a fee and take it from there. The author doesn't pay the freelancer's fee.

JL: **I often get asked how an author should dress for a first meeting with a publishing house and for publishing-related events. Any advice here?**

RC: It's important to make a good impression. Dress your best.

JL: **What questions should authors ask an in-house publicist when they meet?**

RC: In a perfect world, they work together as a team. Typical questions include: To whom have you sent the galleys? To whom have you sent the books? When are you following up with the contacts? I always show my press kits to the author for approval.

JL: **What questions should authors ask private publicists before hiring them?**

RC: They should ask about their fees. Fees are crucial in this business.

JL: **What strategies do you think help sell the most books these days? Do you think book tours are important? A website? Should authors be disappointed if they don't get an author tour or aren't reviewed in *The New York Times*?**

RC: When you look at the number of books published, very few books are reviewed in *The New York Times*, so authors shouldn't be disappointed. The only reason to tour an author these days is so that authors can visit bookstores and make contact with booksellers who can hand-sell their books.

Websites are important also—they give readers a place to go to see what media outlets are booked, and authors also use their websites to produces blogs about their published or upcoming books.

JL: **How much lead time do you need to do a PR campaign?**
RC: At least three to four months.

JL: **How do you see the future of publicity, and can you comment on the state of book reviews as you see it now and potentially in the future? What is working best these days?**
RC: There is so much conglomeration in the newspaper business— one paper owns several newspapers. Many newspapers have let their book review editors go, which is a terrible thing. These days, a lot of newspapers often pick up reviews from the newswire. The truth is, it's hard to get a review unless you can latch on to a hot news item.

Rose Carrano has worked in the publishing industry for over thirty years. She has held numerous in-house positions including administrative, editorial, sales, marketing, and publicity. She started Rose Carrano Public Relations—a full-service public relations and consulting firm serving the literary community—in June 2000. Her client list includes Random House, Kensington Publishing, NYU Press, Barnes & Noble, Middleway Press, Rodale, Skyhorse Publishing, Harper San Francisco, HarperCollins, HarperCollins Children's Books, Black Dog & Leventhal, HCI, John Wiley, Meredith Books, Monacelli Press, Scholastic, Simon & Schuster, Sterling Publishing, Stewart Tabori & Chang, Henry Holt, Ocean Press, Bright Sky Press, Beaufort Books, InnerTraditions/Bear & Company, Icon Editions, Osprey Publishing, New Society Publishers, and Taunton Press.

Personal Branding: Advice for Authors

by Fauzia Burke, FSB Associates

With over fifteen years of experience in online marketing, I can say without a doubt or any reservations that developing a personal brand online is crucial to your success as an author.

Personal branding is new to all of us, but its importance is growing exponentially. So the questions I get asked most often are, "What's in it for me? Why should I invest in building my brand online?" The most important element of a personal brand is that it helps you be yourself and stand out from the crowd. After all, there is no competition for *you*.

The essential elements of personal brand development include: web publicity, blogs, syndicating content for guest blogs, Facebook, Twitter, LinkedIn, and YouTube. The benefits of these activities increase considerably when conducted in a well-planned and cohesive manner. First, it is best to establish goals for developing your personal brand.

Two of the most important goals of personal brand management are:

- To increase brand awareness through consistent social media interactions

- To increase credibility and establish expertise via web exposure

Developing your personal brand takes time, but the good news is that the tools are free and you already have the knowledge. Social media now allows you to share your knowledge and build a following. Once you "know" your readers, you'll have a lot more control over your career and will be able to promote not just your books but also your apps, conferences, videos, webinars, websites, and more. Your personal brand will make you more valuable to your publishers and agents as well. In my opinion, personal brand management is today's resume.

Social media has given us great ways to protect and build our digital reputations. Today we have the ease of searching conversations, the ability to set alerts to help us monitor our names, a constant availability of learning opportunities, as well as a myriad of ways to communicate and interact with others. All of these tools, which were nonexistent just a few years ago, now make it possible for us to be proactive in maintaining, building, and protecting our good name.

Creditability—Web publicity allows others to lend credibility to your work by posting reviews, interviews, and mentions of your book on their site or blog.

Expertise—The benefit of a regular blog is that it allows you to show your expertise and share your knowledge. Four out of every ten Americans read blogs, according to a study by Synovate/MarketingDaily. This trend is increasing daily.

Syndication—Once you have a blog written, it is best to submit it to other sites such as *The Huffington Post*. If possible, you should also submit your articles to other blogs and sites for guest blogging opportunities. Each time your blog gets mentioned or posted, so does your name and the link to your website. Over time, this is the best way to increase the Google ranking of your site.

Relationship Development—More than 500 million active users spend 500 billion minutes per month on Facebook. It is no exaggeration to say that without a Facebook presence, you are at a great disadvantage. Engaging with your readers will lead to higher book sales and career advancement.

Share Expertise—At first, Twitter may seem overwhelming and difficult to use, but as you spend time on the site, you will likely discover the benefits of sharing resources and collaborating with others.

Networking—About thirty-five million people use LinkedIn. It is the most professional of social networks and essential for showcasing your professional experience, contacts, and recommendations.

Show Yourself—The popularity of YouTube is growing hourly; currently it gets two billion views a day. Today, people are looking for an authentic connection with you. Posting a video of yourself allows potential fans and readers to learn more about you, your expertise, and your passion.

Although social media engagement may not provide instant gratification, it should be viewed as an investment of time and money in your career and your future. I have experienced firsthand the benefits of personal branding, both for my clients and for myself. I have witnessed the difference between launching a book for an author who has worked to develop a strong personal brand versus an author who did not invest any resources into building an online presence.

In the coming year, I urge you to devote some time to developing a plan that includes all of the aforementioned elements. Decide how much time you can devote to each aspect of building your brand and also where you will need to invest in receiving help from experts.

Fauzia Burke is the founder and president of FSB Associates, a publicity and social media firm specializing in creating awareness for books and authors on the web. For web publicity and social media news, follow Fauzia on a new Twitter feed: @FauziaBurke. This article first appeared on The Huffington Post Blog November 15, 2010. Reprinted with permission by the author.

These days, it is virtually impossible to sell fiction on a proposal—the publisher wants to see the finished book. But nonfiction can be sold on a strong proposal and sample chapters. These proposals need to demonstrate that you have a great, marketable idea and that you are the "go to" person with the right platform for the book. Here is proposal writing advice from a nonfiction author who has been published by Seven Stories Press, HarperCollins, and Farrar, Straus, and Giroux. It demonstrates how the book has to be "mapped out." Then there is a piece by a novelist about what she did to prepare her work for publication.

To Write a Nonfiction Book Proposal, You May Need to Include a Little Fiction

by Leora Tanenbaum, Author of *Slut!: Growing Up Female with a Bad Reputation*

When you write a nonfiction book proposal, you're caught in a bind. On one hand, you need to lay out a focused, detailed description of your book to hook the interest of an editor who will offer you a contract. On the other hand, chances are that you haven't done most of the necessary research yet because without a contract, you probably lack the resources that would enable you to perform the research.

To resolve this contradiction, you need to distinguish between the inflexible and flexible elements of the proposal. The inflexible elements include your thesis, a succinct explanation of why your book offers something new and timely, a winning title, and at least one sample chapter. For the rest of the proposal, you have to wing it. To some extent, you need to inject a dose of reality-based fiction into your nonfiction proposal.

Don't concoct attention-grabbing assertions or make promises you know you can't fulfill. Do make assertive educated guesses about the way your book likely will unfold. Don't be intimidated by the fact that you don't know everything yet. Do make sure that you are capable of fulfilling all the necessary research required to write the book you promise to deliver. In other words, to write a successful nonfiction proposal, you must do *some* research; then you can make assumptions that will serve as placeholders until you sign the contract and proceed to immerse yourself fully in your eye-opening, can't-put-it-down, beautifully crafted book.

Your proposal, then, is simultaneously a provisional document and a critical road map. You certainly will change many elements as you progress through the stages of researching, thinking, writing, and revising. Yet a strong proposal will guide you through the thicket of the process.

None of my four books in the end truly resembles the proposal my agent circulated on my behalf to various editors. For example, in the proposal for my third book, *Taking Back God: American Women Rising Up for Religious Equality* (Farrar, Straus and Giroux), I wrote in 2005 that my table of contents would look like this:

Introduction: My Story
On Being an American Woman Today
The Role of Women in Christianity, Judaism, and Islam
Devout Women Who Choose Religion
Women Who Said Good-Bye
Reformers From Within
Hot-Button Issues
Rethinking the Divine
Conclusion

The actual table of contents of *Taking Back God*, published in 2009, appears as follows:

Preface
Women on the Verge of an Uprising (introduction)
A Love-Hate Relationship with Tradition
Catholic Women vs. the Vatican
Evangelical Women Spread the Good News About Women and the
    Bible

I diverged—but did not radically depart—from my initial vision. When I wrote the proposal, my plan had been to juxtapose Christianity, Judaism, and Islam and examine obstacles to women's religious equality within all three faiths together. I also had presumed that I could discuss Catholics, evangelical Protestants, and mainline Protestants together under the category of "Christians." But, when I began to work on the book in earnest, I realized that my proposal was quite naive. The three faiths could not be lumped together; the obstacles could not so easily be analyzed from a simplistic "religious" viewpoint; and different expressions of Christianity have far less in common than I had considered previously. I therefore diverged from the blueprint by devoting chapters 3–7 to each separate religious community. My proposal provided an indispensible trail of bread crumbs, but I had to rearrange the crumbs to get to my destination.

Below is the formula you should follow. Acquisition editors are looking for specific ingredients, which you must include. Although you are a creative person, don't be creative with the format. Do not assume that you can skip one or more of the following because your writing is so strong that you don't need to prove anything. Even if you're well-known for drawing outside of the lines, you need to demonstrate mastery of the proposal formula.

Catchy Title—You may very well change your title later. Your editor recognizes this prospect. Even so, you need to grab attention right away. Be provocative.

Voice—As you prepare to write your proposal, be mindful of your writing voice, which is contingent on your audience. If you are pitching a book to university presses for classroom use, write in an academic voice. If your book is geared for *Cosmo* readers, include short, breathless sentences replete with italics and exclamation points. Editors perusing your proposal will assume that your book's voice will match your proposal's voice, so don't mislead them.

Lede—Write an opening paragraph that grabs the reader. Be punchy and timely. Pretend that this paragraph will appear on the jacket of your published book. You want to establish the general theme of your book before you launch into the details.

General Description—Include all of these elements:

1. *Thesis/premise:* Write two to three sentences at most. Remember, once you start the process of writing the book, and certainly once the book is completed, you will need to answer "What's your book about?" as succinctly as possible. Now is the time to crystallize your summary.

2. *Methodology:* How will you gather the information you are reporting? Be as specific as possible. If you will use a journalistic method, describe how you will locate interviewees. If you are a social scientist, state how you collect your research. Do you plan to distribute a survey to a particular population? Include information on both the survey and the population.

3. *Page length/word count:* Provide a realistic length. It's okay if your finished book is off by forty pages, but don't be off by a hundred pages. Most serious nonfiction books run between 250–350 pages.

4. *Audience:* Who are your readers? Be as specific as possible. It's tempting to declare that any thinking person will want to read your book. In fact, narrowing your target audience is a better strategy. If your publisher knows that you're writ-

ing for college-educated religious women in their thirties and forties, you will receive appropriate line edits from your editor and suitable marketing strategies from your in-house publicist. Moreover, your writing will sharpen if you have a focused and targeted community of imagined readers.

5. *Appendices:* Will your book include illustrations or charts? If yes, you will have to provide them and acquire permission to reprint them if the rights do not belong to you. State how many illustrations or charts you intend to include and where in the text they will be placed. Will your book have endnotes? The publisher needs to know. If you want to include an index, be aware that you may be responsible either for creating it yourself or paying someone to create it. Either way, make sure to mention the index here. The same point applies with a bibliography or other resource list.

Why Now?—Why is your book relevant? Why would anyone care to read it? What is at stake? These questions are especially important today, as fewer and fewer books are published in the wake of financial recession. Publishers will not take a financial risk on a book unless it is timely and/or offers something new or different.

When Elizabeth Wurtzel wrote her memoir *Prozac Nation* (Houghton Mifflin, 1994), she related her experiences battling depression while studying at Harvard and working as a writer in New York City. The book is not about the antidepressant Prozac nor about a nation of citizens suffering from depression. Yet Wurzel capitalized on the fact that Prozac, which had been introduced to the American pharmaceutical market in the late 1980s, was much-discussed in the news in the early 1990s. She positioned her autobiography about depression within a relevant and newsworthy framework. *Prozac Nation,* which happens to be a gripping read, went on to form the basis of a motion picture in 2001 starring Christina Ricci. So if you have a worthy news hook, wrap your book around it.

Why You?—What makes you the best person to write this book now? Do not be modest. You need to advertise your "platform": List every achievement and accomplishment you can muster as evidence to prove you're the best person for the task of writing this book. Also mention every shred of experience that demonstrates you can market the book effectively once it is published.

The Marketplace—Research all the books in print (and, if relevant, out of print) on your topic. Do not pretend that similar books do not exist. Do not hope and pray that no one finds out about them. Instead, address them head-on. Describe each book that could be viewed as competition and then explain how your book differs. This section is vital for your editor to persuade others in house that your book is marketable.

By the way, many nonfiction writers believe that being the first to write about Fantastic Subject gives them an edge; therefore, they cover up that others have previously published works on Fantastic Subject. In fact, being the first is not necessarily advantageous, since consumers may be unwilling to purchase a book until the relevance of the subject already has been established. So there is no reason to be anxious about admitting that you are not the first. At the same time, you do need to demonstrate that your book differs from all the others on Fantastic Subject in some essential way.

Table of Contents—Your chapters form a series of linked essays. Each chapter must be able to stand alone but also provide support to your thesis. In general, a nonfiction book should have at least seven chapters. As with your book title, think up catchy chapter titles.

Chapter Summaries—The acquisitions editor needs to be able to visualize your book as a finished product. Therefore, you must be as focused and specific as possible when writing your summaries. Do not assume that an editor will trust you to come up with something wonderful on the strength of a vague plan. She won't. She needs the assurance of your confident, tight, well thought-out blueprint.

Sample Chapters—If this is your first nonfiction book, you must include at least one sample chapter; I recommend including two.

The first should be your introductory chapter. The second should be a chapter that represents the marrow of the book. Demonstrate the way you use quotations and other evidence supporting your thesis, your writing style, and your voice. Do not assume that the acquisitions editor can use her imagination to get an idea of how your book will read. She can't or won't. Using her imagination means taking a risk, and chances are that she can't afford to take a risk and will just reject your proposal.

If you've already written the entire book, do not include it with the proposal. In fact, I recommend that you not reveal this fact until after a contract has been offered. The editor's job is to work with you in a partnership to mold your book into a marketable product. If you tell him that you've done all the work already, ironically you become less, not more, desirable. First, you eliminate a responsibility that many editors not only enjoy but also require to control the direction of the books they acquire. Second, you may give the impression that you won't be flexible during the editorial process. Include your introduction and strongest chapter; you can always spill the full truth later.

Writing the proposal, in my view, is the hardest part of the process of writing a nonfiction book. Crafting a road map when you have only a vague notion of what the road looks like and you're not even sure which road you will take requires presumptions and educated guesses. Your job is to make the best guesses possible based on the minimal research you've completed. Once you've signed the contract and you're on your way, you will be thrilled you have in your possession a map— even if you end up throwing it off the side of the road.

Leora Tanenbaum is the author of four books: Slut! Growing Up Female with a Bad Reputation *(HarperPerennial);* Catfight: Rivalries Among Women—From Diets to Dating, From the Boardroom to the Delivery Room *(HarperPerennial);* Taking Back God: American Women Rising Up for Religious Equality *(Farrar, Straus and Giroux); and* Bad Shoes & the Women Who Love Them *(Seven Stories).*

A novel is very hard to sell these days, especially if it is literary or by an author with a previous track record that is anything but stellar. If you've been published before, editors can go online to a program called BookScan and see reported sales of your books from the chains. They often base the size of the advance on how these numbers look for your proposed book on a similar book. If you are a debut novelist, there are no numbers, which can be a virtue. It's important to submit a very polished, fully written work. You could also send a synopsis and list of potential blurbs. Here, a novelist talks about getting her first book published.

Reverse Engineering: One Writer's Path

by Liza Monroy, Author of *Mexican High* and Writing Instructor at Columbia University

When I was twenty-two and a year out of Emerson College's film and writing programs, I arrived in New York City, fleeing Los Angeles in a reverse *Goodbye to All That,* yet full of dreams of becoming the next Joan Didion. I wanted to write crisp, personally informed reportage, illuminating essays, and novels sewn together from details of personal experience, but I had no knowledge of how to go about doing so or how to get my writing into the world. I'd spent the previous year as an art department assistant for films and commercials in Los Angeles, and my previous entertainment industry experience helped me land a job in the infamous William Morris mailroom. The company has since discontinued the mailroom agent-trainee program in the New York office, but for nearly a year in 2002, I pushed a mail cart through the agency, dropping off envelopes and packages.

I always knew I wanted to be a writer—at William Morris, I was an aspiring client, not an agent—so at work I felt as if I was spying on the literary department, trying to figure out how books got published. I had majored in writing, but the business remained a mystery. I couldn't lock myself in my closet-sized room on the Lower East Side typing away on the novel I'd been obsessing about since high school if I didn't know what to do with it afterwards. Of course, nothing is guaranteed. I didn't assume my books would be published, but I did feel as if I could not write without a knowledge of how to proceed once I had finished a manuscript or a piece. I didn't want to write in a vacuum. Understanding how to get it out there, once the long process of composing and revising was completed two or three times over, was a means of motivation.

My path to writing has been—and continues to be—as roundabout as any career in the arts. There being no clear-cut path to follow is perhaps the only thing about this work that's guaranteed. Though I always knew I would take this road, it turned out to be winding, circuitous. It reminded me of a road William S. Burroughs describes in *The Western Lands* as "devious, unpredictable. Today's easy passage may be tomorrow's death trap. The obvious road is almost always a fool's road." He may as well have been talking about an author's career. Though writing and publishing are undoubtedly businesses, there is no corporate ladder, at least not for creative writers. But there is a flip side. As a job with no clear track, there are many possible ones.

During those days at William Morris, I felt more like a postal employee than anything else. What I didn't yet know was that I was already on my way, the agency experience being a sort of graduate course in the publishing industry. After the first nine months in the mailroom, a kind literary agent in his early thirties plucked me from a handful of applicants to become his new assistant. Working at his desk, I answered the phone, handled his schedule (mostly editor meetings and lunches), printed out submission letters for clients whose manuscripts and proposals were being submitted to publishers, and ensured those manuscripts and proposals were submitted properly and logged for follow-up.

I didn't tell my boss I was an aspiring writer, but I knew that being there would eventually come in handy when the time came. I was getting an unrivaled education in the who's who of publishing, from editors to agents to scouts (a job I hadn't even known existed).

I watched my boss pick writers to contact out of literary journals. He would call, express interest in their writing, and ask if they were working on a book. I came to understand the submission process: the agent would narrow down a list of ten to fifteen editors he thought would be interested in the book he was going to submit, we sent it out, and usually within two weeks we started hearing back. The pass letters came in first, and then, with many projects, *the* call: an editor had made an offer. Listening in on the calls to the clients in which he told them their book had sold were, aside from the free fruit salad and coffee in the mornings, the best part of the job. I dreamed of hearing those words said to me one day about the novel I was then only beginning to think about writing.

When I was twenty-four, in what would be my last year working at the agency, I wrote an op-ed in favor of gay marriage during the height of the gay marriage debate in San Francisco. There was one sentence in the piece explaining that my passion for the issue originated in having married my gay best friend so that he could obtain his green card in Los Angeles, five days after my twenty-second birthday. (We moved to New York City together.) A friend who read the draft suggested I ditch the op-ed and write a personal essay about that experience. I followed her advice, wrote several different versions of the essay, and submitted the final product to all the women's magazines.

It was universally rejected. I was going to give up on it, but I decided to send it to a column I liked in *The New York Times* Style section called *Modern Love*. Once it was rejected from *Modern Love*, I would put it in a drawer and start over on something new.

I submitted it and heard back two weeks later. *Oh, here is the rejection*, I thought when I saw the editor's name in my inbox. Instead, when I opened it, I was pleasantly shocked to find it was a personal note from Daniel Jones saying he would like to publish my essay. A joy of a kind I had never felt before washed over me. This was a moment I would remember for the rest of my life, the moment when I found out I would break into *The New York Times*.

I decided there might never be a better time to go full throttle into something that scared me to death: full-time freelance writing. I woke up one July morning, my first day in "my new job," terrified. What was I so afraid of? I mean besides the obvious not having a stable salary, having to be entirely self-motivated, and all that? I remember that first day so clearly: I walked down the street to the coffee cart I went to every day, bought a coffee and a bagel, walked home, and sat down at my keyboard to the blankest page I had ever seen. My fears came true. I had nothing to write. What was I thinking deciding to be a freelance writer? I was suddenly convinced I had just made a huge mistake. I dealt with this anxiety the only way I ever could: by starting to write. It was, I was sure, a warm-up exercise. A useless freewrite about the man who ran the coffee cart I'd just been to. The quick exercise grew into an essay. A few months later, the result of that hopeless morning became my second *New York Times* personal essay, "When More Than the Aroma Beckons." My point here is that even writing you fear may be futile can become something. Since you never know, there is only one way to find out: keep writing. Write a lot, even if you fear your project might be trivial. I mean, an essay about *coffee?* Then again, it ended up being about more than that. Our obsessions and preoccupations come out no matter what we write. Browsing Hemingway's titles in the gift shop of his Key West house, I came across a quote that was about trusting that the things you needed to say would come through in the work whether or not you remembered to write everything down. It might come through in a detail, a feeling, or some other subtle way.

Supporting myself with freelance fact-checking and copyediting jobs at *Jane* and other magazines, I threw myself into writing my novel on the days I didn't have work. At *Jane,* I worked two weeks out of the month, which helped balance freelance writing and novel time with a steady schedule. I also got married, and having two incomes relieved some of the pressure I felt to make money. Finding ways to lessen that essential, if not ideal, burden—residencies, grants, fellowships, funded graduate programs, or a supportive partner—are absolutely key; it's tough to be creative and productive when you're stressed about from where the next rent check will come. I spent my writing time in a coffee shop and at my home desk with an article and photograph from *Elle* magazine of two women publishers, Cindy Spiegel and Julie Grau, taped above it. By the end of that year, I had a completed draft of *Mexican High*. I finished the last sentence in the big reading room in the New York Public Library and headed home on the subway that evening with the lightest feeling in my chest and the quiet excitement of knowing that, no matter what happened next, I had done it—I had written a novel. I had accomplished the part of the process I could control.

One night, I read an excerpt [of my novel] in a reading series, and a man approached me afterwards. "Is that a full novel?" he asked. "Because my sister is an agent and it sounds like the kind of thing that's up her alley." It turned out he was a friend of a friend's husband. I went home and Googled the agent, whose name I recognized from my William Morris days. She was a big agent. I figured her brother was just being nice. There was no way this agent would want my little novel about teenagers in Mexico City. A few months later, though, around the same time I was rejected from fiction MFA programs at Columbia and NYU, she signed me as a client.

I rewrote the novel again over the course of that summer, and the book was submitted in November. I again applied to Columbia, this time only to the nonfiction MFA, having had a nascent idea for my next book, a memoir based on the *Modern Love* column. Within a few days of the submission going out, *Mexican High* sold to Spiegel & Grau, the publishers whose picture I had over my computer. I was working at *Jane* when I got the call I fantasized about as a twenty-two-year-old assistant at William Morris. I spent the next few days waiting for Cindy Spiegel to call back and say she'd made a mistake and bid on the wrong book. Fortunately, that call never came.

Having sold the novel, I had the luxury of being relatively unfazed when another rejection letter arrived that spring from Columbia. Maybe the universe was trying to tell me I didn't need an MFA. I'd been accepted to a residency, the Jack Kerouac Project of Orlando, to spend three months writing in the house where Kerouac lived when *On the Road* was published and where he wrote *The Dharma Bums*. I was on a roll—not even graduate school rejections could get me down. The following month, though, I got a call from a Columbia writing professor. There had been a mistake in the office, and some applicants received rejection letters by accident; did I still want to come to the program? I thought about it and decided that I did. I was twenty-seven and it was a now-or-never kind of thing. Also, I wanted the MFA degree to make myself more competitive for college-level teaching positions. I saw teaching as the perfect counterpart to writing. My hopeful eventuality was to teach a workshop every semester at a college or university and spend the bulk of my time writing.

My goal, besides the degree, was to improve my craft. By the time I was finally accepted to grad school, I didn't need an agent and I wasn't too byline-hungry. I had proven to myself that I could write and publish. Constantly thirsting for improvement, I just wanted to get better. It turned out I was grateful for the initial MFA rejections. *Mexican High* was published the summer after my first year.

This backwards-seeming route of having a book deal and then going to graduate school was of great benefit. Going to a program unburdened me of all the (mostly self-induced) pressure to learn the business and finding an agent allowed me to put my time in the MFA to the best possible use: focusing on becoming a stronger writer and gaining experience teaching at the college level. Several of my Columbia colleagues have completed, sold, and published books since graduate school, so it's not that I'm knocking the traditional path so much as suggesting that there is no one right way to go about creating your writing career. Bring the same unique creativity you do to the page to designing the larger scope of your writing life to the extent that you can.

There will always be that element which we cannot control. Just as there is no right path, there are no guarantees. As of this writing, my second book is on submission to editors. It wasn't immediately picked up by a publisher the way *Mexican High* was. That was, as my agent described it, a dream scenario—and also 2007 was a much different economic climate. I'm still feeling optimistic, though the landscape of publishing has changed, and it's important for writers to be prepared for any outcome. The fact is that books don't always sell, and then it's about having the drive to go back to the drawing board and do it again. That's why, as Lorrie Moore put it, if you want to be a writer "First, try to be something, anything, else."

During the difficult, challenging times, though, I keep in mind something a very different kind of artist, my capoeira *mestre*, says: "There is no such thing as *I can't*." (My theory is that every writer should also have one obsession that's not writing—for me it's the Afro-Brazilian martial art.) If you find yourself filled with publishing anxiety, return to the page. Remember that you write because you need to, and talent can never be taken away. In a business so heavily reliant on subjectivity, where publishing trends come and go and business goes up and down as the economy does its thing, keep in mind that you became a writer in the first place out of your love of the written word and of books that changed or impacted you in a way you'll never forget. You can't control the business, and the life of a writer is full of ups and downs, highs and lows. What you can control is whether or not you read and write and how much to ensure this interesting and unpredictable path will be a long one. Practice consistently. Believe in yourself and your work, and, eventually, the right agent, editor, and readers will, too. And remember, you are in it for life.

Liza Monroy is the author of the novel Mexican High *and recently completed her next book,* The Marriage Act: A Memoir. *She has written for numerous publications including* The New York Times, Newsweek, *the* Los Angeles Times, Self, *and* Guernica, *and her work has been widely anthologized in collections including* Wedding Cake for Breakfast, The Best of Modern Love, One Big Happy Family, *and others. She teaches writing at Columbia University and elsewhere, and can be found on the web at www.lizamonroy.com.*

If you are writing fiction for young readers, you most likely need to write the whole work or have many very polished chapters to show. For nonfiction you can send a proposal, which should show off your writing and that the concept is fresh and will stand out. The author of over twenty books for young readers shares a piece about her experience writing for this audience, as well as a proposal that eventually became a book with Abrams. Later we will "meet" editors for young readers.

Real Books

by Tonya Bolden, Author of *Maritcha: A Nineteenth-Century American Girl*

"Why don't you write real books?" That's what I was asked years ago during a radio interview tied to an upcoming children's book fair. The show's host, a morning drive time guy if I recall correctly, was doing the event a solid by plugging it, and that's what really mattered. The event. Not the weird question. (And, yes, it stung.)

Why don't you write real books?

I guess that radio guy considered writing for those we call "our future" mere child's play. Perhaps as a child, he had no great books and so didn't know such a book's power to reach, teach, touch: to be a rescue for a troubled teen who finds herself at a crossroads, to be wind beneath wings of a tween about to drop out on his dream. Of course, it doesn't have to always be that deep; there's a lot to be said for feeding the need for wonder and belly laughs.

As someone who, as a child, often answered "teacher" when the question was "What do you want to be when you grow up?" I feel blessed that for more than twenty years, I've been able to spend the lion's share of my time and talent on books for the young—history for the most part.

The number one advice I offer anyone who wants to be in the business of writing for the young is this: Be Ye Flexible. A writing career may begin with talent, but it may not last very long if you are thorny and if you don't cultivate the habit of humility.

Sure, I've gotten testy at times, but I've tried not to be difficult on a routine basis, tried not to make outrageous demands. Unless your name alone is a moneymaker, unless you have produced book after book that has made big bucks, no editor will put up with a prima donna for long no matter how talented you are. If you get a reputation as a difficult person, you may find yourself out in the cold. Publishing is a very small world.

I've known writers who bristle at the idea of anyone messing with their "vision." To be sure, you have to believe in your work and be willing to fight for it, but you also have to be able to take direction, be reasonable. Sometimes writers get tunnel vision; sometimes we take ourselves and our wordsmithing way too seriously. Always remember: it's not about you. More so than in books for adults, it's about the readers—what's best for young minds and imaginations.

And the editor isn't the enemy. The editor wants the same thing you want: a good book. The first time out with an editor can be tricky, even scary, but if you have the good fortune to click with an editor and to work with him or her again and again, you become a better writer. With your defenses down and trust in play, you can focus on craft even harder. What's more, your editor will edit you better as he or she gets to know your style, your strengths, your weaknesses, your quirks. (And writers who are transitioning from writing books for adults to writing books for kids especially need to heed their editors.)

Not all edits are about the art of the prose. Some are more nuts and bolts. For example, a book might be running too long. To add another signature (typically 16 pages) will push up the cost of production and, in turn, the price of the book. If in layouts, I'm asked to cut X amount of words or pages, I might silently sigh, even groan, but then I roll up my sleeves and get to work. After all, the lower the price of a book, the more copies are likely to sell.

Be flexible about ideas, as well. I know some writers and editors believe that the best books spring from a writer's passion for a subject.

While I believe that an overall passion to tell a good story, be it fiction or nonfiction, is a sine qua non, I don't believe that every good book must begin with the writer's passion for the subject.

I was passionate about doing the book that became *Maritcha: A Nineteenth-Century American Girl* (Abrams) because the subject, Maritcha Lyons, was a native New Yorker, as am I. Had I been born in her time, Maritcha is the kind of girl I would have wanted to be (or be friends with). Added to that, many of her role models are people I count among my heroes.

Likewise, I was passionate about doing the book that became *Cause: Reconstruction America 1863–1877* (Random House) because I remember so keenly the sting I felt in my school days when the tidbit I was taught on the subject boiled down to this: Reconstruction was a time when blacks attained some political power and, boy, did things go to hell. I later discovered how warped, how wrong that take was. *Cause* was to some extent a gift to my younger self.

But for every book that grew out of a passion of mine, there's one that did not. That was the case with *George Washington Carver.* My Abrams editor, Howard Reeves, approached me with that idea. I knew the gist of Carver's life but had no passion whatsoever for him. I had, however, always been curious about the man, and that curiosity was enough for me to get on board with the project. Sure enough, when I did the research, the thinking, then recognized for myself Carver's value, I became quite passionate about him, so much so that I took up vegetable gardening.

If you aren't open to other people's ideas, you just might block blessings. You may also have a long pause between one book and the next. That's fine if you are a bestseller, are holding down a day job, or have someone supporting you. But if that's not you and your goal is to live off your writing (which includes the ancillary income each new book can generate, such as royalties and honoraria for speaking engagements), ideally you want at least one contract in the works or in your file cabinet before the current book goes to press. If editors know that you are open to a range of ideas, it is more likely that work will come knocking on your door—and you are more likely to have success when you go knocking on an editor's door for an idea.

I often stumble upon an idea for my next book while researching one under contract. But there are times when that book is off to the copy editor and I'm blank, such as when I've come off back-to-back "heavies," like *Reconstruction*—books that had me at times in tears during the research and crying at the keyboard. There's but so much of that a soul can take. Sometimes I've needed a break. When that happens, it's nice to be able to meet with an editor over lunch, on the phone, or via email and say, "I need something light, something bouncy, something fun. Got any ideas?"

Editors have great ideas, sometimes better ones than writers. "Better" not in terms of intrinsic value but in terms of market viability. More so than most writers, editors see the big picture. They discern trends from fads. They know what their lists do and do not need. They know if the demand for picture books is down while the demand for middle-grade books is up. Bottom line: the agile writer, one who can write across age groups and on a range of subjects, who is open to filling a need, that's a writer likely to stay in the business of writing for the young. Filling needs is how my professional writing life started. And it didn't begin with a book for the young, but with book reviews.

In the early 1980s, a friend from college, Connie Green, asked if I'd be interested in doing book reviews for *Black Enterprise*, the magazine where she was an editor. She recalled that in college I wrote well and was disciplined. Connie also knew of my lifelong love of books and writing (poems and shorts stories as a child, a mad amount of poetry as a teen and young adult).

Book reviews for *Black Enterprise* led to other pieces for the magazine. All that prompted an uncle to recommend me to an elderly friend with a long career in cooking. This woman wanted to do a cookbook and needed a writer to work with her. She already had an agent interested in her idea. I met with this woman and her agent, Marie Brown, who, lo and behold, had been a friend and mentor to my friend Connie when they both worked at Doubleday.

Sadly, that woman's cookbook never happened. But Marie Brown became my first agent. As such, she was soon recommending me for all manner of work for hire, mostly for magazines and newspapers. I was up for anything and everything, operating on the Stanislavsky principle: There are no small parts, only small actors.

I had a day job then, administrative assistant to the writer James Goldman (*The Lion in Winter* and *Follies* among other things) and his enterprising wife, Bobby. It was a great job. And while through osmosis I was honing my writing skills and learning about the business of writing by being around a writer five days a week, the writer I most wanted to be around was me. In 1987, I went out on a limb and left my job. It was now or never I felt, fearing that if I didn't give writing a full-time shot then, I'd lose the nerve.

Leaving the job meant all the more that I couldn't be picky about freelance work. Thankfully, "small" work kept coming, including more book reviewing, study guides for an arts organization, and a chapter on black women writers for a textbook.

Along the way, I was learning so much. About hitting word count. About editing and production. About writing for different audiences. Again and again, I was learning that writing is indeed rewriting, rewriting, rewriting. I wasn't an English major, never earned an MFA. Both my BA and MA are in Slavic languages and literatures (focus: Russian).

Something else I was learning: how to live lean. I'd heard that the average writer earned about $5,000 per year from the craft. I don't know if that was true, but as money came in, I always tucked a little away for dry spells or rainy days. And keeping my overhead low was uppermost on my mind. On this, it's important to note that I never had children. So I didn't have to worry about coin for back-to-school clothes or braces, didn't have to worry about starting that college fund. I could afford to "struggle" and live without frills while trying to make it as a writer.

My entry into books for the young came when Marie Brown pitched me as the person to work with another client of hers, Vy Higginsen. The project was to turn Vy's gospel musical *Mama, I Want to Sing* into a young adult novel. The novel, published in 1992 (Scholastic), didn't do well, but the editor, Ann Reit, took an interest in me. Over dinner one Saturday evening, Ann came up with the idea of my doing a collection of biographies of black women, the book that became *And Not Afraid to Dare*.

Growing up, I'd hated history. What had been served up to me was cold, tasteless. As a book reviewer, I had the opportunity to read so many fine works of history, books that revealed how fascinating history is, how necessary, how transforming it can be when the goal is to offer more than mere information, when the goal is to tell a good story.

While I worked on that collection of biographies, I became even more hooked on history, hooked, too, on making it come alive for young readers. And wouldn't you know it, over the years I've dared to believe that I was writing "real books." But that's where my bragging rights end. Even with more than twenty books to my credit, I continue to stay open to ideas, to cultivate the habit of humility, and, oh, yes, to be careful with the money just in case I hit a dry spell or a rainy day.

PROPOSAL
FOR
MARITCHA

The Life and Times of a Free Black Girl in 19th-Century America

by Tonya Bolden

In *Maritcha*, young readers meet a rarity: a black middle-class girl in slavery days.

Maritcha Remond Lyons, with African, Dutch, English, and Shinnecock blood coursing through her veins, was born in New York in 1848. She was the third of five children born to Mary Marshall Lyons and Albro Lyons, who owned a boarding house (Seaman's House) in Lower Manhattan. It was in Lower Manhattan that Maritcha lived for most of her childhood (on Centre, Pearl, and Oliver Streets—south of the notorious Five Points section and east of the African Burial Ground rediscovered in the 1990s).

For Maritcha, life in New York City was full of delights and pleasures, such as "a gambol over the grassy Brooklyn Heights"; her father taking her, at age eight, to a fireworks display at City Hall Park in celebration of the laying of the first Atlantic cable; and her mother taking her to Crystal Park Palace. Another delight of her life was her maternal grandmother, who "knew personally or by reputation, every colored person in the city." Grandma Marshall also knew an array of white New Yorkers, including Samuel Lord and George Washington Taylor: when they opened a small shop on Catherine Street in 1826, Maritcha's grandmother was a first-day customer: "she hurried over to make an early purchase of a yard of white ribbon to give the 'boys' good luck, for she knew them both very well."

Maritcha's childhood was not without hardships. At one point, poor health had her homebound (and homeschooled) and enduring several "mechanical appliances . . . for the support of my spine for the improvement of my carriage." When Maritcha was back on her feet, there was the everyday prejudice with which she had to contend. Something as simple as getting to Colored School #3 on Broadway and Thirty-Seventh Street was a chore: Maritcha never knew whether the stage coach would stop for her. "Once in awhile, one would respond to my signal, but oftener I was ignored or jeered at." This meant that "oftener" Maritcha walked the several miles to school—"as the exercise did no apparent harm, I was enabled to endure to the end."

What enabled Maritcha to "endure" was her upbringing. Her parents, like most middle-class blacks in the 19th century, were full of race pride and they taught their children to persevere in the face of racism. Mr. and Mrs. Lyons were also committed to the "uplift" of the race. One of the ways they helped their people was by working on the Underground Railroad, leaving Maritcha with memories of "many strange faces [in] our house," where "under mother's vigilant eye, refugees were kept long enough to be fed and to have disguises changed and be met by those prepared to speed them on in the journey toward the North Star."

Maritcha herself became a refugee during the New York City Draft Riots of mid-July 1863. After a mob vandalized and looted their home, like many of other blacks, the Lyons family fled the city, heading north. After a brief stay with friends in New London, Connecticut, the family pushed on to Salem, Massachusetts, where they stayed with their good friends, the Remonds, a family of entrepreneurs and activists. The Lyons family returned to New York, but only for a brief time, deciding to relocate to Providence, Rhode Island. There, Mrs. Lyons had to sue for Maritcha to be admitted to the local high school. During her first two years at this school, Maritcha endured heavy isolation and alienation as the school's only black student. One bright spot was a friendship with Lucia Tappan (a member of the family of abolitionists that included Arthur and Lewis Tappan, founder of the children's magazine *The Slave's Friend* and strategist for the 1838 Amistad case).

In the late 1860s, Maritcha was once again living in New York, where she became a teacher and then an assistant principal of Brooklyn's Charles A. Dorsey School (P.S. 67), which is still in existence today.

Maritcha chronicles Maritcha Lyons's life up until the age of twenty-one (with an afterword summing up the rest of her life). This one girl's story is a window onto significant events and major figures of the 19th century, along with the culture and customs of everyday life in those days.

Helping to tell this story are paintings, photographs, documents, and other visuals of relevant people, places, and material culture. One source for visuals is the Schomburg Center's Henry Albro Williamson Collection, which contains all sorts of information on and artifacts from the remarkable Lyons-Williamson family, from the 18th century to the mid-20th century (see attached Schomburg script of the collection). One of the items in this collection is Maritcha Lyons's unpublished memoir, *Memories of Yesterdays: All of Which I Saw and Part of Which I Was,* dated 1928, a year before she died.

—⊗∞⊗—

Tonya Bolden's books for the young include The Champ: The Story of Muhammad Ali *(illustrated by R. Gregory Christie);* Maritcha: A Nineteenth-Century American Girl, *a Coretta Scott King Honor Book and a James Madison Book Award winner; and* MLK: Journey of a King, *which received a National Council of Teachers of English Orbis Pictus Award for Outstanding Nonfiction for Children. Her* George Washington Carver, *won a Virginia Library Association Jefferson Cup and a Sugarman Award from the Cleveland Public Library. Bolden is a magna cum laude baccalaureate of Princeton University. She earned her master's degree at Columbia University.*

One of the best "platform builders" is to have your work published in a national magazine. If you appear in any of the major ones, your work will be seen by thousands of people, including scouts, editors, and film and book agents. You might be approached by such people to expand your work to a book, or option the rights to a TV show. You never know. In any case, being in such a magazine exposes your writing and your visibility as an author. If The New Yorker *or* Harper's *were to publish a short story, it would certainly help you get a collection published later. No matter the timing, this will help expose your work.*

I had the opportunity to interview EMILY STOKES, *an editor at* Harper's *magazine.*

An Interview with Emily Stokes, Harper's *Magazine*

JL: **How did you get into the magazine industry? How many years have you worked in the field?**

ES: After graduating from Cambridge University, where I studied English Literature, I worked as an arts journalist and an editor for the arts pages of two British newspapers and then took a break for a year to go to school in the United States. Living and studying in America, I realized that most of the literary forms I love best—short stories, memoirs, essays—have been nurtured, even formed, by the American magazine tradition; publications like *Harper's* magazine and *The New Yorker* were exciting to me for the way they juxtaposed fiction and nonfiction, and for their high editorial standards. (I had never heard of fact checking as a profession!) Narrative journalism—reportage with characters and scenes and research done over long periods of time—and short stories don't have many outlets in Great Britain, where there is a lively newspaper culture but relatively few literary magazines and journals. (*Granta* and the *London Review of Books* are notable exceptions.)

Even the *Harper's* magazine internship application suggested the intellectual rigor of the publication; all applicants are required to put together literary excerpts for the "Readings" section, to suggest statistics for the "Index," and to write about their favorite works of literature. The internship lasted four months and taught me a great deal about the meticulous editorial work that takes place at a magazine like *Harper's*, as well as to articulate my hunches about the fiction I thought worth publishing (I was reading submissions for the literary editors). After returning to freelancing work in New York for a few months, I was hired as an assistant editor. I currently work as the assistant to the editor-in-chief, Ellen Rosenbush, and also edit some fiction and criticism. I've been here for nearly two years. Outside my work here, I also write for the *Financial Times*, the *Guardian*, and *Frieze Magazine*, among other publications; I find that writing helps me a lot as an editor (and, for the most part, vice versa).

JL: **Has the industry changed since you have worked in it?**
ES: When I started working at newspapers in Great Britain around 2007, editors were just beginning to realize the infinite potential of the web; newspaper writers were just starting their own blogs, and "Comment" sections were being introduced so that readers could respond to articles online. It's hard to overestimate the implications of this shift. For those serious about newspaper journalism today, delivering a regular Twitter feed is just as important as writing articles. For writers, the Internet offers all kinds of outlets for self-publishing.

For traditional magazines like *Harper's*, the Internet poses many still unanswered questions: how to enforce the same high editorial standards online as in print; how to make money from the Internet? How much free content should magazines offer online to nonsubscribers? Is the magazine still important as an object—a book that you can roll up and put in your handbag? *Harper's* has taken the approach that almost all original print content will remain behind the subscribers' "pay-wall" online, although we offer "tasters" of articles on our home page, and writers often contribute blogs that supplement their articles. *Harper's* is currently preparing a brand new website, and I'm looking forward to seeing how that will change editors' and readers' relationship to the magazine, and how it will affect the average age of our readership. I suspect that we will be able to reach a much wider range of people through our website than we do via the newsstand.

The Internet has provided a great platform for magazines in many ways, but one of my favorite aspects of how publications like *Harper's* and the *Paris Review* have used the web is to create online archives, which are invaluable resources for scholars and general readers.

Oh, and there has been a recession! For most organizations in publishing, this has meant that there are fewer available jobs (even as there are more journalism graduates) and more unpaid internships. It's been a difficult time for those looking to get into publishing, and those in the field have often found editorial staffs becoming smaller and younger.

JL: **What do you look for in submissions? How do you acquire a piece? Walk us through the in-house process.**

ES: At *Harper's*, we receive both unsolicited submissions—fiction and nonfiction—and proposals for pieces that are yet to be written. Unsolicited submissions (unkindly called "slush") are read by our interns, many of whom are writers themselves. They pass on any stories or proposals that they find remotely promising to one of the permanent editors here, who will take a thorough second look.

Every month, soon after the magazine has gone to print, the editors at *Harper's* have an editorial meeting in which we discuss proposals sent to us mostly by writers (rather than agents) or ideas that we have for pieces we would like to commission. The meetings can go on for a while—sometimes two hours—and often the discussion about a proposal will change it a great deal. We might realize, for instance, that the focus of the writer's attention needs to shift, or that the subject is right but the writer isn't well-suited to the piece, or that what had been pitched as a feature would work better as a piece of criticism or an annotation.

My advice to those writing a proposal would be to gain a deep familiarity with the magazine to which they are pitching: is this piece well-suited to the magazine? Is the piece too close to something that the magazine has recently published? Writers should think about why they are better equipped to write this piece than anyone else and should make an effort to write proposals that are written with a sense of style, if possible including characters and scenes. Pitches tend to be anywhere from a paragraph to two pages, although I would recommend three paragraphs as an ideal length.

JL: **What percent of submissions do you accept for the magazine out of the vast amounts you see?**

ES: The percentage of unsolicited submissions that are published is small, but we have found some writers through the so-called "slush" pile, and it is important to us that we remain open to receiving pieces in this way rather than simply relying on agents or writers who have already been published elsewhere.

JL: **Please tell us about a typical day at the magazine.**

ES: *Harper's* is a monthly magazine and so it depends on the time of the month. Things tend to get a little tense as we go to print, and then there is a desk-tidying period immediately after that. We have a few monthly meetings: the editorial meeting, the "Index" meeting (where we brainstorm ideas for "Index" statistics), and a meeting for headlines. Editors' days are spent reading proposals, editing copy, discussing manuscripts, talking to writers, and emailing. A lot of emailing.

JL: **Do you try to publish authors more than once and try to cultivate relationships?**

ES: Absolutely. *Harper's* has longstanding relationships with some of the best writers in America, and we're proud to republish authors over many years.

JL: Do you hold pieces for future issues?

ES: Yes, sometimes for rather a long time so that we can put together the best issue possible, with a range of subjects, styles, and writers. Space is limited, and there is always a list of at least a dozen pieces that are "on hand," waiting to be published.

JL: How much fiction versus nonfiction do you publish?

ES: We publish one short story and one or two pieces of fiction in our "Readings" section; the rest is nonfiction.

JL: Do you seek authors, or are most submissions sent to you by agents or the authors themselves? Do you commission pieces on topics you want to feature?

ES: All of the above. Some of our writers have agents; many don't. We often contact writers whose work we admire to see what they're up to, and many writers contact us to ask if they might send us something to read. We publish excerpts from upcoming books, and we are always looking out for new writers in journals and other magazines. Often, in editorial meetings, we will talk about issues that we would like to cover and brainstorm writers who might be well-suited to write about these issues.

JL: Do you stay in touch with authors whose pieces are not quite right but in whom you see potential?

ES: Yes. If we like their writing style, we will encourage them to submit more ideas or will contact them again if we think of a subject that might work for them.

JL: **Is there anything you would like to see come across your desk that you have not seen before?**

ES: Well, it's always a treat to receive something—lipstick, say—that was intended for an editor at *Harper's Bazaar*! Really, though, I am just always delighted to see great sentences. I get very excited about stories in translation by writers I don't know and would like to be introduced to more foreign authors by translators. It seems ridiculous to me that only three percent of books sold in the United States are translated works; magazines, I think, have the opportunity to change that.

I would also like to see more proposals from women. This is a real issue; *Harper's* is by no means the worst offender, but still we have a great disparity between the number of male and female writers we publish. The question clearly isn't a lack of talent; I suspect it might be about confidence. Probably editors need to spend much more time making sure that they are approaching writers they admire rather than just relying on the best writers to come to us.

JL: **How many people at *Harper's* read submissions?**

ES: Four interns, and then most of the editors (which makes about fifteen).

Emily Stokes is an assistant editor at Harper's *magazine. She studied English at Cambridge University in England and was a Kennedy Memorial Trust scholar at Harvard University. She has written for the* Financial Times, The Guardian, The Times, The Daily Beast, *and* Frieze Magazine.

Your literary career will surely benefit by being published in an independent literary journal. It may have a circulation of say, 3,000 or so, but many are looked at by agents and editors, and literary voices are discovered by having their work appear in a journal. We now are guided by the head of such a publication, one of the founders and the editor-in-chief of Fiction.

To Reach the Literary Editor

by Mark Jay Mirsky, *Fiction* Magazine

When I am asked by writers what I look for in submissions to *Fiction*, I generally look blank. This is because I try to read the stories that come across my desk without preconceptions. I don't have a formula in my head. I know one editor of a prominent literary journal who announced that he could always tell from the first sentence whether a story was worth reading or not. I can't echo that. I do, however, usually know by the bottom of the first page whether or not I want to go on reading. Sometimes it is the language that draws me into the writer's world; sometimes it is the way the plot is already tugging at my attention. What convinces me that a story that has come my way ought to be in the pages of *Fiction* is that I want to live in its world. Why? Because it's full of surprises and riddles that I only half understand. If I want to go back and read the story a second and third time, even though it held my attention through the whole of my first reading, then I sense that I want to publish it.

Since I regard myself as a writer first and foremost, a pang of jealousy is often a necessary ingredient. When the language lapses into cliché, no matter how interesting the plot has been, I don't want anything to do with the writing. If the story doesn't turn on itself in some way—embodying that brilliant title of Henry James, *The Turn of the Screw*, which is almost a motto for every good story—so that the final surprises leave me exhausted (by promising to resolve the questions only to open up additional ones), then I put it down disappointed. I like to paraphrase Robert Creeley when it comes to the process of writing; the poet, whose story "Mr. Blue" is one of my favorites: "I start wherever I can, and I stop when I see the whole thing coming round." Very few stories really accomplish this, so a half-turn of the screw will often do.

To go back and ask again the hardest question, what am I looking for in a submission? I want to be taken into a world that I don't know and find myself asking the same questions that the writer is asking, perhaps not asking with the same intensity or knowing how many of the answers live in the details, but intrigued and feeling that the author cares. I ask of Shakespeare, whose narrative questions continually draw me closer and closer into the text, what should Hamlet have done once his father's ghost has spoken? Should King Lear have let his let power slip away? And in the happier tales that the playwright staged, what is it about Rosalind in *As You Like It* that makes us like her so much, that makes us possibly fall in love with this virtual young woman?

Since American fiction in particular is so besotted with what is called "naturalism," or realistic portrayals of life, it is the strange, the bizarre, and the surreal, which are my particular delights as an editor. After all, I founded *Fiction* with writers like Donald Barthelme and Max Frisch, who were always on the edge, experimenting in fiction, and while I disagreed with some of Donald's enthusiasms, he was in every way my teacher. I try to imagine now what he would want to publish. You can't easily imitate masters of the imagination like Donald, Max, or other favorites of mine like Jorge Luis Borges and Robert Musil—writers who try usually end up with obvious knockoffs. Still, when I feel their spirit laughing in a story I have received, I feel that this new author belongs with us. There is, however, no hard and fast rule for being accepted into the magazine; fiction remains mysterious to me, and I can't entirely explain why I can't get enough of one writer while I remain cold to another. An author who recently wrote in to complain about our online magazine, *Hot Type*, claimed that he found a number of the selections conventional and that he was hoping for more experimental work in the spirit of Barthelme and Musil. Fair enough, but he went on to describe his cutting-edge experiments with computer-generated fiction. I am fascinated by the tension between the machine and the human—and cinematic narratives like *Battlestar Galactica*, texts like Norbert Weiner's *God & Golem, Inc.*, deeply engage me—but experiment for the sake of experiment is not going to woo my attention. If I do err, it will be for the sake of language, image, metaphor, the rhythm its sentences beat out, but finally I want to feel the movement of a plot. "Plot over all!" to paraphrase a dangerous saying.

Finding authors isn't easy. We field over a thousand submissions a year and sometimes two thousand. About a hundred of them come in from agents, and obviously, since the agent has served as a first reader, I ask to take a look at all of these. However, few of these stories serve our purpose at *Fiction* or interest me. The agent who serves on our editorial board, like my managing editors, usually knows what excites me and which authors on her client list I consider the tastiest, so to speak. I batter other agents with requests for work from writers I know and love, such as John Barth and Aharon Appelfeld, but despite the fact that we now pay for submissions, many agencies don't pay proper attention to what we are eager to see in our pages. Some, I suspect, send what they can't market elsewhere. That's foolish—the Barth manuscript we were able to obtain from an agent went on to be placed in *The Best American Short Stories*. Obviously, since I write books and have a substantial teaching schedule and obligations at The City College, which pays my salary, I can't read all the unsolicited manuscripts. This puts me, to an extent, at the mercy of my editorial readers, who sometimes understand what I am looking for and sometimes do not. They try to send on to me all the writers who have had any kind of serious publication in other literary journals and try to read, and to an extent respond to, every submission. Still, it is those writers whom we pluck out of obscurity, previously unpublished, from unsolicited manuscripts whom I am proudest of finding and putting into print. At the same time I try, however, to include several names that have national or international recognition so that readers in bookstores, librarians, and subscribers will pick up the issue knowing that within its pages there is a company of writers who merit attention. And I like, in particular, to discover work that otherwise would have gone unnoticed.

What is the role of smaller journals today? How does publishing in a literary journal help an author's career and expose his or her work? Happily, we send out over 2,500 copies, some to subscribers, libraries (where they have many readers), and agents, as well as some free copies to writers who have published with us. These have a wide reach. To my surprise, several issues ago, a story I wrote about Scheherazade received a glowing review in Turkey. It is not infrequent for a distinguished writer like Joyce Carol Oates to send a note to an author she admires after reading a story in *Fiction*. Or for an agent to ask if a particular writer would like to talk about being represented. (Mary Miller, who was featured in the last issue, received just such a query.) Writers like Robert Stone and T. Coraghessan Boyle had some of their earliest publication in *Fiction*. Did we have any role in their subsequent success? I hope so. I am glad we recognized them. The materials that were not sought out by commercial publishing houses or were rejected by them are some of the treasured pages in *Fiction* that make me glow. How did I find them? Hanging around writers, publishers, agents, and listening—hearing that Harcourt was not interested in publishing Max Frisch's *William Tell: A School Text* and jumping at the opportunity; or finding out that certain pages of Robert Musil's *Diaries* were available and begging for them; or learning that there were over 2,000 unpublished pages of Henry Roth's writing left in workbooks that had not been gathered into *Mercy of a Rude Stream* and that *The New Yorker* would only be publishing a limited number of them, and managing to bring some portion of the rest to light in *Fiction*'s pages. The company of these undeniable masterworks offers some hope to the careers of those who publish alongside them.

I believe, since most writing careers are subsidized by others—universities, foundations, patrons—that publication in *Fiction* does not just launch a writer's life; it sustains it. In the scales of hiring, tenure, promotion, and grants, the magazine's forty-year history and its roster of great authors has real weight. A writer's life (with the exception of a few very lucky ones) is, in professional terms, generally lonely and often unrewarded. Looking back on the company one has kept by publishing in a literary journal is one of the few rewards that never loses value.

Even though the magazine, as a labor of love, comes out less frequently than I would wish, every year brings a number of letters from writers who have finally found a commercial publisher and who write to thank us for launching them into the world of publication. Despite a succession of young student managing editors, the burden of *Fiction* has rested largely on my shoulders and my wife's for many years. Not only the editing and physical production of the magazine, but also the grant applications, the filings with New York State, the IRS, the fruitless attempts to persuade entities like New York City Department of Cultural Affairs Cultural Development Fund, the New York Council for the Humanities, and others that a small literary magazine should be sustained. Luckily, New York State Council on the Arts has been a reliable source of funding for us, and our board of directors has also contributed to the magazine's continued existence. We survive on donations, not subscriptions. That's the truth of most literary magazines, a wisdom I learned from my friend, William Phillips, whose influence on American literature was immense as editor of *Partisan Review*. I remember Donald Barthelme lamenting the loss of "hot type," though the much cheaper cost of "cold type" (which uses photographic paper) is what enabled us to start a publication on very little capital. To go out of print would be to betray him. Donald, while departing early from editorial duties, was watchful throughout his life over *Fiction*, sending us stories and consulting on design. He was shocked that I kept the magazine going; he thought it would fade out of existence after four or five issues. If so, I am convinced that Manuel Puig's career, which was revived with our publication of sections of his *Kiss of the Spider Woman*, would have languished—in fact, I was the one who found him a publisher for the novel. Frisch's *William Tell* might not have come to the attention of Continuum, and Musil's *Diaries* might have waited many more years before being published. Not only do magazines launch and revive careers, they make a world swim into view, a community of writers for the reader. We may be out of the eye of most of "the wide world," but I think we are read by those who are looking for fiction that is worth reading and thinking about twice.

As I try to look forward into the future world of fiction and narrative without losing our commitment to print, I find myself intrigued by the possibilities of the web, ready to take more risks in terms of what we publish in our web magazine, *Hot Type*, which has been in existence for two years. Since at present much of this material is from previously unpublished or about-to-be published writers, it doesn't have the same cachet as work in the print versions of *Fiction*. Still, I notice that some agents are asking us to run work simultaneously, and I want to use the web as a way of striking out in new directions with what we think is fiction and finding narratives that probe the boundaries of what is real and unreal. What we need most is a community of smart readers who like to be challenged, not just coddled. I think that *Fiction* provides for its writers, beyond just helping their careers, an audience of readers who love fiction and are acute enough to enjoy its challenges. If I feel challenged, I think my readers will be as well.

If I had any last words with which to guide unpublished writers, young or old, my advice would be to remind them that the paper and print of a magazine, no matter how handsome, popular, or widely circulated, is just a stamp of love or approval. It's the voice of a group of editors or a single editor and that, again, what a literary editor is usually looking for is kinship and community. It's painful to know that you are excluded, but you and the editor are searching through the medium of writing—in my case, fiction. Often, the editor is himself or herself a writer, and it's wise to know something about what they have written and to respond to it in offering one's own work. The notion of anonymity is precious, but the more likely truth of the matter is that being properly introduced—through an agent, a friend, or through one's own enthusiasm for who and what the editor is all about—counts for much more than it ought to. The romance of being accepted—not because you know someone, but because the writing speaks for itself—is perhaps the most powerful fiction that we have as writers. In this regard, I find myself smiling at a recent note from one of my favorite writers, Sheila Kohler, who reminded me of a few lines I had sent her when her first story came in to the magazine. She had submitted a story, unsolicited, and said that her husband had gone to college with me. I wrote back, "I don't remember your husband, but I like your story." (Of course, I have to footnote her remark by saying that just that touch of the personal may have brought the story out of the vast heap of our unsolicited manuscripts to my attention.)

Whenever a talented student in one of my creative writing courses, at the graduate or undergraduate level, asks how to launch a career as a writer, the best wisdom I can offer them is to volunteer to work on a literary magazine. I was a neophyte when we began *Fiction*, running errands for Donald Barthelme, who was not only my senior but vastly more sophisticated. My association with *Fiction*, however, brought me introductions, interviews, and friendships with some of the world's writers who were then at the zenith of their careers, such as Jorge Luis Borges, Halldór Laxness, and Harold Brodkey. Some I only brushed against, like Saul Bellow, Italo Calvino, Primo Levi, and Joseph Brodsky. Others, when I did meet them, were unexpectedly warm, like Joyce Carol Oates. Sometimes what was most precious was just a letter, a few courtly lines from someone I admired, like Juan Carlos Onetti. I like to think, however, that reading, knowing, and weighing writers whose work I admired and sometimes edited did in fact help me with my own work. Writing is a solitary act, and it takes what my mother used to stress as one of the most important skills in life, "zitsfleisch," i.e., the patience to stick to one's chair and keep to a task until it is finished. It's because of this that the society of writers is so important, and the best place to experience that community is not in a professional organization or a political cause, but in the common endeavor of writing—a community most happily encountered in a magazine where one has a chance of being read by one's fellows and recognized.

Mark Jay Mirsky founded Fiction *magazine in 1972 with Donald Barthelme, Max and Marianne Frisch, and Jane DeLynn. The author of thirteen books, among them the novel* Blue Hill Avenue—*cited by the* Boston Globe *as one of the 100 essential books of New England—he is the editor of Robert Musil's* Diaries *in English. He is the former chair of the English Department at The City College of New York. His latest book is* The Drama in Shakespeare's Sonnets: "A Satire to Decay." *(Fairleigh Dickinson University Press).*

With the advent of new media and social media, it is increasingly important to have an online presence, and it is useful for the author to be familiar with these venues. We turned to a talented young journalist who has been published online and whose first work of nonfiction, Running the Books, *was published by Nan A. Talese Books, and he is now working on his second book. He began as a reader at the* Atlantic *and shares that experience with us, too.*

Some Advice for the First-Time Author

by Avi Steinberg, Author of *Running the Books: The Adventures of an Accidental Prison Librarian*

At some point in college, I decided that I wanted to be a writer of short stories and novels. As I was too socially phobic to join the literary scene on campus, much of what I wrote went unpublished (which, of course, is just fine with me now.)

During a postgraduation editorial internship at *The Atlantic*, I gained my first look into the world of publishing—and for the first time began to think about the business of writing, not just the art of it. At *The Atlantic*, each intern was assigned to assist a particular senior editor (this, in addition to tending the slush pile, opening mail, and, if you were really lucky, doing some fact checking). To my great pleasure, I was assigned to the literary editor, Benjamin Schwarz. My job consisted mostly of managing the endless flow of review copies of new books. Every afternoon, it was my responsibility to gather up the cases of freshly delivered books and take them to Ben's office. This meant that his office wasn't actually an office but more of a warehouse of books; the entire space, the floor, sofa, chairs, and desk were covered in teetering towers of books. Every once in a while we'd talk on the phone. (Ben didn't live in town, so we rarely met face to face.) I'd read him the titles, and he would tell me whether to discard a book or keep it for possible review.

The scene in the office filled me with dread and awe. As a reader whose tastes tended toward dead authors, I hadn't realized just how many new books hit the market on a regular basis. It was overwhelming. Seeing these books, all together, swallowing up the editor's office and, in turn, being tossed aside or occasionally given a reprieve, gave me my first realistic picture of what it actually meant to write books for a living: it meant that copies of this thing that you poured your heart and soul into would eventually wind up the fourth book from the top in the fourth pile on the floor of an office, awaiting its fate—and that was only if you were among the lucky ones who were published at all.

What I learned, in short, was that being a writer would entail rejection of an unprecedented sort. And the kicker: rejection would happen even if you were successful. Like any editor, Ben had to make tough decisions about which books to review. Inevitably, this meant that even excellent new titles would be passed up. The piles in Ben's office told me that the hard part of being a writer wasn't the writing itself, as I'd imagined, but the effort to find readers.

In a strange way, it was a relief to make this discovery. Since rejection was so common and extended to even great writers, there was no shame in it. There was no use in taking rejection personally; it was par for the course. As a young twentysomething with not much to lose, this gave me a bit of confidence—but confidence to do what, exactly? Beyond filling endless numbers of pocket notebooks with mad scribblings, I had no idea what it actually meant to be a "writer," what it meant to pursue a career as a writer. Here's what I did know, or thought I knew: that pursuing writing in an academic setting—in an MFA program, for instance—would be a disaster for me. At that point in my life, I needed to venture far away from any campus.

During this time, I made an unavoidable and, in a sense, necessary error: I applied for a staff editor position at *The Atlantic*. At the time, I regarded the job, which was mostly a fact-checking gig, as a door into publishing and ultimately to becoming a writer. As luck would have it, I wasn't offered the position (it didn't help that in the interview I had rather naively insisted that my ultimate goal was writing, *not* editing—not the best thing to say in an effort to land a job as an editor). With my newfound enthusiasm for rejection, I tried to take the news in stride. Still, I couldn't help but feel that I'd been shut out of a rare opportunity to get my foot in the door. As it turned out, though, *The Atlantic* had done me a major favor by kicking me to the curb. As a publishing novice, I didn't understand that an editing job, even a good one, can stall a writer and a writing career. This surely isn't true for every aspiring writer—there are some notable exceptions—but it was the case for many of my friends, and I'm fairly certain that an editing job, at that delicate moment, would have had negative effects on my own fledgling literary efforts. For a wannabe writer, editing other writers can be a frustrating and potential disillusioning endeavor. Worse, it siphons one's literary energies. After a long day or week of copyediting, it would be almost impossible to get excited about, much less focused on, my own writing. The best thing for a young writer is . . . to write.

Now that the editing job had fallen through, I was forced to find something else. As luck would have it, *The Boston Globe* had a few exciting and steady freelance gigs. (This was 2004, an era ago in publishing terms.) The pay was low, the benefits nonexistent, but the opportunity to develop interesting thousand-word feature articles for the weekend metro section was, at that point, the exact apprenticeship I was looking for. After a few weeks exploring the city for stories, interviewing people, doing research, and bringing everything together as elegantly as possible on a short deadline, I realized that I was doing precisely what I needed to be doing as a writer-in-training. I realized, in other words, that I was lucky to be doing this and not sitting in an office at *The Atlantic* editing other people.

After a busy year or so writing for *The Globe*, I decided to look for more secure work, something with better pay and benefits. Again, I considered an MFA—what if I could get funding?—but again I rejected the notion. (After tasting the world of paid writing outside of the academy, I felt more secure than ever in the decision to keep my distance.) I chose to take a low-risk move and apply for a job that was not in any way related to publishing. The basic idea, whether true or not, was that at the end of a day working at Starbucks or in construction or as a teacher, I would be physically tired but I'd also be excited to open up my laptop to work on fiction. The job I ended up getting wasn't one I'd ever considered before nor even knew existed: a librarian in a prison.

Fast-forward. After almost two years working at the prison library, I was beginning to realize that my plan to "write on the side" wasn't panning out. I decided that it was time to plunge back into the publishing waters. Although I'd walked into the prison job knowing that it would, among other things, be a valuable learning experience for a writer—a different side of life in the city, a new vernacular, etc.—I hadn't quite grasped the idea that the prison itself was my subject. After working there for a while, however, I realized that there truly was a big story in the prison library itself, a story that ranged both wide and deep. For the first time, I seriously considered writing a book. To my surprise, the book I envisioned was nonfiction.

The *Boston Globe* work that I'd done before taking the prison job had, in some important respects, prepared me for the task of proposing a book. My work at *The Globe* had taught me to write tight, disciplined copy on deadline. I'd learned how to pitch stories to harried editors. From these well-seasoned editors, I learned the fine art of brevity. While these skills were immensely valuable to me, the time had come for me to unlearn this newspaper training. I was trying to write in a new mode (for me). Until then, I'd written either fiction or traditional newspaper journalism. The book proposal I had in mind was something between these two modes: it was fact-based, like newspaper journalism but, unlike it, it also placed a premium on authorial voice. It filtered facts—real people, real experiences—through my highly subjective eyes and my own life experiences. This memoir would be told in a freewheeling, quirkier, and much more personal voice than anything I'd written for *The Globe*. It could explore varieties of experiences and use a greater range of language than traditional newspaper writing permitted. It took some time for me to get comfortable with the new mode.

At this point, I made another tactical error. I was impatient. Because the book was so clear in *my mind* and I was so eager to shop it, I jumped the gun. The voice I was using for the story was tentative and bloodless. It read like some kind of mix between a humorless newspaper piece and an academic article. I knew that it was hitting the wrong notes, but confident that I would get it right soon enough, I began shopping it to agents.

This is not a good idea. Even if you have the greatest idea in the world, it isn't wise for a new writer to approach an agent with half-baked work. Agents are looking for something to sell, and I wasn't offering anything that was ready to go. I got extremely lucky and found myself talking to an agent who recognized the potential of the story, who had the patience to read early first drafts and urge me along. Other agents, even those who were interested in the concept, passed on it, probably because the prose wasn't proposal-ready. The best approach for a young writer is to take the extra time, even if it's a painful few months, to create a truly polished proposal before hunting for agents. If you give an agent reasons to pass on your proposal, chances are he or she will. Proceed only when both the concept and the execution are white hot.

A quick word on hunting for agents. I generated a list of agents by scouring the "acknowledgments" section of books that were similar in sensibility to the one I was working on. In this section, authors often thank their agents by name. I also shook every tree I could and let every person I met (and not just people in the literary world) know that I was in the market for an agent. I cross-referenced all of the names from my list of seven agents in the annual *Guide to Literary Agents* by Chuck Sambuchino. This book was useful in a variety of ways. The book helped me (1) determine whether a given agent was indeed looking for new clients, (2) confirm that the agent had experience with and interest in the kind of book I was pitching (narrative nonfiction, memoir), and (3) obtain submission guidelines, which tend to vary from one agent to the next. After a batch of query letters, I received three interested responses and three passes; one was no response. Of the three who were interested, one passed after reading my sample chapters (again, the half-baked prose problem) and the other two were ready to proceed. I met with each and felt that I had a good rapport with one, so we partnered up. Chemistry is very important. An agent might have a good track record, but if you don't get along with him or her as a person and as a potential business partner, then you should think twice about joining forces. It's important to meet with an agent and decide whether you will work well with this person, whether you understand each other. Like any relationship, communication is key: make sure this happens from the outset. This means listening carefully and asking questions.

Even after I secured an agent, I still struggled to shape and polish the proposal. After some months, my agent finally indicated that it was ready for market. I expected another longish period of waiting. But within a week or two, my agent presented me with three incredible options: Algonquin, the Nan A. Talese imprint at Knopf Doubleday, or an imprint at HarperCollins. In October of 2010, my memoir was published by Nan A. Talese/Doubleday as *Running the Books: The Adventures of an Accidental Prison Librarian*.

It's hard to overstate the importance of reading *about* books to the process of writing a book proposal. It is crucial for a new writer to begin to develop the skill of talking about books in the same language that people in the publishing industry talk about them. Reading interviews of agents and editors online is a good place to start. Remember, behind every book is an editor and an agent. Again, these people are mentioned in the "acknowledgments" section of a book. Track down a few recent books in your genre (it is most productive for you to focus on books in your field—if you don't write YA fiction, then the views of people who work in this field will be of minimal use to you). Find the editors' and agents' names in the back of these books, then search them online—many of these people have either written articles or been interviewed about their views on the business. Listen carefully to how they talk about books—both the books that they work on and about the field in general. They are in the trenches every day; you won't get a more up-to-date view of things.

It is also valuable to make a few conscious "case studies." Walk into a bookstore; search Amazon. Pay attention to how books are classified and packaged: Which shelf would your book appear on in Barnes & Noble? In what genre would it be sold on Amazon? Study the covers of books: the back cover, the blurbs, the author's bio. Pay attention to the publisher and imprint of books and begin to trace their differing sensibilities. Among the books that are similar to yours, what strategies do the publishers use to lure readers? What kind of language is used? It is important to know about marketing because you will need to show publishers that your book is market-able. Pick a few recent books in your field and try to read *everything* that has been written about them, from publisher's press releases to major reviews to blog mentions to Twitter and Facebook chatter. Acquaint yourself with Amazon, Barnes & Noble, and Goodreads reviews. Try to understand all the ways and means that a particular book has been presented, and not presented, to readers. To what extent does the language of the reviews echo, or not, the book's marketing rhetoric? Was the publisher's marketing strategy effective? Don't dwell on bestsellers; a more nuanced and realistic view can be seen by analyzing the experience of books that were well-received but still under the radar or which were overhyped. At the first stage of publishing, the proposal stage, a first-time author will gain an edge by thinking not only about how to write his book but also how to talk *about* his book.

Publishing a first book is all about developing an audience. Some first books already have an audience. *Julie & Julia* by Julie Powell was based on a popular blog. A book proposal that comes with an existing audience is a dream for a publisher. But usually, a first book is a first book—it is the author's first major effort to find a wide readership. Social media give writers a more direct link to a larger potential audi-ence than ever before. A writer who makes good use of Facebook and

Twitter and a variety of other social media tools isn't simply promoting her book; she's developing relationships with readers, person to person, all over the world. These relationships will grow and expand.

Unless a first book made a major splash, or in the rare occasion that it was marketed aggressively, the reader-outreach effort rests on the shoulders of the author. It is an ongoing campaign, best waged online. This doesn't necessarily mean you should become a blogger. It all depends on how much you are publishing and how satisfied you are with this published material. If you are, for example, happily publishing regularly with online magazines, it might be better to forgo blogging—which is time-consuming—and instead get more involved on Twitter. This allows you to stay connected and to be a part of the conversation, and to reach readers directly and in a focused way— but without spending too much time working on an entire blog post. On the other hand, if you aren't publishing regularly or aren't satisfied with what you've been able to place in a magazine, a blog can give you that platform to get your best stuff out there, to speak in your real voice. The point is this: It is crucial that you do the kind of writing that you want to do and that you find a home for this writing. Better to write a few really solid pieces and try to circulate them around than to constantly carpet bomb the world with your words. One cool article is infinitely more valuable than a bunch of rushed blog posts.

I wrote a few essays for *The Paris Review* online on topics that I found interesting and that I knew would have wide appeal (e.g., on the accidental art of the airline safety card). These pieces made the rounds online. The final two essays generated scores of comments and more than 1,350 tweets and counting. One tweet from Roger Ebert, which linked to the airline safety cards article, reached more than half a million people. Links in popular blogs like Andrew Sullivan or *The New Yorker*'s Book Bench and many others also bumped up the page views. A link to Amazon at the end of the article gave motivated readers a chance to buy my book *on the spot*. The number of people who encountered that Amazon link to my book is probably greater than the number of people I will meet on a first-book tour—and without the motion sickness. (Which isn't to disregard the importance of doing readings and supporting bookstores, but a struggling writer has got to be practical!) I've received many personal emails from readers who enjoyed my *Paris Review* pieces. The essays have also connected me with other magazine editors and opened up the possibility of reaching additional untapped readerships. The takeaway: A well-placed, well-conceived online item can go a long way in connecting a writer with readers of all kinds.

It is worth noting, as well, that this particular series of articles was not on the subject of my book. For obvious reasons, much of the writing I did when my book first came out related directly to the book's subject, including articles on the theme of prison libraries in *The New York Times Magazine, The Huffington Post,* and *The Daily Beast*. But the *Paris Review* pieces moved me past that subject and, in a sense, reintroduced me as someone who writes on a variety of subjects. Again, the most devoted readers are those who are interested in the *author* not just in a given subject. By diversifying one's subjects, a writer casts various nets.

An email I received from a reader says it all. In a message over Facebook, this reader wrote: "I'll be honest with you, I'm not someone who reads about prison. I wouldn't have thought to buy *Running the Books*. But I really loved your recent article [on airline safety card art] so . . . I bought your book and really look forward to reading it." When I asked this man whether he was a regular reader of the *Paris Review*, he told me that he'd never even heard of it until he'd received the link to my article from his friend, who had retweeted Andrew Sullivan's blog post. The readers are out there; it's only a matter of finding them or, better yet, letting them discover you.

Avi Steinberg is the author of Running the Books: The Adventures of an Accidental Prison Librarian *(Nan A. Talese/Doubleday). He is currently at work on a travelogue of the* Book of Mormon, *which will be published by Nan A. Talese/Doubleday in 2013.*

Appearing in an online journal is a wonderful thing for your visibility and reputation, as is starting a blog. Here are three pieces by people who have been active in the online world: ALANE MASON, the founder and publisher of Words Without Borders; MARCELA LANDRES, founder of Latinidad e-zine; and JEFF RIVERA, an author and blogger.

An Interview with Alane Salierno Mason, Founder and President of Words Without Borders

JL: **When did you found Words Without Borders, and what is your mission?**

AM: The idea began to crystallize in 1999, and we launched the magazine in 2003. The *Words Without Borders* mission is to promote global understanding and bridge cultures through the translation, publication, and active promotion of contemporary world literature; to open doors for readers around the world to the multiplicity of viewpoints, richness of experience, and literary perspective on world events offered by writers in other languages.

JL: **Why did you want the journal to be online?**

AM: That was the most practical, least costly, and most accessible way of doing it. Literary translation was seen as—well, was, in actuality—a fairly elite project, and to broaden its audience we wanted to democratize it as much as possible while maintaining high quality. So it was important to us, the founders and original funders and board members, that the work be widely available to all readers, rather than in what would otherwise have been a high-priced, low-circulation print journal.

Also, the Internet made it possible to communicate with authors, translators, and publishers in other languages in a timely enough fashion that such a magazine became possible—in a way, for the first time. You have to admit that the medium seems to fit the message.

JL: **How did you start it? How is it funded?**

AM: I started it by talking about it to a lot of people and establishing a network of advisors, then by finding a "fiscal sponsor"—Bard College—that would take the project under its wing and vouch for it, so to speak, to potential grantors. Then I wrote a grant application to the NEA [National Endowment for the Arts] for a seed grant, which required matching funds. The first matching grant came from the Flora Family Foundation. The NEA remains a critical and enthusiastic funder. So are the Lannan Foundation, the Reed Foundation, Amazon, and many private individuals.

JL: **Who reads *Words Without Borders* and how can one subscribe? What is your circulation? Do you intend to expand that?**

AM: Our readership is truly international. At least half is located outside of the United States. Some might be Americans working or studying abroad, but others are clearly people of various nationalities and languages reading each other via the lingua franca of English.

Currently we have approximately 30,000 unique visitors a month, and that is growing by about 20 percent a year. *Words Without Borders* is available for free online, and we ask for reader support in the same way that NPR [National Public Radio] asks for support from its listeners. You can subscribe via the website to a free monthly newsletter alerting you to new material posted there, or you can follow *WWB* on Facebook and/or Twitter. And you can subscribe to e-reader editions for any e-reading device. The e-reader editions are a recent development, and my feeling is that they will greatly expand our audience.

JL: **How do you find authors to publish? Do the submissions come from agents or directly from the authors?**

AM: Many come directly from translators; others from agents, foreign publishers, academics; and others from our broad network of advisors.

JL: **Are there any new authors discovered by the journal that you are excited about?**

AM: I have a particular favorite in Goli Taraghi, whom we published in our very first issue of *WWB* in 2003 and whose collection of stories, *Pomegranate Lady And Her Sons*, I am hugely looking forward to publishing with Norton in 2013. I am also especially fond of MuXin's stories and Najem Wali's. But I have too many other favorites to count or mention.

JL: **Do you have any new plans for the future? Will there be a print version?**

AM: *WWB* is launching an exciting education project to facilitate the use of our materials in high school and college courses, and to engage students in learning about foreign literature by setting up in-person and virtual visits of foreign authors to their classrooms.

In print form, we have generated five anthologies: *Tablet & Pen: Literary Landscapes of the Modern Middle East*, edited by Reza Aslan; *The Ecco Anthology of International Poetry*, edited by Ilya Kaminsky and Susan Harris; *The Wall in My Head: Words and Images from the Fall of the Iron Curtain; Words Without Borders: The World through the Eyes of Writers;* and *Literature from the 'Axis of Evil': Writing from Iran, Iraq, North Korea, and other Enemy Nations.*

Alane Salierno Mason is a vice president and executive editor at W.W. Norton & Company, where she has edited prize-winning and bestselling works both of fiction and nonfiction. She has published reviews and essays in Vanity Fair, The Boston Review, *and other publications, and translated Elio Vittorini's* Conversations in Sicily *(a New Directions Classic). She is the president and founder of* Words Without Borders, *a not-for-profit organization dedicated to the translation, publication, and promotion of international literature (www. wordswithoutborders.org), hosted by Bard College and funded by the National Endowment for the Arts and other public and private donors. Please contact them if you want to submit to or support them.*

An Interview with
Marcela Landres, Latinidad

JL: As an avid follower of your e-zine *Latinidad*, it is clear that you are providing multiple services to the Latino community and beyond. Can you tell us what you offer and how often your e-zine comes out?

ML: I teach writers not only how to hone their craft, but also how to make themselves more marketable to agents and publishing companies. My passion is helping Latino writers manage the particular challenges and opportunities they face, but the majority of the writers with whom I work are not Latino and come from all classes, cultures, and colors. Some of the writers who hire me have agents and are under contract with publishing companies, but are dissatisfied with the level of editing given to their manuscripts and want me to do a deeper, more substantial edit. Others have been published and are taking their careers in a different direction, such as making the move from children's to adult books, and want guidance on how to smoothly make this transition. A good percentage are unpublished and seek professional feedback to make sure their work is submission-worthy before they send it out.

Primarily, I edit literary and commercial novel or memoir manuscripts and provide critiques of proposals. In addition, I offer phone consultations. *Latinidad*, my free e-zine, which is published once a month, focuses on specific resources to do just that.

JL: **You were at a large publishing house. What prompted you to found *Latinidad* and how and when did you do it?**

ML: I used to work at Simon & Schuster and loved it. One of my objectives when I was at there was to find and publish Latino writers. In order to do this, I reached out directly to them and over time developed an extensive database of their email addresses. Whenever I received an email that I felt was of interest to Latino writers (e.g., announcements about contests), I would forward it to everyone on my database. Robin Blakely, a publicist who was instrumental in making one of the books I acquired—*Move Your Stuff, Change Your Life* by Karen Rauch Carter—a bestseller, offered to help me create a website to better connect with Latino writers. Since I have a high regard for Robin, I took her up on her offer and marcelalandres.com is the result.

Once the website was up, Robin encouraged me to publish an e-zine, as it is one of the most effective means by which to build traffic. I was already regularly emailing announcements in a piecemeal manner to everyone on my database, and an e-zine would just be a more structured way to provide the same information. Thus, *Latinidad* was born.

JL: **How do you fund the e-zine?**

ML: I publish *Latinidad* via yahoogroups, which is a free service. The e-zine doesn't cost a penny to publish, and only requires an investment of my time, which I'm happy to provide.

JL: **How many subscribers do you have?**

ML: *Latinidad* has over two thousand subscribers from around the world, plus it is syndicated in latinola.com.

JL: **Tell us about the book you wrote and how you are selling it as an e-book.**

ML: When I was still at Simon & Schuster, I would travel around the country to writers' conferences to present workshops to writers. A month or two before each event, I would email an announcement about the workshop to everyone in my database. Invariably, I would receive an email from writers who could not attend the workshop requesting—and offering to pay for—a video or audio version of my workshop, or a hard copy of my notes. After years of such requests, I sat myself down and wrote *How Editors Think*, which is essentially the written version of my most popular workshop of the same name. Down the road, I will write e-book versions of all my other workshops. At the moment, my *How Editors Think* e-book is available for sale exclusively on my website.

JL: **I see you conduct workshops. Can you tell me about these?**
ML: When I first began to work at Simon & Schuster, I asked every agent with whom I came in contact to send me manuscripts by Latino writers. With rare exception, they would reply, "That's a great idea! Where can I find Latino writers?" After a few years of this, I realized that in order to publish Latino writers, I would need to find them myself.

Shortly after I had this epiphany, I made a list of the directors of every writing conference and MFA program in the United States. I created a flyer with the words "Latino Writers Wanted" in big, bold letters, briefly described the kinds of fiction and nonfiction I was seeking (specifically novels with a contemporary U.S. setting and realistic Latino characters, and nonfiction in the categories of inspiration, spirituality, self-help, New Age, pop culture, relationships, and sexuality), and invited writers to submit their proposals directly to me, but only if they first emailed me so I could send them submission guidelines. Then I wrote a letter introducing myself to the directors, and requesting that if they had Latino writers at their conference or MFA program, that they share the enclosed flyer. I mailed off the letters and waited for the submissions to pour in. While a few submissions trickled in as a result of my mailing, the most rewarding and unexpected result was invitations from conference organizers asking me to present workshops. I said yes to every invitation, and in this way my speaking career was launched.

I quickly learned that while there is an industry devoted to teaching writers how to get published, most of the people giving this advice are writers. Meanwhile, the kind of person who ultimately decides what does and does not get published—namely, acquisitions editors—generally are not providing advice to writers. As a result, writers tend to have some misconceptions about what editors really do for a living. If I had a penny for every time a writer came to me after one of my workshops and told me that I was the first person to tell them the real deal about book publishing, I'd be Bill Gates.

JL: **In your e-zine you provide great information about contests, job events, etc. How do you stay current?**

ML: Much of the information I publish in *Latinidad* I receive from writers, agents, editors, and publicists who are seeking my help in spreading the word. I don't charge to post the announcements, so everyone has an opportunity to share, though I tend to include only information that would benefit my readers. In addition, I read the *Publishers Lunch* e-zine as well as *Publishers Weekly*, *Writer's Digest*, and *Poets & Writers* magazines. Every time I come across an article or ad that would be of interest to writers in general and Latino writers in particular, I make a note of it and down the road will share it either through my *Latinidad* e-zine or—if it is time sensitive—via Twitter or Facebook.

JL: **How do you find clients and subscribers to the e-zine, and how do you reach the Latino audience?**

ML: Most of my clients find me. Some attend my workshops and decide then and there that when they're done writing their novel, they will hire me; a year or two or three later when they reach "The End," they email me and request a consultation. Others discover my website after Googling "editor." A few connect to me via the online directory of the EFA (Editorial Freelancers Association). Of course, a significant number are referred to me by good old-fashioned word of mouth.

JL: **Can you recommend any literary journals or any other resources for Latino authors?**
ML: Almost every issue of the *Latinidad* e-zine includes a Q&A with someone offering advice to writers. For example, the April 2012 issue focused on tax tips for writers.

Back issues of *Latinidad* can be found by visiting groups.yahoo.com/group/marcelalandres.

In addition, I highly recommend the excellent DVD by Jotham Burrello called *Submit: The Unofficial All-Genre Multimedia Guide to Submitting Short Prose*. It should be required viewing for every writer seeking to submit work to literary journals.

JL: **What do you see as the future of Latino publishing?**
ML: Until a Latino writer makes a significant and enduring contribution to a publisher's bottom line, the larger houses will invest a modest amount of time, energy, and money publishing Latino books. In the meantime, small and university presses such as Coffee House Press, Akashic Books, and the University of Arizona Press will continue to publish the better Latino books.

Marcela Landres is the author of the e-book How Editors Think: The Real Reason They Rejected You, *publishes the award-winning e-zine* Latinidad, *and is an editorial consultant who helps writers get published by editing their work and educating them on the business side of publishing. A member of the Women's Media Group, she has acted as a judge for the PEN/Beyond Margins Award and was formerly an editor with Simon & Schuster. For more information, visit marcelalandres.com. Her e-book is available for sale exclusively at marcelalandres.com/E-book.html.*

An Interview with Jeff Rivera, Author and Blogger

JL: How did you become a blogger, and for whom do you blog? When did you start?

JR: I fell into blogging by accident. I've always written, whether it is stories or my journal, which I have kept since I was in the eighth grade. I started blogging for an online publication called *American Chronicle*. I knew that I was going to be moving to New York from Miami and I wanted a way to start meeting people in the publishing industry; I thought: What better way than to start interviewing people? Everyone loves to be interviewed and I was naturally curious (some would say nosy). I had just come off of successfully self-publishing my first novel and having it acquired by Warner Books, so I had a little bit of credibility. I wanted to know in particular what it was like for Latinos in the book publishing world. From there, I started writing for Mediabistro—a couple of how-to articles. How I lucked into that I don't know, but I did and I saw an opportunity with the website's blog, GalleyCat. I knew that as a person of color, there was very little coverage for us, so I wrote the editors and proposed that I start blogging for them. They told me they'd "get back to me" and, lo and behold, a couple of weeks later they did.

I started out blogging for free and eventually it was bumped up to a paid gig. I still blog for GalleyCat on occasion but used that opportunity to start blogging for *The Huffington Post*, which opened even more doors to sites such as *Publishing Perspectives*, Examiner, and now *Entertainment Weekly*. The smaller opportunities came through luck, but once things got going, the larger opportunities were not flukes. If there's one thing I'm good at, it's taking a small opportunity and using it to open more doors.

JL: You seem to focus on covering publishing. How did that come about?
JR: Publishing naturally was an interest to me because I'm first and foremost an author. I'm also by nature an enthusiast for marketing and publicity and I think I'm equally passionate about those.

JL: Do you know how many people follow you?
JR: That's a great question because I shut down my Twitter account, but I do have a few thousand Facebook friends. More impressive have been the reactions to some of the stories I've broken like that of Seth Godin leaving traditional publishing—that led to mentions in everything from *The New York Observer* and Fast Company to the *LA Times*. The story I recently broke with Jackie Collins sparked over 120,000 other stories about the fact that she would be e-publishing her stories. I was grateful for the two of them for giving me those scoops.

JL: How did you become an author? What do you write?
JR: I've been writing since I was in the second grade, but mostly just little stories. I always dreamed of being a novelist and would go into the school library and just imagine myself one day having that happen. I then got led astray—was attracted to the neon lights of the entertainment industry and writing screenplays, but after constant rejection, I decided I was going to write a novel. Having never written one before, I decided to base it on one of my screenplays. I didn't want any more rejection, so I decided to self-publish and built a large enough online following that it led to landing an agent and then a book deal.

JL: Has blogging helped with your overall platform as an author?

JR: Very much so. The network of people to which I've been introduced was all spawned by blogging, not only big shots in book publishing, but also celebrities and people in film and television. Here's the thing: You may not earn a lot from blogging, but if you use it as a way to meet the people you want to meet and build relationships, and do favors and ask the questions you want to ask and learn from the best, it will open up other opportunities. I don't think I make any more than a few thousand dollars a year blogging, but I do know that blogging has led me to gigs that have made me a much more substantial income.

JL: **Do you read other blogs? If so, which ones?**
JR: Yes, very much. I love reading GalleyCat and Mediabistro, of course, and I love reading blogs on Deadline.com, *Hollywood Reporter*, and *Entertainment Weekly*. Seth Godin's is fantastic and my new favorites are blogs on Inc.com.

JL: **Tell us about some of your favorite interviews you have done.**
JR: My favorites are with the big celebrities and major producers and authors. I always get a kick out of those because even though I do quite a few, I'm still very much a kid from Hillsboro, Oregon, inside who can't believe I get to talk to these people. Many of them have become close friends, colleagues, and clients, and even call me to ask me for advice, which is just a trip. I loved doing interviews with Nicholas Sparks, Jackie Collins, James Patterson, Fergie, Enrique Iglesias, Stan Lee, Hugh Hefner—so many great, amazing people and legends.

JL: **What do you think was the most exciting thing in publishing in the last year?**
JR: The most exciting thing I've seen is the huge wave of indie authors who are starting to get their feet wet and who are finding tremendous success. It is the future, whether people like it or not.

The thing is, you can dance in both worlds. Some books I write are more appropriate for indie publishing, and others are better suited for traditional. You don't have to only choose one, and you don't have to badmouth the other; there's plenty of pie for all.

JL: Can you suggest any resources for writers, any blogs, journals, books, etc., that have been useful to you?
JR: Definitely Mediabistro.com is great for writers and I love Alan Rinzler's blog as well. I also like reading Joe Konrath's blog, and do so regularly. Seth Godin's is a must-read every morning along with Inc.com's.

JL: What do you think is the future of blogging?
JR: There will always be some form of blogging whatever they might call it in the future. There will probably be more video blogging or vlogging, as they call it. It's an excellent way to voice what you're passionate about and to open doors for yourself and build a reputation that can lead to a lot of great things, if you play your cards right.

Jeff Rivera is an author and inspirational media personality. He has appeared on national television, radio, and print in such outlets as The Boston Globe, Publishers Weekly, Right On! Magazine, Rotarian Magazine, *TMZ, WABC, WNBC, WCBS, SITV, American Latino, and NPR. He also writes or has written for Mediabistro, GalleyCat,* Publishing Perspectives, Digital Book World, *Examiner,* American Chronicle, School Library Journal, *and* The Huffington Post *and has been invited to speak and inspire groups all over the world from South Carolina to Nigeria. He has been on panel discussions for* The Library Journal, *Authors Guild, the Harlem Book Fair, and many others.*

Very few publishers of adult fiction will accept a partial manuscript or an unwritten manuscript with just a synopsis or proposal. Sometimes they will offer on such minimal material in the case of a well-known author or one who has just won a huge prize, or if you already have a big name and are writing the next book or two in a franchise, or your name and work is already a brand. Beyond that, not too many offers are being made on fiction without a complete manuscript in hand. These days, we ask authors to prepare a full manuscript that is as polished as possible. We also suggest they include a synopsis and sometimes a personal statement and a list of who might blurb the book.

The advances are certainly more modest for most authors these past years. Yet, if a publisher really sees the potential, it seems they will spend a lot of money. They have to be convinced of the marketability. "First fiction" may be easier to sell because there is no sales history and there is an excitement about a debut. Story collections still sell, but it is not easily. They need to be very polished and, for the most part, should have appeared in magazines—the more prominent the better. Having a strong link thematically is a plus. Getting your fiction into The New Yorker, *or any other high-profile journal, can be a huge advantage.*

If you want to be sold to large commercial houses, the bar is very high in terms of what they have to envision being able to sell— certainly 20,000 or more. So the smaller houses, university presses, and midsize houses are taking more risks, and we are seeing some very big successes with them. Here is a piece by an editor at a mid-sized house.

With Fiction
I Am Looking for Art

by Kathy Belden, Bloomsbury Publishing

The publishing process for fiction and nonfiction can be quite similar in the broad strokes, but there are distinctions. Non-fiction is typically bought based on a proposal; for fiction, a complete manuscript is most often required. With fiction I am looking for art; the best nonfiction can be artful, but a good idea executed well enough can find readers, a market. I hold fiction to a different, higher standard. My first thoughts are about the language. The ideal: language that captures my attention from the first sentence, the first paragraph. It is rare for me to change my mind after this early impression. If the language isn't there—I'm not there. And what that means, whether it's a certain quality or charisma or spareness or lushness, is completely subjective and may vary. Two of my favorite novels publishing within a year of each other are stylistic opposites, and their voices have little in common. But both speak to me personally; both sound utterly like themselves and unlike anyone else. Beyond voice, I want to see that the novelist is exploring something larger than language—and that, too, can mean many things, from deeply personal human insight to larger societal issues. Acquisition of fiction is highly individual, as you may have gathered by now. But you have to attract just one editor, and a process begins that can last as long as a career, over many years and books, with wonderful friendships at its core.

PRIMARY POINTS OF CONTACT

Once you have an editor on the hook, art and commerce meet, and this can typically be a somewhat uncomfortable alliance. You have been toiling on your own, committed to your vision, and now the marketplace begins to assert its voice in the form of a book editor. But it doesn't have to be unsavory or unpleasant. In the best circumstances, with good communication and a genuine effort at building a relationship, editors (publishers, by extension) and authors can sustain each other over time. An editor's devotion to a writer's work can have immeasurable benefit. And long-term author relationships can inspire and instruct on a personal level, and professionally bolster an editor's list and career.

It begins with that first book. Here I'll discuss the most important points of contact between author and publishing house during the publishing process: acquisition, editing, and publication. Editor and author are in touch throughout and there are other important moments of intersection, but these are the broadest and most essential.

ACQUISITION

For editor, author, and agent, acquisition is among the most thrilling moments. All of my fiction submissions come through agents—and thankfully so. Over the years, agents and editors work together and we develop an understanding of each other's tastes; we develop relationships. Submitting to the right editors is part of the art of agenting. When an agent hits it right, it can lead to an acquisition. Make sure your agent has contacts that are appropriate for your work.

For the editor, every new book brings new hope, a new opportunity, and, on the most basic level, new business for the publishing company. But the editor is only one of many people who must be convinced by a novel's merit. For the editor, it will likely be a personal response, but book publishing is a business, at every scale, large and small, and so the marketplace and the book's sales potential are real considerations.

Once an editor has made a decision about a book, she takes it to the editorial meeting. These meetings, often held weekly, are a forum for discussing new business. Every editor pitches her new projects here. At the table also sit her fellow editors, the publisher, as well as people from sales, marketing, and publicity. This is the first instance of many when the editor acts as the salesperson, convincing others of a book's merit and market potential. We discuss everything from the mechanics of the work itself to the author's sales track record and connections in the larger literary world, as well as any prizes or fellowships or related publications that would add luster to his or her reputation. These may be the boxes we have to tick off as we discuss a new work of fiction, but don't be discouraged: on as many occasions as not, an editor's passion can convince her colleagues a novel is worth a look, even if the author is a complete unknown. As is often heard around these meeting tables, "It's all in the read."

Once an editor has the support of her colleagues, and all or enough of those at the table agree the title is worth acquiring, discussions of format and advance begin. Format is important at this stage for a couple of reasons. Hardcovers bring in more money and enable the publisher to pay more toward an advance. But if there isn't a market for the hardcover or the market is smaller and could be increased by publishing in a lower-priced format, then we have to consider original trade paperback. Today, with the introduction of e-books, the old model of hardcover first, paperback one year later, is shifting. We're publishing more original trade paperbacks for debuts and young voices, even for more experienced novelists with challenging sales track records. And that's a fine choice despite most writers' desires to be published initially in hardcover.

Our goal is to publish in the best format to reach the most readers—and writers have to do their best to feel good about either format. Format has little to do with literary market. Many high quality and successful books have been published first as paperbacks. Grove Atlantic, for example, has its Black Cat imprint, which publishes strictly in original trade paperback, fiction and nonfiction, and its list includes Anne Enright's Man Booker Prize–winning *The Gathering* and Michael Thomas's *Man Gone Down*. Pulitzer Prize–winner Jhumpa Lahiri was first published in paperback as well. There's no shame in this format, and in today's risk-averse marketplace, sometimes a lower price point is more desirable, but this is something we consider and reconsider with author and agent as publication approaches because the marketplace is currently in such a state of flux, more so than it has been for decades.

Once format is determined, we talk about how we would value the book based on some quick calculations: projected number of copies sold multiplied by retail price multiplied by royalty percentage. In most cases, an editor would also create a profit and loss statement, which takes into account other factors as well (production costs, additional income opportunities, returns, overhead, etc.). In an ideal scenario, the advance reflects what the author will earn so the publisher doesn't have to write off any unearned advance. (Although in some circumstances, particularly with higher sales, the publisher can still make a fine profit on a book with some amount of advance write-off.)

After the group settles on a number and the ultimate decision maker gives her okay, the editor is free to make an offer, often in consultation with her superiors. At times, the editor is cleared to a maximum amount and is able to negotiate as she desires. On other occasions, the discussion continues with every increase in the offer until the final amount is agreed upon. The process leading up to the auction could take days, depending on demand, or weeks. Some books are quickly bought with an aggressive preemptive offer the agent and author can't ignore. Some go to auction, where multiple publishers offer in rounds until one publisher wins out. Some manuscripts are sold in best-bid auctions, in which every publisher is asked to make the highest bid from the start. There are more amorphous processes as well with multiple players and layers. Or on some occasions, there's just one bidder and the editor and agent go back and forth until an agreement is made. In this scenario, the agent and author have less leverage, but this doesn't mean that the book has less potential. Sometimes one editor sees what others do not. So feel good no matter how the process plays out and what your advance is. Books are unpredictable "products," and there's no reason not to feel optimistic at this stage (more on expectation management below).

WHAT TO THINK ABOUT WHEN CONSIDERING A BOOK PUBLISHER

The advance is the most obvious component when considering a publisher. It's not always financially easy to be a writer of fiction and to make a living wage, so any publisher would understand the need for money. (I would warn you, though, that most novelists slave away to supplement their incomes beyond their advances.) In some instances, it's clear: One publisher outbids another. This is the measure by which we value the work. More money equals more value. But there are other factors. As an editor who has worked at the largest of houses and the smallest, and ultimately landed happily with a mid-size publisher, I'd suggest it's worthwhile to thoughtfully consider more than just money before entering into this important relationship.

Great books come from publishers of every size. Many of the best books, certainly many of my favorites, have been published by the largest publishers; the Big Six dominate the industry.

While large publishers have resources and influence, not every book is best served by that scale. I would also suggest that before agreeing to any deal, an author speak with his or her would-be editor. Editors act as in-house advocates for the book and will see the book through the whole process, from acquisition through publication. She's an important person to have on your side. Getting even some small sense of this person through a phone call or a meeting will help determine if you and she will be good working partners and, most important, whether you share a vision for the book editorially. Also, inquire about the editor and publisher's track record and experience with books like yours. There are certainly occasions when it's a benefit to be different, but typically publishers have strengths. Know the publisher's list. Make sure your book fits well and that the publisher has had success at the appropriate level in the past.

Ultimately, the better the fit, the better the publishing experience. When I say *experience*, I don't necessarily mean sales or attention. That's what we all hope for at this stage, of course, but whether all goes as hoped or not, ideally your faith in your editor and publisher will be such that you can feel some measure of confidence that best efforts were made all around, no matter the results.

EDITORIAL PROCESS

Editing is the defining moment in the author–editor relationship. Some manuscripts need a lot of editing; others very little. Since I began working in publishing, I've heard tales of editors who don't edit—and yet every editor I know does, particularly at my current place of employment. It's one of the essential services a publisher provides, and every writer should expect it. Your editor will be looking at the novel's structure, plotting, character development, etc., as well as the language. Every novel could use the feedback of an experienced general reader. Your editor should be something more than that; your editor should be your *ideal* reader. She will see what your other readers will see—the beauty and the flaws.

To avoid frustration, always ask your editor questions. Ask for transparency in the process; it helps reduce anxiety on your end and tension between author and editor. At this stage, I'd suggest asking about timing: the time it might take to edit, the time you'll have to revise. We can't always provide feedback as quickly as a writer might like. If you have scheduling needs, share them up front. Often there's a stack of manuscripts in need of editing, and as much as we hate to make writers wait, some patience may be required. It's not a lack of desire to quickly satisfy everyone's needs; it's simply a function of workload and time. (I don't think most people realize that editors do all or most of their reading and editing on their own time, outside of the office. The workday is filled with meetings, email correspondence, agent lunches, conversations with agents and authors, and advocating and interacting with other departments.)

The author can opt to listen to his or her editor or not. We're making suggestions, for the most part, not demands. It's your book and we're trying to help you make it as strong as it can be. I never expect an author to fully agree, and I often expect that the author's improvements will be better than what I might suggest, particularly with fiction. You are the artists. But at minimum, if your editor suggests there's an issue, whether you agree with the solution or not, consider it, or consider that something may be amiss and look to revise in the manner you think most suitable. And always feel free to ask for clarification, to request feedback on all or a part of the manuscript during the process, and to continue the discussion by phone, email, or in person. Generally, editors will adjust the way they work to suit the writer's particular needs.

After author and editor have agreed the manuscript is ready to go, two additional and essential phases of editorial work take place: copyediting and proofreading. Bless the detail people! They save us all. The copyeditor looks at grammar, spelling, consistency of style, formatting, etc. Fiction may require special instruction for the copyeditor. If an author has stylistic particulars that may not conform to the house rules, the editor should alert the copyeditor to respect the author's style. If a writer cares about type design, express this now. The author reviews the copyedit, agreeing to or stetting any changes, and then the manuscript goes to a typesetter where the first pass pages or loose galleys are produced. Once finished, these are sent to the author and proofreader simultaneously for review. This is typically the last opportunity the author has to interact with the text. Ideally, by this point, few changes are made, but it's the author's right to revise if necessary.

PUBLICATION

Even if all goes swimmingly well up to this point and everyone involved is thrilled with the manuscript, results speak loudest. Results are measured in two ways: sales and attention at publication. Sales count the most, but ours is a game of perception as well. Sometimes attention, in the form of reviews and other media coverage, suggests better sales than have actually occurred, and even people in house are fooled into thinking a book has sold more than it has.

A lot of thinking, talking, and work lead up to publication, and there are important people behind the scenes assuring the book's success. At some point, almost a year before publication, editors begin to present books to sales, publicity, and marketing. This is done on a seasonal basis, one list at a time. (Publishers publish in two or three seasons, depending on the company.) Presentations are done in writing, with tip sheets (in-house documents that describe and provide details about the book and author) and then catalog copy, and with impassioned extended pitches at the sales conference and meetings. Typically, authors get involved at the catalog copy stage. In all of my positions, at houses large and small, authors suggestions about copy are taken quite seriously.

After these professionals take in the content of the list, plans are made, sales reps start selling, and publicists are assigned. Once bound galleys are produced from the first pass pages (if they are still produced—some houses have made the shift to electronic galleys), anywhere from four to six months before publication, your book will leave the confines of the publishing house. Bound galleys are sent to potential blurbers, to reviewers nationwide, and to sales reps who will share them with booksellers. This part of the process is probably the most mysterious to outsiders. Even more than a time of mystery, this can be a time of acute anxiety for the writer. For many months, there's little going on that the writer can see. But this is where the importance of relationships comes in. Your editor should enlighten you; if she doesn't, ask questions. Most of us on the publisher side have gone through this so many times, we take the details for granted; but your questions will remind us to share our insights, which will hopefully help quell the prepublication jitters. Also, there's plenty for a writer to do to help out during this period: work with the editor to secure blurbs, create a website and Facebook page, develop contact lists, join reader-based online communities, talk to local booksellers, etc. It's a fine time, too, to remind yourself what this whole process is about: the work. For some, starting the next project can be a grounding and wonderfully distracting experience when facing the unknowns of an upcoming publication.

In addition to your editor, you will now get to know your publicist. My advice: Treat your publicist well, visit the office if you can, and meet the people who will work on your book. We all work harder for people, more so than pieces of paper. And many of us work harder for people we like. (Being a hard-ass hurts more than it helps.) Don't assume if the book isn't getting attention it's because the publicist isn't doing his or her job. After working for nearly a decade at a small independent publisher where I publicized the books I edited, I learned for certain that a publisher cannot force the wider world to take interest. Books come with magic or they don't (with degrees in between). We can maximize the magic, but we can't manufacture it. The market, alas, speaks, and it doesn't always say what we want to hear. I still remember when at my first publishing job I had the discouraging (albeit naive) realization that not all good books sell. A shocking moment, but there are ways to remain optimistic about the industry and your own work despite this.

The publicist will manage author tours, media outreach, and reviews. Fiction is still driven by reviews, and in a few lucky instances, off-the-book page interviews and profiles, and very occasionally radio. Although the decimation of print media has reduced the number of outlets over the last decade, old media is still best at driving readers to books, particularly fiction. Facebook, Twitter, blogs, websites, and other direct-to-consumer approaches are rapidly developing, all of which are handled by marketers and the author. It's essential to engage in this realm, but its effectiveness at driving sales is still even less quantifiable than old media. All of these methods, however—old and new—help generate talk—word of mouth—another essential way to move books into people's hands.

GENERAL ADVICE

I would guess that a large percentage of writers are unhappy with their overall publishing experience. Publishers screw up, without doubt. But in my experience, authors may enter the process with unrealistic expectations. For many years, when Oprah ruled the roost, almost every author would ask if we'd pitched Oprah or if we'd heard from her producers. Out of the thousands upon thousands of books published during that period, probably fewer than one percent would have even reached the hands of her producers. I'm not suggesting writers stop hoping for the big break or advocating for themselves (or agents on their behalf). There is, of course, a place for optimism—which is precisely what keeps me in a business that's plagued with disappointment. But most literary novels sell modestly, and good review coverage is not guaranteed. Remember that careers can be built up over time—everything you can accomplish beyond nothing is something. One name-brand writer didn't achieve any sales success until his thirteenth book. Thirteenth! It's a great gift to have the skill and the imagination and the discipline to write fiction. Allow yourself to feel good and to enjoy the publication process, whether you're the writer who hits with the first novel or, if like so many before you, it takes the lucky thirteenth.

Kathy Belden has worked in the editorial departments of Crown Publishers, Four Walls Eight Windows, and now Bloomsbury. She's an executive editor and has had the privilege to work with Jesmyn Ward, Gordon Lish, Michael Kimball, Jon McGregor, Mitchell Jackson, and many others.

When an editor acquires nonfiction, it is important that he or she has a strong proposal to bring to the editorial meeting. The proposal should include the author's bio, pitch, platform, and a marketing section. Many houses also want to see some sample chapters. While it is not the final writing, the proposal is a chance to show off the quality of writing. A chapter or two of the book with the proposal will help the editor see the arc of the book and also the way the book will read. The editor will want to know why you're uniquely qualified to write the work. If you already know who might blurb your book, that is useful, too.

Here is a description of the acquisition process as told by an editor at Nan A. Talese Books.

Publishing Nonfiction: A Look Behind the Scenes

by Ronit Feldman, Nan A. Talese/Doubleday

The publication process can be mystifying for a first-time author. There's a lot that goes on behind the scenes once an agent presents a project to an editor. But just what does an editor do? Think of the editor as the author's in-house advocate. She's the person who will read the author's initial proposal, fight to acquire his or her talent, enhance his or her book's content, and help position the book in the marketplace. In the paragraphs below, I describe the publishing process from my perspective—as an editor at a small literary imprint of a large publishing house.

THE SUBMISSION

Most of the submissions that I consider reach me through literary agents who are familiar with the types of books I acquire. I've never acquired a book through another avenue, although I will occasionally consider an unagented work if it comes highly recommended from a friend, or reach out to an author myself if he or she has written an article that I think could be expanded into a book.

The memoirs I review are generally fully written because their appeal lies in the execution. Most other nonfiction projects are submitted as proposals, which are comprised of a project overview, an author bio, chapter summaries, one or two sample chapters, and market selling points. Proposals vary in length, but when the author is previously unpublished, I prefer to read something on the longer side, around 50–70 pages, so that I can get a better sense of his or her approach to the material.

There are a number of criteria I use to evaluate a proposal: Does the subject interest me? Would it appeal to a general trade book audience? Does the project fit with the artistic vision of my imprint? Are the sample chapters engaging? How timely is the topic, and is it still likely to be of interest at the projected time of publication (generally nine months after the edited manuscript is accepted)? Who is the target audience? Will the book fill a previously unexplored niche in the marketplace? Does the writer have the right credentials to pursue this project (e.g., experience as an investigative reporter, access to previously overlooked archives)? Does the writer have a platform that will help sell the book (media contacts, awards, previously published articles, etc.)? Is this an idea I can easily pitch to my company's sales force? What is the hook?

To give an example of what sells, I recently acquired a book about the conflicting personalities and politics of first cousins Alice Roosevelt Longworth and Eleanor Roosevelt based on an 80-page proposal that described "a tightly focused double biography of two extraordinary women and their tangled lives" that would "provide an unusual window into the twentieth century." The project enticed me for a few reasons. First: subject matter. The co-authors described two famous and influential cousins—one a first daughter and the other a first lady—who had an "oil-and-water relationship." Second: the execution. The writers, a deputy editor at *Newsweek* and an amateur historian, wrote vibrant and engaging sample chapters that showed their talent for establishing character and building narrative momentum. Third: the unprecedented nature of the project. The authors noted that while some of the material had been referenced in passing in other books, this would be the first biography to tell the story in depth. Fourth: source material. The authors had been promised interviews with many people who knew one or both of the women. Even better, they had been granted access to Alice's letters and diaries, which have never been made available to the public. And finally: audience. I researched other recent Roosevelt books and found they had respectable sales, suggesting an enduring interest in the family.

I evaluate memoir according to many of the same criteria, although I usually have more material from which to draw an opinion. While I don't expect to see work that's ready to hit the printing press, I do prefer a project that's in relatively good shape: strongly conceived, strongly structured, strongly executed. Regardless of my opinion, it's to the author's advantage to present his or her best work possible because even if I believe the project can improve through editing, there's a whole contingent of cost-conscious people who need to sign off before I can acquire it.

THE P&L

When I find a project that excites me, I call or email the agent to register my interest and perhaps arrange a phone call with the author if I have any questions about his or her approach to the material. Then I solicit second reads from my colleagues in the hopes of being able to make an offer. My direct supervisor—the editorial director—has the most crucial say in whether I can buy a work. It also helps if I can get the support of our paperback copublisher, although that division has been increasingly cautious about committing to a project at the acquisitions stage. Since e-books have begun to cannibalize paperback sales, the paperback publisher will often refrain from financial involvement until seeing how a book has fared in hardcover. I might also solicit feedback from readers in outside departments including foreign rights, subsidiary rights, publicity, and sales—anyone who might like and support the project.

Once the editorial director is convinced that we should proceed with an offer, I ask our business department to run an acquisitions

P&L (profit and loss) statement, a projection of the book's financial profitability, to see if we can afford to publish it. The P&L takes various potential costs and revenues into account. On the negative side of the ledger are the plant and manufacturing costs, company overhead, author's royalty, production costs, advertising costs, and promotion costs. On the positive side are the wholesale price, projected subsidiary rights income (from selling volume rights for large print, audio, etc.), and projected number of sales. The sales number is purely speculative, but to make the projection as realistic as possible, I base the figure on the sales of a recent "comp title," a comparable book in the same format (hardcover, paperback) and genre (fiction, nonfiction). To obtain sales data for books released by outside publishers, I rely on Nielsen BookScan, a company that tracks cash register sales from a number of major booksellers. The best comp titles are those that have been successful, but not anomalously so. *Eat, Pray, Love*, for instance, would never pass muster as a comp title. The books we rely on tend to have more conservative sales, which, for a large publishing house, might be between 10,000–50,000 copies.

Once the P&L numbers are crunched, we have a better idea of a book's profitability and a clearer picture of the author's potential earnings. If the numbers look good, the editorial director shows the P&L to the publisher and asks him to approve the terms of the offer.

THE OFFER

Once the publisher authorizes an offer, I call the agent to convey the news and dish the details: the amount of the advance, the desired publishing territories (i.e., world, North America, United States, etc.), the desired subsidiary rights (i.e., first serial, book club, audio), the royalty rate, the payout structure, the manuscript delivery deadline, and the terms of the option (the right to have an exclusive look at the next work). The agent discusses the offer with the author, then calls me back to either accept or negotiate. The agent might ask for a higher advance, different territories, or a more favorable payout structure. (Typically, the money is paid out in quarters—on signing, on delivery and acceptance of the final manuscript, on publication, and twelve months after publication.) Sometimes the agent will ask if I can include a bonus, an additional sum paid to the author if the book meets certain conditions, such as earning out its advance or becoming a *New York Times* bestseller. To change any of these terms, I need to get the approval of my business manager, who will consult the P&L to determine if there's leeway.

The offer process works a bit differently if an author has serious interest from more than one publisher. If that's the case, I have two options: I can wait for the auction, which the agent sets for a specific date and time; or I can give the agent a limited amount of time (usually between twenty-four to forty-eight hours) to respond to a preemptive offer, which, if accepted, would prevent an auction from taking place. If the project does go to auction, there are two ways the agent can conduct it. In a "best bids" auction, the participating editors submit their most attractive offers up front, along with additional information that might entice the author, such as marketing plans. In a "rounds" auction, each editor makes a bid, with the highest offer treated as the floor that the other bidders must exceed during a succession of rounds.

No matter how the offer is made, if the deal is accepted, I (a) rejoice and (b) send the agent a deal memo outlining the terms of our agreement. At the same time, I request a contract, which usually takes about four weeks to produce, as the request has to route through numerous individuals before it can be drafted and checked against the agency's boilerplate. When the agreement is ready, I arrange for signature and countersignature by the author and publisher. And, finally, I release to the agent the portion of the author's advance that is due on signing.

While all of this is happening, I introduce myself to the author and send him or her our manuscript formatting guidelines and an author questionnaire. The guidelines explain how to style and prepare the final manuscript and supplemental material (bibliography, endnotes, art, etc.), and the completed questionnaire will help the publicist and marketing manager plan a promotional strategy further down the road.

EDITING

Over the months or years it takes an author to complete a manuscript, I'm usually in touch with him just a handful of times. I may check in to get a progress report and to make sure he or she is on track to meet the deadline, but I often won't see any written material until the full project is complete. Once the author delivers the manuscript, I go to work. Each project has its own unique strengths and weaknesses, but I use a similar set of questions to tease them out: Does the story have momentum? Are the claims well-supported? What areas are confusing? Is any material repetitive or inconsistent? Is there dead weight that could be cut? Material that should be reshuffled? Scenes or characters that could be fleshed out? Overused words or phrases? I mark my specific notes, comments, and line edits on the manuscript, and convey my general concerns in an editorial letter. But the conversation doesn't stop there. I usually see a few drafts of a work before it's ready for copyediting, and over that course of time, ideas are volleyed back and forth. While the author knows the material and the ideas he wants to convey (to use a computer metaphor: the back-end coding), the editor sees what's actually on the page (the interface). It stands to reason that the best content is produced when the channels of communication are left open.

There are a couple of other points I consider at this juncture. First, the title and subtitle: Do they sum up what the book is about, and will they attract the widest audience? And second, the publication date: When will the market be most receptive to this particular book? The latter is usually a company-wide decision, as there are a multitude of considerations, including media attention, seasonal tie-ins, and bookstore placement. *Snow-Storm in August*, for instance, a narrative history involving Francis Scott Key and his crusade against abolition, was selected for July 4 so the publicist could make use of the book's patriotic theme. An illustrated gift book, *Encyclopedia of the Exquisite*, was published in November to capitalize on holiday sales. It's also important to remember that certain types of books sell better during certain times of the year. And we look at outside publication schedules to avoid pitting similar titles against one another.

PRODUCTION

Once the revised manuscript is ready for production, I release the D&A (delivery and acceptance) payment to the author via the agent, and send the manuscript along with any art to a production editor who will oversee the material's progress into print. If the project contains any potentially libelous content, I will send an additional copy to our legal team for vetting. Over the next few months, the author will see the book at several stages. He will review the copyedited manuscript, which will have been checked for spelling, grammar, punctuation, clarity, and consistency. He will also see the sample interior layout. And, finally, he will look over the typeset pages, which are simultaneously read by a proof-reader. If the book includes an index or art insert, the author will see these, too.

Bound galleys are usually produced from the first set of typeset pages and are used for a variety of purposes, including the solicitation of blurbs. I create a blurb "wish list" in conjunction with the author before sending out requests. Of course, if an author has a personal connection to a specific author, he's more than welcome to reach out himself—but he should run everything by his editor first.

LAUNCH

Just before the manuscript begins to cycle through production, my focus shifts to presenting the book to the company. The first step is the launch meeting, where the editors present their respective books for an entire season. This happens fairly early on—about a year before publication—and having the author's completed questionnaire by this point is helpful. The launch meeting serves a different purpose for each department. For publicity, marketing, and art, the presentation enables them to choose assignments and brainstorm ideas. For sales, it's an opportunity to review decisions about the book: the title, price, publication date, comp titles (which, at this stage, are used to entice accounts to place orders), catalog copy, etc. Soon after the launch, I distribute the final manuscript to the individuals who will have a hand in the book's publication and I prepare additional material for the field reps who work outside of the office: an excerpt of the text and an audio presentation that is similar to my launch speech. I also attend meetings about the cover design, which will eventually be presented to the author for feedback.

PUBLICITY AND MARKETING

Three to four months before the on-sale date, our publicity and marketing people start to trumpet the book to the media. Galleys are sent for review consideration and to targeted groups who might generate buzz for the book. These might include book bloggers, relevant associations or organizations, and social networking sites that conduct galley giveaways in exchange for early reader reviews, such as Goodreads and BookBrowse.

If an author is local and wants to meet the publicist and marketing person, I encourage him or her to drop by the office. But either way, the publicist will keep the author apprised of our efforts and will let him or her know of any confirmed reviews or interview requests. Occasionally, an author will choose to hire an outside publicist to manage some aspect of the book launch that's beyond our purview (e.g., a book tour—which we rarely coordinate for new authors). I also encourage the author to create a strong presence online— through a website, Facebook page, Twitter account, or a blog. If he or she is interested in writing op-eds or articles related to the content of the book around the publication date, the publicist can help pitch those ideas to newspapers and periodicals.

PUBLICATION

While the publicist pitches the book to the media, the sales reps meet with book buyers to take initial orders and the digital department converts the final typescript into e-book format, ensuring that the coding can be read by a variety of devices.

About a month before the publication date, finished books arrive from the printer and are sent to the accounts. By this point, we have a good idea of the amount of media coverage a book will receive—but whether the attention will translate into sales remains to be seen. The publication payment is automatically released to the author via the agent on the publication day. And then I keep an eye on the sales data: both the net sales (our sales to accounts) and actual point-of-sale data (cash register sales). Since accounts are permitted to return unsold inventory after three months, it's difficult to see an immediate picture of how a book is faring. But, hopefully, in time, all the hard work has paid off.

Ronit Feldman is an editor at Nan A. Talese/Doubleday, an imprint of Random House's Knopf Doubleday Publishing Group, where she has worked since 2005. She has edited nonfiction by Jules Feiffer (Backing into Forward: A Memoir), *Avi Steinberg* (Running the Books: The Adventures of an Accidental Prison Librarian), *Jefferson Morley* (Snow-Storm in August: Washington City, Francis Scott Key, and the Forgotten Race Riot of 1835), *Jessica Kerwin Jenkins* (Encyclopedia of the Exquisite: An Anecdotal History of Elegant Delights), *and Mark Lamster* (Master of Shadows: The Secret Diplomatic Career of the Painter Peter Paul Rubens), *among others. Her fiction authors include Jonathan Odell* (The Healing), *Elizabeth Black* (The Drowning House), *and Allison Amend* (A Nearly Perfect Copy).

The smaller publishing houses have been producing many wonderful new voices and doing a fantastic job at it. While their resources are small, their passion and the fact that every book has to count have made for some excellent publications and some innovative campaigns. Here is an interview with one such publisher—ERIKA GOLDMAN—who has published a Pulitzer Prize winner and a National Book Award finalist just in the last few years.

An Interview with
Erika Goldman, Bellevue
Literary Press

JL: **In the past, you have worked at large publishing houses. Now that you are running a smaller one, what would you say are the differences? Are there things you can do now that you could not do before?**

EG: One of the best things about running a small press is that everyone gets to do a bit of everything but, needless to say, that can be tough as well. With only two full-time people in the office and the help of part-time assistants and consultants, we're all deeply engaged in all aspects of the publishing process, and, at the same time, since we're so busy, we can get spread pretty thin. We can't shunt work off to another department—we're it! It's great, though, to have the freedom to exercise and implement our editorial vision throughout without being dictated to by the bean counters and marketeers.

JL: **How did you get into publishing and what makes you stay? Tell us your about your publishing background.**

EG: Although I was advised in one of my first interviews out of college never to say that I wanted to be in publishing because I love to read, that's exactly why I got into publishing. What makes me stay is the positive reinforcement and intellectual stimulation I get from working with authors on their texts. It can be a wonderfully creative and engaging process.

JL: Do you think the book itself is in jeopardy? How have you been involved with e-books?

EG: There have always been relatively few readers of serious literature (for our purposes, "the book"), and publishing has been in a state of upheaval since I started in the business in the early '80s. And, while the digital revolution is clearly having a profound impact on global culture, I can't help but believe that the book will endure (I'm counting digital books as books here). Those of us who care—writers and readers—care passionately. And young people join our ranks every day. We'll have to become extinct before books do.

Since we've had the option readily available to us, we've been making all our books available as e-books as well. I haven't personally shifted over—I'm too much of a book-as-object fetishist—but I have nothing against people who read on e-readers. It does make it difficult to see what people are reading on the NYC subway, though, to my great regret.

JL: Clearly things have changed, and both authors and agents are more open to working with smaller publishers. How do you see this shift?

EG: I see this shift as a necessary, and even healthy, one. Small presses are more often motivated by their love for and commitment to what they publish rather than profit (though of course they need to find ways to survive). They tend to invest in their authors over the long haul rather than simply pay lip service to the idea as do the larger houses. And they are good at hand-selling their books, building a true community of readers. As larger houses take fewer risks on writers seen as quirky or noncommercial, more agents and authors are coming around to understanding that a dedicated small press may actually be able to serve them better.

JL: **Please tell us about your publishing house and what you look for in submissions.**

EG: We're a mission-driven, small independent press. Our mission is to publish literary and substantive fiction and nonfiction at the intersection of the arts and the sciences. We're having a great time redefining what that means with every title that we publish. Our goal is to promote science literacy in unaccustomed ways and offer new tools for thinking about our world.

JL: **Are all your submissions agented, or have you published any works without an agent? How do you find books?**

EG: Many of our authors have agents, but not all of them. We find our books through our relationships with writers and agents, but people cold-contact us, too. We also meet writers at conferences and meetings where book people gather.

JL: **What kinds of advances do you pay?**

EG: We pay an advance of $1,000 across the board, with no exceptions, against standard trade book royalties. Most of our books are published as paperback originals.

JL: **What rights do you typically acquire?**

EG: Our typical contract covers all publishing rights, but if an author has representation that has specific expertise in certain areas or territories, we'll negotiate.

JL: **Do you have to answer to anyone when you acquire a book or do a Profit and Loss statement?**

EG: We're lucky enough to have a very light structure that makes us responsible for our own acquisition decisions and their consequences—as long as we stay within our budget. Since most of our books are straight text and our publishing parameters are fairly similar, we don't do P&Ls for acquisition, but rather only for postpublication budgetary analysis.

JL: **Some authors are under the impression that if a book gets a small advance, the publisher will not promote the book. Tell us about how you promote books. Do you think there are any limitations for smaller presses in terms of what they can do for a book?**

EG: I've never put so much thought, energy, and resources into book promotion as I do now. We work with a publicity and marketing consultant, Molly Mikolowski, who's the best in the business. We follow up on all (reasonable) leads and expect our authors to be full collaborators in the marketing process. Authors have to be active self-promoters these days, no matter who their publisher is. We feel our money is much better spent on creative, flexible marketing, and publicity campaigns that will build word-of-mouth and longer-term interest. And, unlike larger houses that tend to focus their publicity and marketing efforts on the first trimester after publication, we're in it for the long haul to build a strong backlist that will sustain us into the future. That involves ongoing academic front- and backlist marketing as well.

Of course, we can't put thousands of dollars into advertising campaigns, but I've never met a publisher, commercial or otherwise, who believes that limited marketing budgets are well spent on advertising. So far, I can't say that we have a typical marketing budget—we invest in marketing when we see a sensible opportunity to do so.

JL: **Who is an ideal author for you?**

EG: I enjoy working with authors who want to be full participants in every aspect of the process and who are practical and realistic. I believe in sharing information and, where needed, educating authors about the publishing process so they know more or less what to expect.

JL: **You have had some remarkable successes, such as publishing Paul Harding's *Tinkers*, which, as you know, won the**

Pulitzer Prize. Did you ever imagine the book would do so well? Can you describe the entire process from acquisition to the book winning the prize to managing all the foreign sales and printing and promoting hundreds of thousands of books? How did your company rise to the incredible demands of this success?

EG: While I felt that *Tinkers* had literary prize potential because it's such a remarkable piece of writing (and it was nominated for other prizes before it won the Pulitzer), I would have had to have delusions of grandeur to have even contemplated the possibility of the Pulitzer. The book did very well for a first novel before the Pulitzer, but after the prize, it took off and has now sold over 450,000 copies. That's the power of the Pulitzer Prize for Fiction. Even if the book deserves it, we're incredibly lucky.

The book had fantastic support from passionate fans within the publishing community from the start, and they reached readers who spread the word. People fell in love with the writing. Devoted sales reps, independent booksellers, and reviewers all championed the book, eventually bringing it to the attention of the Pulitzer committee. And we were lucky to have Perseus, which owns our distributor Consortium, step forward and volunteer to front the costs of the post-Pulitzer reprints, which we couldn't have afforded otherwise. So it was an incredible network of supporters that helped make *Tinkers* a success and allowed us to benefit from that success.

JL: **What exactly changed when the author won the prize?**
EG: The prize changed the game for us entirely—it was the key to our survival, as we would have likely gone under otherwise. As a mission-driven nonprofit with very few titles under our belt, we had been (and still are) reliant on philanthropy. The market crash of 2008 caused some of our major donors to withdraw, and we were hanging on by a thread. I had even had some tough conversations with Paul Harding about the possibility of our having to close down before

his book was published. So the prize gave us a future and put us on the map. We're making our way back up to eight titles published per year, which I feel is just right for our size and staff capacity.

JL: **After a great success such as that, is it hard to then have the author move to a larger house? Do you think after all the money the author has made in royalties from your company, there would have been a way to keep the author with you? Do you see this as inevitable with small publishers?**

EG: If we are lucky enough to succeed with a book, I expect the author to consider all of his or her options for the next book. We're just too small to offer competitive advances (though we pay standard trade book royalties)—it could potentially bankrupt us and would be irresponsible on our part to try to play with the big guys. Most of our authors aren't independently wealthy, and given the chance, they're obliged to consider moving to a house that will pay them an advance that reflects their marketplace value. If a larger house can ramp up their success further, more power to them. We stand to benefit from that in a boost to sales of our book. When a book succeeds for us, our author will be fairly compensated through their earned royalties—as was Paul Harding.

JL: **You recently published a National Book Award finalist and the winner of the Sami Rohr Prize for Jewish Literature. What do you think is contributing to this great success other than your obvious great eye? What is your editorial process?**

EG: Our vision, our mission, and our passion for good writing drive our editorial process. All I can say is that it is immensely gratifying to me that we've been recognized by these honors for publishing what we love and believe in.

JL: **How do you see the future of your press and smaller presses in general? What are the challenges?**

EG: I see a rich future for the small, independent press world and couldn't be happier to be a part of it. The greatest challenge that we all face, if we're lucky enough to survive the long odds, is to preserve our creative energy and focus.

Erika Goldman is publisher and editorial director of Bellevue Literary Press (BLP), an independent nonprofit book press. Located within the NYU School of Medicine, BLP publishes literary and authoritative fiction and nonfiction at the nexus of the arts and the sciences. Since its first small list appeared in 2007, it has received several major literary prizes: The Sojourn *by Andrew Krivak was a 2011 finalist for the National Book Award in fiction and winner of the first annual Chautauqua Prize,* The Jump Artist *by Austin Ratner was 2011 winner of the Sami Rohr Prize for Jewish Literature, and* The New York Times *bestseller* Tinkers *by Paul Harding was awarded the 2010 Pulitzer Prize for fiction and the PEN/Robert Bingham Fellowship for Writers.*

The field of literature for young readers has been exploding since the great success of Harry Potter. *We all have also seen grown-ups reading the blockbuster YA series and sneaking in to* The Hunger Games. *The Young Adult literature accounts for a large percent of the business done in the industry. We will hear from* CAITLYN DLOUHY, *the editorial director of Atheneum/ Simon & Schuster,* HOWARD REEVES, *an editor-at-large of picture books and other books for young readers, and the former publisher of Abrams. We will also share an interview with* SHARYN NOVEMBER, *a top editor of science fiction and fantasy.*

Children: The Toughest Audience You'll Ever Love (to Write for)

by Caitlyn M. Dlouhy, Atheneum Books for Young Readers, Simon and Schuster Publishers

Stop and consider for a minute—when you think of the books that truly meant something to you, the ones you think of first when someone asks you about an important book in your life, chances are you are going to remember something you read as a child or a teen. When little kids love a picture book, they want it read over and over again. There's something they're connecting with—the rhythm, the personality of a character (be it a dog or a conniving duck or a dinosaur or another kid), or the way something scary is handled (there's a reason there are so many spooky-thing-lurking-under-the-bed books)—or they love dipping safely into another world. Parents can present a preschooler with pretty much any book and coax the child to read it with them *once*, but the over-and-over factor is pretty much dictated by the child. It's been said that if you have an animated enough voice, a kid will listen to the first page of the phone book being read, but they're not going to want the second!

When those kids get older, they're still looking for something to connect with—the characters, a type of story, a world other than their own—where characters are having to contend with similar issues or utterly unexpected situations. The big difference is that middle-graders and teens (that is, readers between the ages of eight to eighteen) have a lot more say in what they read. They might reread a book a few times, but more often than not, when they really like a book, they want a similar experience in the next book. There's a reason why series and trilogies are so popular. And when they absolutely adore a book, that's a book that might become the precise book they think of when they stop and consider for a minute, twenty or forty years later, which books they best remember. It is also usually the one they most needed at the time when they read it, a book that helped them make a little bit more sense of a world that didn't quite make sense, that reminded them there were others experiencing similar challenges, and that let them escape for a while when things seemed unbearable.

For me, those books would be *The Outsiders* and *A Separate Peace*. When I was younger, all of my friends were reading Judy Blume novels, but I was one of those kids who was easily embarrassed, and there was no way in heck I was going to walk around with *Are You There God? It's Me, Margaret* (which, I must admit, I can't wait to have my own daughter read). Nope, I'd much rather hang with Sodapop and Ponyboy and worry like mad about them (and crush on Ponyboy) and wish my life in the tiny town I grew up in were half as exciting. But you know what? It *was* exciting when I was reading a book like that. *A Separate Peace* was one I read and reread, trying to figure out why, *why* Gene would shake that branch, why, why, why, and then, with each read, hoping against hope that maybe this time Finny wouldn't die, even though, of course, I knew he would. As relationships grew more complex during my high school years, I was fascinated by the complex dynamics between people in books—for instance, how certain characters could be such good friends, yet that layer of jealousy never went away. And the stories have lingered—a part of my DNA—for decades now.

Stories matter. Stories can make massive differences in kids' lives. The letters kids write to authors are jaw-dropping. One boy wrote to Sharon Draper that he wished she would adopt him because he would help her take care of Melody (the little girl with cerebral palsy in Sharon Draper's *Out of My Mind*) and make sure she was okay. Another wrote to Phyllis Reynolds Naylor to say she'd never have let anyone know her stepfather was sexually abusing her until she read about a similar situation in one of the Alice books and realized it was okay to tell, and that she should and had to tell. Kids read Jack Gantos's Joey Pigza novels and think, there's a hyper kid just like me and he's okay! Books for tweens and teens can be a blast to read—exciting, harrowing, informative—just like books for adults are, but there's always the potential for something more, to *matter* at a whole other level.

Children's book authors used to be considered the second cousins of the literary world. The response to an author saying "I write for children/teens" was often "Oh, how nice." It was considered easier, simpler. Folks who didn't have the chops to write for adults wrote for kids. (Curiously, people who don't know much about publishing wonder when I'll be "promoted" up so that I can work on adult novels.) Whether it's the popularity of books like the Harry Potter series, *Twilight*, or *The Hunger Games* that has made adults reading kids' books more acceptable; or the fact that the tween/teen market is the fastest growing literary marketplace; or that "adult" writers realize how badly they've underestimated children's book writers and finally recognize them for being every bit as challenging, skilled, vibrant, or a combination of all of this plus some stardust; or because the advances have gotten better—it certainly seems as if there have never been more "adult" writers now wanting to write for kids. Interestingly, there are also a lot more agents who either specialize in representing children's authors and illustrators, or agents who once solely represented adult authors who are now taking on writers for children.

There's no tougher audience, I'll tell you that much. Most tweens/teens are not going to put up with anything that doesn't grab their interest from the get-go. They smell a message from a mile away (so please check all didacticism at the door). And most of all, they don't want stories told from an adult lens. One of the notes I write most often as I'm line-editing a manuscript is "Authorial! Please re-cast." A great writer for kids *has* to be able to tap into the voice at the age of the audience. The perspective has to stay age appropriate…a twelve-year-old character isn't going to be able to philosophize about the death of his dog the way a thirty-year-old would…and if you thread in a thirty-year-old's philosophizing into a novel for twelve-year-olds, the reader just isn't going to buy it, and they are going to put that novel right on down. You have a whole different level of responsibility when you write for a younger audience; not to hyper-bolize, but what they read can affect who they become. Additionally, you have to be able to create just as compelling a plot as in any adult novel, equally intriguing characters, and a style that will appeal to an audience who just isn't going to keep going another fifty pages "in case it gets better." And, generally, all of this has to be accomplished in usually a much shorter page count (*Harry Potter* notwithstanding). If an adult novel is poetry, a kids' book is a haiku.

There are differences in editing as well, and most children's book editors do so with an absolute sense of who their audience is—we become the kid who will be reading it and have our bull★★★t radar on at all times. For me, voice is deeply important. I can help a lot with plot, with character, but I can't infuse a voice into a manu-script without one—that's something that is uniquely the author's. I know that if an author can create a great voice for one character, he can do it for another. I once had an author on her third or fourth revision, and one character just wasn't singing. The others were daz-zling, but this poor character felt straight out of Hollywood casting and was keeping the novel from feeling pitch perfect. I couldn't come up with a voice for the character, but I could make suggestions as to how the author could think about the character differently. One suggestion led to the author making a seemingly small change, but it turned into a remarkably powerful one—she changed the color of the character's hair. The character had been a blue-eyed blonde, and the author had gotten mired in the clichés attached to blue-eyed blondes. But the minute she made that character a redhead, out came this utterly unexpected but true-blue voice, and suddenly the entire manuscript was humming.

A common sticky area for adults who write for children for the first time also has to do with voice—the adult voice. The adult voice sometimes creeps in, either leaving a young character far wiser than her years and thus not entirely believable, or having an adult character figuring out solutions for the problems the young main character faces rather than letting the young character work through them herself.

A children's book editor usually is, and should be, bloody demanding. Most are looking for the richest characters, most compelling stories (whether fiction or nonfiction…nonfiction is, after all, a story, just not made up), and the most powerful writing. Funny. Sly. Fantasy. Historical. Futuristic. Complex. Spare. Angry. Heartwrenching. Verse. Edgy.

So you still think you wanna write for kids? Have you read any kids' books lately? Middle-grade novels? Teen novels? Get reading. First of all, you're going to have a blast. Second of all, it will help you see the differences between the writing geared toward adults and the writing aimed at kids. *Jim the Boy* is about a boy but written for adults. *M.C. Higgins, the Great* is also about a boy, but it is written specifically for kids. The difference is the perspective. In *Jim the Boy*, the interpretations are adult, bestowed upon Jim in a way that Jim could never have actually interpreted them at that age. In *M.C. Higgins*, you get raw, honest, kid reactions. Take a look at how *The Lovely Bones* (adult) is handled compared with *What Jamie Saw* (teen), or *Snow Falling on Cedars* compared with *Kira-Kira* or *Hatchet* vs. *Into the Woods*. Read! Read *Holes* and *Moves Make the Man*. *Out of the Dust*, *Love That Dog*. *Dark Dude*; *Chicken Boy*; *Bud, Not Buddy*. *Sarah, Plain and Tall*; and *Catherine, Called Birdy*. *Shooting the Moon*, *Walk Two Moons*, *Moon Over Manifest*. *Copper Sun*, *Chains*, *The Grand Plan to Fix Everything*. *Leonardo's Shadow*, *The Tale of Despereaux*. *The Graveyard Book*, *Looking for Alaska*, *Where Things Come Back*, *The Underneath*. *Higher Power of Lucky*, *Shooting Star*. *Inexcusable*, *Thirteen Reasons Why*,

Witchlanders, The Watcher, etc. If you want to write about a thirteen-year-old, read books geared toward thirteen-year-olds. What you'll also see is that you can write about anything. *No* subject is off-limits. It's all about presentation—being respectful of your audience, leaving the salacious parked by the door next to the didactic.

So you've read a slew of kids' novels—probably more than you thought you would because they're pretty fantastic, right? And you've gone on to write your manuscript. And you've reworked it again and again. And you're ready to—no, not put it in a drawer, hoping that an eager children's book editor will come aknockin' looking for a manuscript they can publish, but send it on to an agent, or, if you can find one (and there are still a few of us about), directly to an editor. Be advised, however, that an editor who still is open to receiving "slush" might find several thousand submissions coming in each year; it can take quite a while to get back to you! While a majority of the projects we take on come via agents, we also find manuscripts through writers' conferences and recommendations from writers who we are already publishing.

Once you have completed your research and have started writing, the next step is to think about what you're going to show an editor/agent. If you're writing fiction, know that it's very rare that a middle-grade/YA editor will take on a new author based on just a few chapters. It's easy to make a synopsis sound stellar, to compare your work to John Green's or Laurie Halse Anderson's, but to write the whole piece so that it truly is stellar and worthy of the comparisons is a whole other talent, and precisely the talent for which we editors are ever hunting. For nonfiction, however, a solid outline and several chapters could suffice.

Then, look for agents who actually focus on children's titles or who have a good track record with a few great children's writers. The good ones are going to know the best editors for your particular manuscript. Try to get a sense of what different editors publish. Oftentimes, an editor is mentioned in a book's acknowledgments. If you think a particular book is in the same range as yours, check out who that editor is.

We get a ton of submissions. Most *aren't* the stuff from which editors' dreams are made. We read a lot. We read a lot of not-so-good stuff. We get cranky. So, when something's even hinting at outstanding, we take notice. Some editors want a manuscript to be in close-to-publishable shape. Others (me being one of them) respond to the voice, to what the story could be based on the promise of what's already there. Either way, if it's already outstanding or shows every promise of reaching outstanding, we'll likely make an offer. Sometimes it's an offer of notes—the manuscript isn't quite publishable, but if you're willing to do XYZ, I can get a sense of whether or not you are someone who can rewrite, and I will be more certain that you're capable of improving your piece. Other times, it's an actual offer, as in an offer for a book contract.

There's a hazy area in between the reading and the offer (either kind) that takes place in most publishing houses. It's called the acquisition meeting, and that's where, more often than not, an editor brings a manuscript so that other folks in the publishing house can also read it. Those other folks could be publishers, sales reps, publicists, library/education marketing folk, designers—all, some, or one, but usually at least a few. The enamored-of-a-manuscript editor will pitch it to the acquisition team, letting them know all the brilliant reasons why this brilliant project should be acquired. Then everyone weighs in. Publicity will have thoughts on unique ways they can promote the book. The library/ed managers will remind everyone that a book about the underground railway, for example, will be a perfect tie-in for middle school curriculum. A sales rep might say the indies (independent bookstores) will love this or that B&N will pass (not necessarily the kiss of death, by the way). The publisher might also let the editor know, for instance, that another house is also publishing a novel about a girl who is in a car accident and who can no longer tell when she's awake and when she's in a dream. Sometimes everyone loves the manuscript. Sometimes no one gets it. Sometimes it's a mix. But it's not "acquiring by committee"—it's more that it's important for an editor to have a sense of how the project could be received in house because the ultimate hope of any editor is that every new book and author she brings in will be enthusiastically supported by her colleagues.

It's usually at these meetings where the advance (the amount the author would be paid up front, before the book is published, which would be earned out against the royalties the author will receive once the book starts selling) is determined. There is no cap on the amount of the advance offered. Once your advance "earns out," that's when—happy day! —you'll start receiving royalty checks. The advance is, in fact, an advance against royalties. We provide the publishers with a profit-and-loss statement in which we make our best guess as to how the book will do in the first year of sales and try to give an advance that would equal the royalties that first year would bring the author. Sometimes we're right on the money (pun intended), sometimes we're off . . . but if the book doesn't sell as well as we'd predicted, the author never has to return any of the advance. However, if the book sells better than expected, then the author will start receiving royalty checks earlier (refer to the aforementioned "happy day!"). If the book doesn't sell as well as expected, it's likely that if the author had received a hefty advance for that book, he will have to lower his expectations for the advance on his next book.

Once the editor's desired book project is given the green light, then the editor gets to make one of her favorite calls—to the agent and the author to tell them that we love their manuscript, and we're going to make an offer. If I love a manuscript but know it's going to need a tremendous amount of revision, I will let the agent and author know that immediately, just to ensure that they're on board and willing to do the work that's needed. The offer would include the advance (usually paid in halves, though sometimes in thirds or other combinations—the first disbursal occurring on signing the contract and the second on turning in the final edited manuscript), royalty, and subsidiary rights for all the formats we would like to publish the book in, including hardcover, paperback, e-book, book clubs, and audio.

Once everyone finishes happy dancing, the editor puts together the request for a contract paperwork (the result is a 15–20 page contract—brace yourself!), while the author (I assume!) is letting everyone know he or she is about to be published. Mind you, that "about to be published" phase usually takes longer than an author anticipates because once the contract terms are agreed upon, then the editor will read the manuscript again and pull together notes from which the author can revise the text. Editorial letters can run from a few pages to a dozen pages long, all depending on what type of work the manuscript needs. I have yet to have a manuscript come in that didn't need some revision, and most need a good deal. Remember those writing professors who've told you that rewriting is as important as writing? Yep, true! You'll revise. The editor will read. The editor will likely read a second time. The editor will likely need to write a second editorial letter. Might do some line editing as well. The author might be thrilled for the chance to make the manuscript even stronger. Alternatively, the author might feel annoyed (or curse or rant or throw objects at a picture of the editor). Hard as it might be, you'll achieve your best work if you can leave your ego at the door, at least in part. Editors are making suggestions in order to help you bring out the best in your story; we certainly don't want to create extra work for ourselves or for you. But our commitment is in large part to our readers—we want the best for them and have a pretty good sense (okay, oftentimes a really good sense) of when your story can be even better than it already is. Eventually, most authors calm down and realize, yeah, that character really does sound like a forty-year-old man rather than a fifteen-year-old teen, and they revise again. The editor will read again. Chances are the manuscript will be in pretty darned good shape at this point, so the editor will likely do a heavy line edit this go-around. (If the revision doesn't fall into the "chances are" category, then yep, you guessed it, another editorial letter will come.) After that, usually the manuscript will be ready to turn in to the copyediting department. The author and editor get several weeks off (from the manuscript) for good editorial behavior while the copyeditors have at it, and the author gets the second half of her advance.

Once the manuscript is back from copyediting, both the editor and author go over the copyeditor's comments. Copyeditors save our tails . . . that's all I'm saying about copyeditors. Then the book is given to a designer to set the pages, and upon the first set of those (called first-pass galleys) is the last time we should be making any wholesale changes to the manuscript—somehow you see things differently when you read the pages set in type as "real" pages. And by now it could already have been a year, or three years, after you signed that contract, all depending on how much work the manuscript needed—but the good news is that by this point you are really close to having your book published.

And when it does publish, your book could just be that remarkable one that some kid, somewhere, years later, will say was the book he or she remembered best from when he or she was a kid.

Caitlyn Dlouhy is the VP/editorial director of Atheneum Books for Young Readers, an imprint of Simon & Schuster Publishers. An MFA program in Fiction Writing also taught her a lot about editing, and she publishes both picture books and novels. Just a few of the novels she's had the great pleasure of editing include the Newbery Medal–winning and # 1 New York Times *bestselling* Kira-Kira *by Cynthia Kadohata; the National Book Award Nominee and Newbery Honor Book* The Underneath *by Kathi Appelt; Edgar Award-winner* Dovey Coe *by Frances O'Roark Dowell; Michael L. Printz-honoree* Nothing *by Janne Teller; Coretta Scott King Author Award-winner* Copper Sun *by Sharon Draper, and PEN Literary Award– winning* Weedflower, *also by Cynthia Kadohata.*

Children's Picture Books: The Format Changes but the Process Remains the Same

by Howard W. Reeves, Abrams Books for Young Readers and Amulet Books

Before this book is even published, the picture book as we know it may be obsolete. It will be electronic rather than printed on paper. Some people propose that both the electronic version and the traditional version (printed on paper and bound) will live side by side, just as audio books live alongside the printed book. But will the picture book go the way of the recorded album/CD: entertainment that is easily downloaded from a source, for a fee, and kept electronically and viewed on demand? "It's not really an either/or conversation for me, but rather, it's about which direction, print or digital (or both) is right for each title," said Junko Yokota, director of the Center for Teaching Through Children's Books.[1]

Picture books are very often read at nap time or bedtime, when parents/caregivers want a child to nestle down, relax, and nod off. Electronic books with bells and whistles—icons to click on, sounds

---

[1]Habash, Gabe. "TOC 2012: Children's Books Must Exist in Digital and Print." Publishers Weekly. February 14, 2012. http://www.publishersweekly.com/pw/by-topic/childrens/childrens-industry-news/article/50631-toc-2012-children-s-books-must-exist-in-digital-and-print.html

to be heard, additional material such as a short animation or a puzzle to solve—stimulate the mind and keep the brain buzzing. Parents understand that holding a plastic device in one's hands that not only contains electronic books, but music, games, and other eye-opening media will not help a child prepare for sleep. A traditional bound book with text and printed pictures, where the only stimulation is tactile—the turning of pages—is relaxing, calming, and sleepworthy.[2] Granted, many picture books have escalating plots and riveting climaxes, but just as many are purposely published as bedtime fodder.

So what does the children's picture book market look like today? There are electronic books, printed hardcover and paperback books as well as audio books. There are brick-and-mortar bookstores (both independent stores as well as national chains) and stores that are not book-centric but sell books (such as department stores, museum stores, gift stores, stationery stores, and the like). There are Internet stores. And, of course, there are lending libraries. Along with these, children's books also are sold at book fairs—usually within schools where the child chooses what he or she wishes to buy—and chances are your child knows Scholastic fairs and book clubs, where children and their teachers/parents/caregivers choose books from a catalogue. As certain stores close up shop, others move in to fill their niche. Also, many school systems or teachers within a system incorporate trade children's books into their curricula to give a more well-rounded, honest, and appealing perspective to world and historical events than textbooks often offer. Therefore, as we move further into the twenty-first century, the status of picture books and children's books appears to be relatively secure.

There are definitely places to buy or borrow books in more than one format, but how do these books come to be? No matter the format, acquisition by a publisher is relatively similar. Book concepts may come about in several ways, but primarily an editor receives

---

[2] Bosma, Julie, and Matt Richtell. "For Their Children, Many E-Book Fans Insist on Paper." The New York Times. November 21, 2011. http://www.nytimes.com/2011/11/21/business/for-their-children-many-e-book-readers-insist-on-paper.html

submissions from agents as well as solicited material from established authors, friends of these authors, and other noted folk; or an editor reviews material in the company slush pile (the very large collection of unsolicited manuscripts that arrive at a publisher's office each day); or an editor has an idea for a book and commissions an author and/ or illustrator to work on the project.

Editors sign up books for different reasons, usually based on the commercial appeal of a subject or author, or personal interest. For instance, an editor may wish to sign up a project based on the status of the author. Perhaps he or she is a well-known celebrity (such as recent books by Madonna or Jerry Seinfeld) or a successful writer of adult literature (like Jan Karon or John Irving) or an established children's book author who is published by another house. An editor's own interests also play a role. I like history and nonfiction; therefore, I publish a lot of picture books about artists, like Andy Warhol, or pirates, such as Jean Lafitte. I also have edited books about civil rights, the revolutionary war, and dinosaurs. At the same time, I love picture books that offer humor or have a very exciting twist or an innovative art style or design. A successful book is typically one about which an editor is passionate and which he or she can get the sales and marketing departments excited about.

Editors read a great deal: stacks and stacks of manuscripts. Picture book (or storybook) manuscripts are not as intimidating as long nonfiction or novels since they should only be a few pages long. Printed picture books are usually thirty-two, forty, or forty-eight pages in length, so the manuscripts run from a page or two (double-spaced) to perhaps five or six pages, depending on the depth of the story. Nonfiction picture books of the same printed page length have manuscripts that tend to be longer as they often include captions, a time line, or other back matter such as bibliographies and an author's note. When they are printed, these nonfiction picture books may also be longer than storybooks—often having as many as fifty-six or sixty-four (or more) pages—so their manuscripts may be as long as twenty to twenty-five pages. Of course, these are all approximations; every manuscript is different.

When preparing a manuscript to submit to an editor, please don't format or design the manuscript, add artwork, or set the text off in decorative boxes—instead of helping the editor, you are creating more work for him or her. For one thing, it is often difficult to download these large files. And, eventually, if the manuscript is contracted, the editor has to unformat it before it is given to the designer. Typically the artwork is not included in storybooks or fiction picture books when a manuscript is submitted for consideration; editors and art directors contract an illustrator later in the process for the work. In the case of nonfiction books, the artwork may be archival art or reproductions and these likewise will be obtained after the manuscript is contracted. However, for nonfiction, you may wish to supply a sampling of the type of images you imagine being used to illustrate the book.

When I am looking for new material, sometimes the subject immediately says "not for me," such as self-help books or books that deal with problems or disabilities. Other times, I can read a few lines and find that the story just doesn't pull me in (and there aren't that many lines to do the job in a picture book!). Other times, I read the whole thing, know the project isn't for me, but know someone in the house who likes the genre or theme, and I pass the project on to him or her. Or I read the manuscript, love it, and wish to sign it up. Many projects are brought to an editorial meeting to be discussed and to get a consensus. This is particularly helpful when I am on the fence about a project and need other points of view. At an editorial meeting, we discuss the literary merits of the work along with why we think the project has commercial appeal.

Most fiction (novels) these days comes from agents. The manuscripts are very long, usually 200-plus pages, so an agent helps an editor by being the first reader. Agents learn your tastes and send you manuscripts they believe will be of interest. Picture book manuscripts often come from agents, but often new authors can still be discovered in the slush pile. As previously noted, picture book manuscripts are relatively brief, so it is easier to read many in one sitting and be able to green-light or red-light a book after reading just a few sentences or paragraphs. Even though this means I can read more proposals, I still find most of my nonfiction manuscripts via authors who send them to me directly (some have agents, many do not) or by commissioning the work myself. If I have an idea or know of an upcoming event or anniversary, I often call authors to ask if they are interested in writing on the subject. At the larger houses, there seems to be less interest in reading unsolicited materials. They tend to lean more toward the recommendations of agents.

Once I have decided I wish to acquire a project, I have to get it approved, first by the publisher and then at an acquisitions meeting (we call ours "pub board," i.e., "publishing board"), where it is discussed by a committee that includes various people from different departments: sales and marketing, the publisher, a few editors, production, and the editor presenting the project. The focus is primarily on the commercial appeal and sales potential of the project. Editors prepare a profit and loss form (P&L) that gives all the project's production information (the trim size, page count, number of color images, and special effects, such as glitter on the cover or lift-the-flap devices in the interior) along with the unit cost to print and bind the book, the proposed retail price, the proposed first print run, and anything else relevant to the project. Through experience and/or looking at comparable titles already published by the company or by another company, editors can come up with a retail price and propose a print quantity. Not surprisingly, how well an editor believes a project can perform is often more ambitious than what the sales and marketing people believe it can do. There is a lot of discussion, and often editors are sent away to redo the P&L with different specifications. Just as often, the pub board committee may decide the project simply is not financially feasible and the project dies on the table.

When a book is given the green light by the pub board, then the editor contacts the author/illustrator or his or her agent or other representative to make an offer and negotiate terms. In the case of picture books, I often acquire a manuscript written by one person and then contract illustrations to be created by another. The author may suggest an artist or style but may not be aware of certain publishing trends or problems, or how a particular artist works (e.g., is he or she often late delivering material), which will have a great deal of impact on the final book and its potential market. Typically, I will contract an illustrator, and often the author and illustrator will never meet or speak to each other. I want to give the illustrator as much freedom as possible to create the images, so I find it best not to have an author dictate what goes on each page or what the exact setting is or whether the characters are boys or girls or humans or animals, etc. However, I always share the sketches and final art with the author, and ask for their feedback.

I love books that stimulate the mind and can enthrall a child. Picture books can be entertaining for adults, but if the story or humor or experiences are not those that a child can understand, then the book has missed its mark. Picture books are primarily for readers four to eight years old, so they have to reflect the world that age group understands. These children don't worry about mortgages or retirement; they are not nostalgic nor do they reminisce; they aren't dating, having dinner parties, or falling in love. They do play house and dress up. They do have tea parties. They have backyard adventures. And they love their teddy bear and their mommy and daddy—children this age are still very fond of their parents and have not separated yet from them. A successful picture book entertains the adult reader as much as the child (because there is nothing worse than reading an incredibly dull book to a child), but it never loses sight of the child.

When I edit a picture book, I always read the manuscript aloud. Picture books are read aloud to young children, and sometimes older children also use them to practice reading. So when I edit such a book, I read aloud because then I can hear the words as a child would and immediately notice when the language is jarring or awkward.

Interestingly enough, what looks good in print often sounds bad when spoken. Conversely, alliteration, rhyme, and silly-sounding words all work together to create a more riveting read, so writers, too, should read their manuscripts aloud.

The production process is a group project: author, illustrator, designer, copyeditor, and editor. Everyone plays a part, and there is a lot of going back and forth as the book goes through each stage: manuscript, sketches, final artwork, designed pages, color printed proofs, and the final book. There is also jacket copy to write and the cover image of the book to discuss. The jacket image is typically the only "advertisement" a book receives. You don't see many billboards for books or books advertised on television or in magazines because it is very costly. Only authors who generate a great deal of revenue warrant such expense, such as Jeff Kinney, Stephen King, or J.K. Rowling. So publishers work to make sure the reviewers will write about the book or that "talkers" will blog about the book. You also hope a bookstore will show the book face out and not spine out, but in-store real estate is costly, so few are shown this way. Therefore, the cover is discussed by the artist, designer, and editor, as well as by sales and marketing. Everyone needs to be happy with it so the cover has the very best chance of getting noticed when out in the world by itself. However, I always ensure that the spines of the picture books I edit have more than just text (author/title/imprint), such as a tiny piece of art or a beautiful design. I call this "spine identification." When a consumer runs his or her finger along the spines of books on a shelf, a little fairy or elephant or puppy may entice the consumer to pull the book out and look at it. That is more than half the battle: getting the consumers to hold the book in their hands and turn pages. If you can get them hooked, they will very likely buy it.

Whether picture books are printed on paper or offered electronically, the process of acquiring, creating, and distributing the book does not change that much. Editors still have to acquire and create content and make the book fit the needs of the retail market, such as the proper format for the electronic device (currently they are all different) or the proper dimensions and specs for the bound copy. And just like they don't have to format their own manuscripts to submit them to editors, writers also don't have to worry about formatting them for e-books since it is done by the publisher. Of course, publishers and retailers all want the book to sell well. But the overriding hope of all editors is that the picture book will appeal to children and get them excited about reading, as well as open their minds to worlds beyond themselves and their own imaginations.

Howard W. Reeves is editor-at-large at Abrams Books for Young Readers and Amulet Books. He was formerly founding editor and publisher of both imprints. Reeves was also a founding editor of the Walt Disney Publishing Group, primarily for the Hyperion Books for Young Readers imprint. He is on the faculty of the School of Visual Arts MFA Design program and lives in New Jersey.

Sci-fi/Fantasy, Children's, and Young Adult Books

An Interview with Sharyn November, Viking Children's Books and Firebird

JL: **You are an expert in the field of fantasy and science fiction and have been at Firebird and Viking for years. Tell us about the state of the genre and why you love it.**

SN: It has been fascinating watching children's and young adult (YA) fantasy explode over the past fifteen years or so, starting with *Harry Potter* and continuing with *Twilight* and *The Hunger Games*—to mention three touchstone series, each of which sparked an explosion in its respective genre. It's almost as if the genre has evolved with the age of its characters—from school stories to adolescent romance to tales of independence in the world.

What I love is how many new voices and stories there are. There are writers and characters of color, new twists on old themes (fairy-tale retellings, steampunk, magical realism, angels and demons, vampires, werewolves, and urban fantasy), and a bridging of the gap between children's and YA literature and that of (and for) adults. We see this in the writers—and the readers. Reading YA fiction has become an adult pleasure, too.

Over the past few years, science fiction has entered the mix, starting with dystopian and postapocalyptic settings. It has expanded to include hard science fiction, characterized by rigorous attention to scientific details or accurately depicting worlds that more advanced technology may someday make possible. These stories are often set in space, on other planets, or in the online and/or gaming world. I am always surprised and delighted at the evolution of science fiction and fantasy.

JL: **What do you look for in a submission?**

SN: I love manuscripts that surprise me—that take off the top of my head (to paraphrase Emily Dickinson on poetry). A strong voice, an unexpected take on a familiar subject, an unusual subject, a sense of humor, a dead-on instinct for story. I look for a writer I would read for pleasure.

JL: **What were your last three acquisitions?**

SN: I've really enjoyed stepping out of my comfort zone with Gordon McAlpine's *The Misadventures of Edgar and Allan Poe*, a middle grade illustrated series about the great-great-great-great-grand-nephews of Edgar Allan Poe. It's witty and fast paced and layered with literary allusions (although you don't have to know the references to get the jokes, which allows it to speak to both children and adults). I call it "smart, funny fiction for smart, funny tweens."

I am over the moon about *Althea & Oliver*—a first YA by Cristina Moracho, who recently got her MFA. It can best be described as *The Time Traveler's Wife* meets *Weetzie Bat* à la Sarah Dessen. Her writing is just gorgeous, and she flirts with magical realism without making a commitment (to take the analogy all the way).

Finally, I've just signed up a new novel by Nnedi Okorafor. We published her *Akata Witch* last year—it's a YA fantasy set in Nigeria with an entirely unique set of tropes and parameters, and it has just been named an Andre Norton Award finalist. Nnedi won the 2011 World Fantasy Award for her first adult novel, *Who Fears Death*. She has the most remarkable imagination.

JL: **How do you acquire a book? Take us through your editorial process.**

SN: It's probably easiest if I give you a list of the steps:

1. Read a manuscript I love.

2. Get second reads to confirm that others love it, too—my assistant, my teenage readers, folks from sales and marketing. In-house support is vital.

3. If they agree with me, I give it to my boss so she can read it. Assuming she likes it, I run a profit and loss statement based on a variety of advances, discuss it with the agent, and talk with the author to make sure that we click (the editorial process is alchemical). Sometimes we need to come up with a marketing plan or another kind of promotional commitment. This process can take anywhere from one week to several months, depending upon the project (the author may need to do a revision), people's schedules, and so on.

JL: **Are there other genres you like to publish besides fantasy and science fiction?**

SN: Of course! Contemporary middle grade and YA, historical fiction that feels as if one is *right there* (like Ellen Klages's *The Green Glass Sea*), and the occasional nonfiction book.

JL: **What percentage of your authors are agented? How do you find your authors?**

SN: I find authors in a variety of ways—sometimes through agents, from referrals through other authors, by reading widely (books, online work, journals, anthologies, chapbooks—you name it—I'm an omnivore), or by approaching someone whose work I've loved in other genres. And, of course, authors approach me. I would say that 90 percent of my authors are agented.

JL: **Is it important to you that an author has an MFA?**

SN: Absolutely not. It's nice to know that someone has made that commitment to his or her writing, but it's not a prerequisite. You would be surprised to learn how few children's and YA authors have MFAs.

JL: **Do you find that some of your authors have previously written for adults and what, if anything, do they have to concentrate on, change, or adjust to make the shift?**

SN: Many, if not most of them, have—Elizabeth Hand, Charles de Lint, Nancy Kress, Nina Kiriki Hoffman, Kelly Link, Pat Murphy, Ellen Klages (and that's just the beginning of the list). In every case, these authors' adult work already had appeal to younger readers and/or remarkably accurate teenage/child characters. Appealing to that audience requires a shift: more immediate action and narration, a closer focus on the main character (because, of course, we are seeing everything through the protagonist's eyes, and that protagonist now has a less experienced perspective—and cares less about an adult perspective), and away from any hint of condescension toward the audience. What surprises adult authors, I think, is how *little* they need to change their style. There are fewer taboos nowadays, and readers can handle a wide range of stylistic challenges. Think of what *you* read as a teenager.

JL: **Who are your favorite authors?**

SN: I always consider this a trick question, so I'll answer a varation on the theme: Who are my favorite writers *now*? Diana Wynne Jones, Randall Jarrell, Laurie Colwin, Lloyd Alexander, Nancy Farmer, Ursula K. Le Guin, Garth Nix, Tamora Pierce, Karen Hesse, Paula Fox, and just about every writer with whom I've worked.

JL: **Is there a fantasy (no pun intended) project that you would like to do?**

SN: The one that all editors would like to do is: find a book that is the perfect balance between literary and commercial that gets multiple starred reviews, wins awards, and makes *The New York Times* bestseller list. (And transforms into a gorgeous interactive e-book. And yes, that is a joke!) My dream project . . . Well, I want to hear a story that I'll never forget. Because story is at the bottom of it all.

Sharyn November is a senior editor at Viking Children's Books and the editorial director of Firebird. She is a two-time World Fantasy Award finalist for her editorial work, and Firebirds Rising, *her second anthology for the imprint, was also a World Fantasy Award finalist. She lives outside of New York City, and her website is www.sharyn.org. She is always looking for new stories and storytellers.*

When the economy began failing, many terrific editors lost their jobs and became agents or independent editors. Of course, there have always been outside editors, but their numbers have increased in recent years. Some are part of groups and market themselves as such; some groups put out newsletters and visit agents to drum up business. Many refer work to other independent editors if the work is not right for them. Some have groups and newsletters. They all have their own rates, so be sure to ask them up front what kind of work they think is needed on your proposal or manuscript and how much it will cost. If you already have an agent, you can ask your agent about the editor and the fees. The demand and abundance of editors has also gone up because the publishers are so risk-averse, and all works have to be very polished when they come in. The editors are also often under intense pressure and don't have as much time to edit. Many of these editors have websites.

Now we meet with a newly independent editor who also worked in house at Random House.

A New Chapter

by Judy Sternlight, Independent Editor

I didn't start off in book publishing. After graduating from Brown University, I pursued a career in theater and communications. I worked several jobs to stay afloat in New York City, including corporate communications, proofreading, acting gigs, freelance writing, and teaching and performing with Some Assembly Required, my improvisational theater company. All of these jobs, and the experience of managing a freelance career, gave me skills that I would one day rely on as a book editor. And the fact that I was a voracious reader would also prove helpful down the road when I had to make decisions on which books readers might be hungry for.

Oddly enough, my background in improvisational theater has been especially useful. Spontaneous performances (without a rehearsed script) teach you how to hold an audience's interest with high-stakes situations, strong characters and relationships, emotional truth, good timing, dynamic pacing, and satisfying endings. Improv is based on teamwork, intuitive thinking, and an eagerness to follow other creative minds to unfamiliar places, all of which apply to publishing.

Teaching theatrical technique to actors was also great practice for working with writers. The editors I most admire use positive reinforcement, just as my theater company did. Performers and authors are inclined to relax and improve more rapidly when you point out some things that are already working before you tackle what needs to be strengthened next. And, of course, presenting books at launch and sales meetings—the editor's best opportunity to get the whole publishing group excited about upcoming titles—is basically a performance. I loved it when there was heckling to respond to, or at least some provocative questions to answer, because it woke up the room and made everyone listen.

ENTERING THE WORLD OF PUBLISHING

I got my first publishing job through a lucky break. Ready for a career change, I took a temp job for a taste of this mysterious and intimidating world. I spent several weeks in the sales department at Random House and was impressed by the intelligence, good humor, and passion of the people I found there. I was also blown away by the free books (which are sadly less abundant these days, thanks to the economic downturn). At that time, I was moderating a book club through my alumni association and David Ebershoff, the head of the Modern Library imprint at Random House, had agreed to come and talk to us about his first novel, *The Danish Girl*. When I told him I was hoping to find a job in editorial, he invited me to interview for an entry-level position. Getting a "day job" with health benefits—one that would involve smart, inventive people and storytelling—was a huge gift at just the right time.

In my early publishing years, I worked with legendary editors Jason Epstein and Samuel S. Vaughan, as well as Ebershoff, who was a rising star at Random House. These three editors had radically different personal styles, but all three were expert communicators. I learned a tremendous amount by reading their editorial letters to writers and looking at the notes they scribbled into manuscript margins, as well as fielding (and let's be honest—eavesdropping on) their phone calls to authors, agents, and colleagues in all of the departments that supported the books we produced.

I made some early mistakes. On my first day, I took a phone message from a prominent agent whose nickname turned out to be Binky and not Spanky. There are so many names to remember, but the longer you're in publishing, the easier it gets. I also humiliated a prominent fiction writer; while escorting her into the office, I accidentally ejected her from the revolving doors in our old building. Red lights flashed and a security recording boomed through the elevator bank, announcing that she was not authorized to enter. She was very miffed, which may explain why she turned down my invitation to introduce one of our Modern Library Classics. But none of my early mishaps proved fatal.

As a novice editorial assistant (answering phones, making photocopies, scheduling appointments, and drafting rejection letters), I had a dreamy idea about what book editors did all day. I pictured them editing books for hours at a stretch in their book-lined offices, as well as reading and evaluating promising manuscripts from literary agents. I knew they broke up their days with scintillating lunch dates, and I pictured them attending glittering literary events and dinner parties at night. It seemed like the perfect job. But I quickly learned that there was much more to being a successful editor.

Most editors at big publishing houses spend their days flying through meetings and trading phone calls and emails to discuss publicity, marketing, sales, cover and interior designs, foreign and subsidiary sales, and production issues on their forthcoming books, and then conveying key messages and requests to authors and agents. Expense accounts are tighter than they used to be, but lunch dates are still common. Add to this the high-stakes game of acquisitions—pitching possible new titles to the publishing team, and engaging in heated auctions and negotiations—and it becomes a real juggling act. It's a thrilling life, and a demanding one. And it means that the job of detailed editing and book development is a much smaller part of the in-house editor's daily routine than you might expect. At Random House, I did most of my real book editing late at night and on weekends.

As I settled in, I began reading and evaluating manuscripts, and taking on my own editorial projects. The Modern Library Paperback Classics list was expanding, and this gave me and a group of younger editors the chance to take charge of our own titles. It was a golden opportunity that involved brainstorming with veteran editors about which world classics should be inducted into the canon and which of today's prominent writers should introduce these works to "a new generation of readers." I still remember the excitement I felt when suggestions I made in those meetings became real books on bookstore shelves. After about six years, I became the main acquisitions editor for The Modern Library. In consultation with the publisher and our illustrious Modern Library Board, I edited definitive editions of American and British classics, and commissioned original anthologies and fresh translations of major works from acclaimed scholars and celebrated literary translators of Russian, French, Italian, Spanish, German, Sanskrit, Farsi, and Urdu.

I also acquired new titles for the Random House and Ballantine imprints, specializing in literary and international fiction, with some narrative nonfiction, murder mysteries, and women's fiction thrown in. On top of this, I worked on reprints with Jane von Mehren, the expert trade paperback publisher, scouting out hardcover titles from other publishers that might thrive on our paperback list. The fact that my duties were split between acquiring for Random House, Ballantine, and Modern Library and keeping an eye on what other publishing houses were up to put me in a rare and enviable position. Most editors don't get the chance to acquire such a wide range of titles. This worked in my favor when I left Random House and set up my own, independent editing business.

FINDING INDEPENDENCE

When publishing companies combine divisions, people get reshuffled and laid off. This happened to me at the start of 2009, shortly after one of my books, Peter Matthiessen's *Shadow Country*, had won the National Book Award. Many editors have been laid off once or twice, bounced back, and found terrific new opportunities, so I didn't panic; I immediately began to freelance, thanks to an outpouring of support from some wonderful literary agents I had worked with. But when leads came in for jobs in corporate publishing, I hesitated to follow up on them. What was stopping me? It was the sudden realization that I loved working from home as an independent editor. I had been laid off at just the right time, after building up enough credentials and cultivating a big enough support network of industry professionals, to strike out on my own. I founded Judy Sternlight Literary Services and haven't looked back.

As an independent book editor, I am now much closer to living out my book editor fantasy than I was when I learned and polished my craft at Random House. My job has been streamlined down to my favorite parts of editorial: working directly with authors and agents on promising manuscripts, enjoying fun and productive lunch dates without having to race back to the office for meetings, and attending more literary events without feeling like I am neglecting my authors. But I could never have started my own literary services company (or have pulled in such talented clients) without those hectic years at a big, prestigious publishing house.

For years, freelance editing flew under the radar in main-stream publishing. But today, independent editors are a driving force and a safety net in this rapidly changing industry. As publishers tighten their belts and reduce their editorial departments, fewer in-house editors can dedicate the time and focus to helping writers bring out the full potential in each book. They have too many other responsibilities, and there is financial pressure to avoid long waiting periods between paying for a book and publishing it (earning that money back for the house). This is one reason why publishers are less willing to take chances on promising manuscripts that need development.

As a freelance editor, I enter the process earlier than in-house editors (who still play a vital role at the publishing house by selecting, fine-tuning, and championing their books to colleagues and industry "big mouths"). Writers hire me directly, often at the suggestion of their agents, to help them develop or refine their manuscripts. Usually, they work with me before the book is submitted to publishing houses. By helping authors strengthen their manuscripts before agents send them out, I give agents a better chance of selling them and of getting higher advances. Sometimes I'm called in when a promising book has already been rejected by a few editors or when a title that's already under contract needs an extra boost.

I work with clients at various stages in their careers, from talented aspiring writers to major, prize-winning authors. I always ask to read some pages and chat with prospective clients before I take them on. It's important that I connect with the material and the author and have a strong gut feeling that I can help bring the project to the finish line. If it's not in my wheelhouse or doesn't suit my personal taste, I'm not doing that writer any favors by taking on his or her book. And sometimes, if a project isn't right for me, I can suggest a more suitable editor.

My most frequent assignment is an editorial analysis, also known as a "read and review." For works of fiction (my specialty), this means reading the entire manuscript and giving the author a long editorial letter suggesting specific revisions. For nonfiction, I sometimes work on book proposals, which offer a good road map of the whole book but only include one or two actual chapters. Nonfiction projects may also involve developmental editing—helping an author to flesh out a story—or taking a full manuscript and helping the writer to nail down the narrative arc, the best voice, or the right emphasis for the book's natural readership.

Usually, my authors (or their agents) return the revised manuscripts to me for a second round. Depending on what the book needs and what the author can afford, this might mean a second editorial analysis or it might mean a full line-edit of the manuscript. And when a book is due to be published and is on a crash schedule, I'll sometimes step in to do some book doctoring—selectively rewriting and reorganizing a book in consultation with the author and other key players. Each assignment is unique, but in every case, the author and I become a team, working closely together to make the book the best it can be.

NETWORKING

In addition to actual book editing, a crucial part of my job is to maintain my network of contacts and friends in the business and to stay on top of publishing trends. I happen to love doing this, which is lucky because all of us in publishing—even writers who craft their books in isolation—need a strong support network to sustain a successful career. This means setting up occasional dates—lunch, breakfast, drinks, whatever—attending publishing events to trade ideas, and learning the particular interests of agents, editors, writers, literary organizations, and other experts in the industry. Sometimes I come up with useful ideas for other people, and sometimes they return the favor, sending great projects or people my way.

Along these lines, I recently joined forces with four publishing veterans to form 5E, a think tank of independent editors. While I no longer have office buddies to confer with, I frequently touch base with this group for advice. And when we get a query that seems better suited to another editor, we pass it along. Collectively, we have more ears to the ground, and this helps us to stay on top of the latest developments in publishing, such as the recent e-book explosion, the shrinking of traditional media and bookselling outlets, the opportunities provided by social media, and success stories involving authors and agents who are exploring a wider range of publishing options.

Making a career in publishing is not especially lucrative for most of us, but for anyone who loves books and storytellers, it can be vastly rewarding. It's not a nine-to-five profession; in fact, it tends to become more of a lifestyle than a job. Authors, editors, agents, and others in the industry become good friends, and successes and setbacks can feel deeply personal. Helping to bring great books into the world—whether they are captivating works of fiction; wise, practical books; or thrilling nonfiction narratives that shed light on important ideas—is hugely gratifying. I can't think of a more exciting field.

At Judy Sternlight Literary Services, Judy edits literary fiction, mysteries, historical and women's fiction, and selected nonfiction titles. As a Random House editor, her authors and translators included Rita Mae Brown, Ana Castillo, Peter Constantine, Edith Grossman, Bret Anthony Johnston, and Peter Matthiessen. Her books have won the National Book Award, the Sophie Brody Award for excellence in Jewish literature, the Commonwealth Writers' Prize for Europe and South Asia, the PEN Beyond Margins Award, and other accolades. For more information, visit: www.JudySternlightLit.com.

A book can be sold in so many ways and so many forms. There's the text itself in hardcover or paperback, and "ancillary" rights. Publishers aim to "exploit" any rights granted to them, and agents do, too, if they have retained them for the author. We now have an explanation from an expert, Jennifer Thompson, of what rights come into question as derived from a book.

What Are Subsidiary Rights?

by Jennifer Thompson, Perseus Books Group

Subsidiary rights are all the different rights to a book that can be licensed for broader dissemination of the work. On the domestic side, it includes serial licenses to magazines or newspapers, electronic and e-books, audio, reprint (including paperback, special deluxe editions, and omnibus), book club, large print, permissions, and dramatic (including stage and film). In addition, there are world English and translation rights. When a publisher is granted all rights, they have the possibility of exploiting any of these rights for which they have the capacity, most commonly paperback, e-book, and audio rights. Most large publishers do publish their own paperback and e-book editions and possibly audio, but few will exploit the remaining serial, book club, large print, or dramatic, not to mention translation (though occasionally a large house will publish in Spanish for the U.S. market) options. Thus a rights team, whether in house or at an agency, will sublicense any and all rights it can for the most complete and effective publication possible.

Any right granted domestically can be granted for world English or in any language when the rights seller believes it is in the best interest of the work. The maturity (i.e., sophistication and depth) of the given market should determine the subrights granted. For example, typically in Great Britain, most subrights are sublicensed because the British market has solid serial, e-book, audio, and book club demand. Whereas, in more emerging markets, granting serial or e-book rights to a publisher who has no means to exploit the rights makes little sense. An issue that has emerged with e-book and electronic rights is whether or not there is any advantage for a U.S. publisher to grant those rights to a British or Australian publisher when, given technology, it is easy enough for the originating publisher to exploit the rights itself. Individual publishers have their own strategies and, not surprisingly, the larger publishers are more apt to retain these rights for themselves in the bargaining process.

AGENT OR PUBLISHING RIGHTS TEAMS

When and why do agents grant world rights? A few agents in the industry have a policy of never granting U.K. or translation rights. They have robust rights teams within the agency (or a boutique agent has ample experience), and the agents and the authors get to keep a larger percentage of any monies earned in foreign rights deals. Other agents have either a very small rights departments or no department at all, and regularly sell all rights. Most often, the sale of world rights is determined by several factors, such as the rights capacity of the acquiring publisher, the ambitiousness of the offer, the strength of the proposal, and the amount of work that an editor expects to take on, as well as the overall strategy of the acquiring house and their willingness (or lack thereof) to take on a book without certain rights. Some publishing houses are much more aggressive about pursuing rights than others because they see it as a mitigation of risk as well as part of an overall publishing strategy. Most mid- to large-sized publishing houses have aggressive international distribution and, if not a publishing branch in London, then, at the very least, a strong U.K. presence. That doesn't automatically mean a publisher will keep rather than license U.K. rights, but it makes the question more competitive and arguably provides the strongest outcome for a given book.

TRENDS IN THE DOMESTIC MARKET

Until about eight or ten years ago, the U.S. paperback reprint market was quite robust and a source of large subsidiary rights deals. But more and more publishers came to realize that they could reach the paperback audience with similar effectiveness but with much greater profitability to themselves. Book clubs have also seen a significant decline in the past five years with many publishers shrinking or shutting programs. Serial (especially the first serial) is another area that was once a reliable licensing source that has now become the exception rather than the rule. Most magazines commission original pieces, and serial is often seen as last-minute filler. Having said that, serial placement can still be a wonderful source of publicity and marketing for a publication, and serious rights departments continue to see the intrinsic if not financial value that placements bring. On the positive side, audio publishing, for which many had predicted problematic decline, has held steady or gained strength. Most significantly, electronic and e-book publishing has exploded, creating new opportunities as well as a major shift in publishing away from traditional outlets such as mass market publishing and book clubs. The current standard royalty rate for e-books is 25 percent. As I said before, e-books are not purely or even mainly a subsidiary right that is exploited by a rights team, given that most publishers produce their own e-books, but I mention it here because it is a piece of the changing landscape that authors should understand.

TRENDS IN THE INTERNATIONAL MARKET

As with the domestic market, there have been real changes in the international market in recent years. Even before the international financial crisis, publishers had become more cautious about translation projects and more focused on their own domestic authors. Advance sizes have decreased significantly particularly for midlist titles, and the financial crisis of 2008 exacerbated the decline. Not surprisingly,

China has been a consistently growing and robust market, though the average advance size continues to be relatively modest for most titles. Poland is another area of strength. They did not join the euro-zone and felt much less of the impact of the crisis than other European countries. Brazil is also a bright spot in international publishing. Their strong economy, bolstered by a focus on education, means a growing readership. According to *Publishing News Brazil*, there were 670,000 people at the Rio Book Fair in September of 2011, of whom 145,000 were children, and there were 2.8 million books sold. Compare that to Book Expo America 2011 whose attendance, according to *Publishers Weekly*, was just over 21,500.

While e-books are currently around 15 percent of the U.S. book market, varying by genre and publisher, and they are predicted to be at 12 percent of the U.K. market by 2015 according to DigiWorld by IDATE, they have yet to break through in a significant way in any translation market. Even so, translation publishers around the world are preparing for that inevitability and licensing e-book rights whenever U.S. publishers are willing to grant the rights. One concern rights sellers should consider carefully before granting these rights is the rapidly changing standards within e-books. It is not in the original proprietor's interest to grant e-book rights to a publisher at the current 25 percent of net standard if the publisher is currently unable to make use of the rights, given the knowledge that within two years that rate may have changed to the 50 percent (for which many agents and rights holders are strongly advocating). One solution is to grant these rights for a very limited term when and if there is an active e-book strategy in place, and when there isn't one, to add into the contract a right of first refusal clause for the licensing publisher.

BENEFITS OF LICENSING RIGHTS

When one begins to consider subsidiary rights, the benefits seem obvious, so it is unfortunate when they are undervalued and underexploited. Fortunately, today most agents and publishers understand the value both of risk mitigation as well as potential additional revenue streams beyond the intrinsic value of finding a wider audience for a given work. Though it is much less common than in the past, an advance can be earned back by a publisher before a book has even been printed if there are strong international sales based on the proposal of the book. There are also instances when a book performs better in international markets than it does domestically. Ultimately, the more ways a book can be licensed, the more readers it can find and the better off the author and the publisher will be.

Most authors are quite happy to have foreign editions of their books. But some have concerns about the quality of a translation or the visual appearance of the book. These fears can be addressed in the negotiation stage of the sublicense contract with things such as translation approval or jacket consultation. While subrights teams should be, and generally are, working with reputable publishers in whose interest it will be to produce the best possible translation of a book, it is fair to request approval of a translation if an author is fluent in a given language or has a contact willing to assist in a timely manner. As for the fears about the aesthetics of a foreign edition, again, an author can request approval. However, it is good to keep in mind that the publishers in a given country know their market infinitely better than an outsider, and it is in their interest to sell as many copies as possible given their investment.

THE NITTY-GRITTY OF A SUBRIGHTS SUBMISSION

Domestic Submissions

The required timing and material for domestic submissions varies depending on the right. For audio rights, sales are often made based on a strong proposal because the intention of the audio publisher is to have the audio available around the time of original publication. Serial has two different time frames: first serial, which runs before the publication of the book; and second serial, which happens anytime after. Serial pieces obviously must be stand-alone passages and are often selected from early material by the submitting rights person usually in coordination with the author or editor. Reprint opportunities generally happen after the original publication of the book, and in most cases, this occurs when the originating publisher believes an interested reprint publisher has the motivation and capabilities to breathe new life into a particular book, which the originating publisher wouldn't or couldn't match. Large print opportunities tend to depend on the success of the original publishing plan. If a publisher buys rights before the original publication, it is because it is convinced that book will be a lead title and large seller. Often large print deals come after an original publishing success. Domestic right splits are generally 50/50, except for first serial which is 90/10 in the author's favor.

International Submissions

A submission to U.K. editors is much like the submission of books in the U.S. market in terms of timing and material. For the most part, a U.K. publisher will expect to publish a British edition at the same time as the U.S. edition is published. To publish later means to lose the publicity opportunity of reviews and media generated in the U.S. market at the time of publication. Further, in the age of Amazon, it means a potential loss of sales for eager readers who could order the U.S. edition. In terms of the material used for a submission, British editors may have higher expectations of the proposal's quality, not because they have a higher ultimate standard, but rather because they are not the originating editors and thus in most cases, they have much less (if any) input into the editorial process that shaped the books. Therefore, a proposal that is sufficient for a U.S. license may need to have some more polish or additional material for a successful U.K. submission. In the past four or five years, the British market has retracted significantly, particularly for licenses from the United States. Publishers are looking only for the "big" books.

While exceptionally strong proposals with hot topics, ground-breaking ideas, or exceptionally fresh fiction (particularly if there was a heated auction for the U.S. sale) can generate numerous translation licenses, it is becoming more and more the case that books are licensed when a full manuscript is available to be evaluated. This may be in part a response to a common experience of many editors who have overpaid for a book that did not deliver what the proposal promised or what they imagined the book would be. It is also surely a result of shrinking budgets and the necessity to make every single book count. The frustratingly simplistic mandate for "fewer bigger books" is being repeated the world over. In any case, as translation publishers are buying later in the publishing process, rights sellers are able to boost their submission with early reviews and blurbs.

Subrights Agents

An integral part of most every subsidiary rights team, whether in an agency or a publishing house, are the subagents who are on the ground in the major international markets around the world. The standard international agent fee is 10 pecent. That is in addition to the standard splits, 80/20 for Great Britain and 75/25 in translation (both in the author's favor). These earnings go against the advance. One might be tempted to think it is not worth having another person taking a cut of the payment, but if the subagents do their jobs well, they add tremendous value and their fee is more than worth it. Subagents are on the ground in steady contact with local publishers, gaining expertise by living and working in a given market. They will know a much wider range of publishers than a rights director based in the United States. They can monitor the health of local publishers and the quality of publication much more accurately from the ground, follow up on royalty reporting and payments, and will have a keener sense of what the market will support for a given title. Multiply that by fifteen or twenty agents, and it's clear that subagents add crucial expertise to any rights team. Of course, it is important for rights departments to choose wisely, manage closely, and be strong advocates for their authors with subagents who may represent many different lists.

Once a deal has been agreed upon, it generally takes between three to six months for a contract to be fully executed. This is sometimes sped up, particularly with British and Australian publishers, if there has been a recent deal between the parties and any contractual sticking points have been hammered out already. On the other hand, with contracts in China, the process may go even more slowly due to the need for official government approval, which is dependent upon having a finished published U.S. edition of the book with a copyright line identifying the copyright holder. As advance payments are due upon signature of the license, advance collection is no faster. One further complicating factor that authors need to be aware of in the collection of advances is the need for current tax forms granted by the U.S. government. If the deal is done by a publishing house, it must be a 6166 form, and if the deal is negotiated by an agent, the author herself must apply for an 8022 form. These forms are important because they allow the acquiring foreign publisher to pay the advance without removing the local taxes. If a payment is collected without a form in place, the local authorities will take up to 20 percent of the promised payment. The application process to the U.S. government takes between two to four months, and can be delayed even longer by an incomplete or erroneous application and, not surprisingly, one may not know there is a problem with the application until the forms are expected back. Depending on the tax laws of the country in question, the forms that prevent the double taxation between the two specific entities (whether it be two publishers or the foreign publisher and the author) will usually be valid for several years. However, any time a new foreign publisher reaches an agreement for a title, the form must be applied for and put in place. The application cannot be filed until December of the preceding year. So for 2013 forms, applications can only be submitted by the U.S. government in December of 2012. This means an advance owed in the first three months of the year will not be paid out until March at the earliest and more likely later, unless the proprietor is willing to forgo the amount deducted for local taxes.

REALISTIC EXPECTATIONS FOR AUTHORS

Because global markets—apart from China, Poland, and Brazil—tend to be shrinking, (particularly in the number of acquisitions from the United Sates or Great Britain), it is increasingly difficult to count on translation deals. Authors need to be realistic about what to expect when a book is published. A chance that a book will be licensed in ten to twenty languages is now the great exception rather than the rule. Foreign editors are much more careful about what they select, and books that are clearly addressing an American audience are very difficult to sell. Fiction continues to sell abroad and, not surprisingly, books that have high profile sales in the United States are the books that get the most immediate and widespread attention for foreign editors. YA books have been steady and growing as well in recent years. Topics for nonfiction titles that are extremely difficult to sell internationally include American foreign policy, politics, environmental issues, local histories, most sports, cookery, diet, and health care. Nonfiction areas that do work include popular science (particularly new advances in science), mathematics for the lay person, world history, and biographies or autobiographies of international figures. It often happens that a book will have few or no international licenses by the time of its U.S. publication, but as very strong reviews come in and sales take off, translation editors will either consider or reconsider a book that may have seemed "too American" in the early stages. There are also occasional surprises where a book has a mediocre publication in the United States but takes off in one or several countries.

INTERNATIONAL PUBLICATIONS

The general rule is that a book is licensed to an international publisher, and that publisher is responsible for finding a translator. Most have a pool of trusted translators with whom they like to work, though very occasionally, a translator will push a book to an editor. The standard time granted for a translation process is eighteen to twenty-four months from the signing of the license. If a publisher isn't able to manage to find a translator within that time frame, it can be considered in breach of contract and rights revert to the proprietor unless an extension is requested and granted. More and more these days, television and radio are becoming important ways to market and publicize books in many countries, and an author's ability to speak a foreign language in order to do an interview is useful. Obviously, language abilities are not crucial to most sales, but many publishers still hope to set up interviews, by phone or email, with an author around the time of publication. In very rare cases, generally when advances are quite high, publishers will invite an author to do a book tour. In most cases, it is not within the publisher's budget, but if an author happens to be traveling to a country where his or her book will be published, most houses will be very happy to set up some events around publication to raise the profile of the book.

Subsidiary rights provide multiple opportunities to widen the reach of a given work and enhance any book publication, providing new revenue streams and growing a fan base.

Jennifer Thompson has a BA from St. Olaf College and a master's in international affairs from Columbia University. She began her publishing career at Farrar, Straus and Giroux and went on to work for Maria B. Campbell Associates as a literary scout. Following this, she became a rights manager at Random House. For the past nine years, she has worked for the Perseus Books Group, where she is a co-director of international rights.

If your book has movie or TV potential, your literary agent will speak with you about also working with a film agent. Typically, when you sign with an agency, you grant them the rights to make a movie deal, a TV deal, or even a dramatic stage deal. These rights are highly unlikely to be granted to a publisher, so they are retained by you, the author, to be offered separately. Large agencies often have their own film agents and expect you to work with them if you are their client. The downside is that if their people don't want to represent it, you may be limited by that. The upside if they like it is that they have a lot of clout. A boutique agency may also have film representation and work with a specific agent for these rights. They may also have more flexibility about using any film partner who gets and loves your work. Some film agents might be more literary, and others are more genre-oriented and only want the next Hunger Games. *Be sure to ask your agent how this works with their agency and make sure you ask to speak personally with the potential film agent who winds up representing those rights. The usual commission of a co-agenting arrangement is a total of 15 to 20 percent, with 7.5 percent going to each agent. Your literary agent is the liaison and oversees the contract for you. You can always hire an entertainment lawyer to do the deal or read the contract, or you might want both, as a film agent knows all the people in the industry and might even get an auction going whereas the lawyer may be more of a straight contracts person and not a negotiator. You might ask your primary agent how they handle all of this before you sign with him or her. We now meet a brilliant film agent who represents many agencies, from book to film rights, as well as individual screenwriters.*

When a Book Becomes Something Else

by Michael Cendejas,
Lynn Pleshette Literary Agency

As a literary agent in Hollywood, I often find myself saying to people that I don't handle any talent, which usually only gets a laugh from those in the entertainment business. What I mean by that is that I don't represent actors, but writers—writers who are imbued with a great talent for storytelling and who are the impetuses behind all films.

A film or television series begins at its source, whether from an original idea or from existing material: a book (either fiction or nonfiction), a short story, an article from a magazine or newspaper, a play, even another film or television series, and these days from the Internet, blogs, and e-books. Each of these sources, or "properties," is characterized by certain rights that must be acquired from the author or owner/proprietor in order to move forward.

Let's assume you've written a novel. You've peddled it around, and through sheer determination, talent, and a little bit of luck, you've found yourself a literary agent (probably in New York) who's going to get your manuscript out to publishing houses for, hopefully, auction and eventual sale. At some point during this process, your agent will send the manuscript to someone like me in Hollywood to determine what kind of interest there might be in your novel for film or television. At the same time, any announcement of a sale might attract Hollywood scouts whose sole business it is to keep tabs on the literary market and report back to studios and producers. Film scouts also troll *Variety* and *Publisher's Marketplace* for news of book deals suitable for film.

That's where I come in, as your Hollywood film agent. Together we talk and determine the best course of action for getting interest in your material for film or television. Then I set out finding the right pairing, whether a producer, screenwriter, director, actor, studio, or financier. I make calls upon calls, send emails after emails—all for the purpose of getting your material out. This is called the "submission."

As the responses start coming back, we may find someone who falls in love with your work and is determined to get it made. Let's hope we find a few of these buyers to make the sale brisk and lucrative, though many times it can also be slow and pitiful. In any case, someone wants to make an offer.

The offer can come in two ways. A straight, outright sale or "purchase acquisition" of your material is when a purchase price is negotiated and agreed upon by all parties. This is paid by the purchaser immediately. Mostly, however, the offer comes in the form of an "option," which gives the purchaser the right to acquire or buy the rights to your material at a certain point down the line.

The option consists of an agreed-upon period of time, "the option period," for a set amount of money or "option payment." The option period is typically 12 to 18 months, and when the option expires, an additional period is usually granted. When negotiating the option agreement, the purchase price is also determined as well as the back-end or profit-sharing percentages to which you will be entitled once the film or television series is made.

Most important, when you are thinking about selling your novel for film or television, what you're really talking about is what rights you're giving away ("rights granted") and those rights you are keeping ("reserved rights").

Rights granted are those rights that the buyer needs in order to develop and make a film or television series, usually called "motion picture and allied rights." Reserved rights are those rights that you retain as the author, such as publication, live television, live radio, and, hopefully, live stage.

At this point, your head might be spinning from all the terms and conditions that go into a contract for a film or television series—without question this is only the tip of the iceberg. Whole books have been written on the subject. The point is that you should trust your literary agent who sold your publishing rights to find the proper agent for you to sell your film or television rights, and together you can make informed decisions. The most important thing is that the agent has ideas about how the book could work as a film and loves it.

Once you've optioned or sold the film or television rights to your material, that's when the real work (and wait) begins, such as finding the right screenwriter to adapt your material. Finding the director. The actors. Sometimes even more financing. It's a collaborative effort and, sadly, one that usually doesn't involve you. For example, one film we worked on—*Brokeback Mountain*—took eight years to come out.

So, at that moment when you're seated and watching the words and thoughts that you struggled to put down on paper come alive for the first time on screen, your only hope will probably be…that they got it right.

Michael Cendejas has been a partner at The Lynn Pleshette Literary Agency in Los Angeles for more than ten years, corepresenting such prestigious works as Annie Proulx's Brokeback Mountain, *Scott Smith's* The Ruins, *Lisa See's* Snow Flower and the Secret Fan, *and Ron Rash's* Serena, *to name just a few.*

You may be very technologically savvy, but many of us who did not even have computers when we were in college have to make a special effort to stay current on everything going on in this rapidly changing field. For years we have known that e-book rights were going to become a real business, but it took a while to get going. You may wonder why the build was slow, what is actually happening now in the field, and where things may be going. To that end, I interviewed STEVE KASDIN, an expert in the field of e-book publishing.

An Interview with
Steve Kasdin, Director of Digital
Strategy at Curtis Brown, Ltd.

JL: **Not long ago, there was much talk about the e-book, but not much action. Walk us through what has actually happened in the last few years in electronic publishing.**

SK: E-book devices have been around since the late nineties, but at that time there was virtually no consumer interest. I don't think it was so much about the devices themselves (primarily the Rocket e-book) but the fact that very few books were available in electronic format, and downloading content was complicated and somewhat intimidating. Sony introduced an e-reader in 2006, but the online store had very few books. People bought them primarily for reading documents; they were, in fact, very popular in the publishing industry, where everyone had to lug around large, unwieldy manuscripts until the e-reader was developed.

In November 2007, Amazon introduced the Kindle. What Amazon did that no one had done before, and what made the Kindle so successful right from the beginning, was it focused on the customer experience. For more than a year before the Kindle was introduced, Amazon worked with publishers to get content; they pushed the publishers to make as many of their books as possible —both frontlist and backlist—available in electronic format. Then they created a very easy, friendly way for consumers to buy and download the books. So when Kindle finally launched, they had about 100,000 titles available literally at the push of a button.

On the other side of the equation, the content side, this opened up a whole new world. Books that were out of print, or even never published, could be digitized and sold to the public, bringing in new revenue opportunities to the authors and publishers.

JL: You handle electronic rights at your agency. Can you tell us exactly what you do and where you see the role of an expert such as yourself?

SK: Now that authors can take to the marketplace older, out-of-print, or previously unpublished works to which they control the electronic rights, they are finding that there are many options for them. I work with the authors and agents to determine the best way to bring these e-books to the market, depending on their preferences or needs. Do they just want the highest royalty? The widest distribution, perhaps internationally? The most marketing? Can they supply their own cover and/or conversions? A conversion—creating a digital file by scanning a print book—generally costs about $200 for a text-only book (no charts, graphs, or illustrations); not a lot for a single title, but with a series it can add up.

There are basically three types of options for authors: publishers (traditional or electronic only), direct to retailers, or distributors/aggregators. Publishers, whether electronic or traditional, basically buy the rights for a specified period of time, create a book cover, pay for conversion costs, and market and distribute to retailers. Going directly to retailers can bring in a higher royalty, but it's a lot more work for the authors; they have to supply their own cover, other artwork, marketing, etc. Distributors are somewhere in between; they don't acquire any rights, they just distribute the books for a percentage of the revenue. They'll create covers and convert files for a price, usually out of the first proceeds. I help our authors make these choices.

JL: **Can you explain what these recent lawsuits with the big publishing houses are about?**

SK: There are currently two significant lawsuits worth paying attention to. The U.S. Department of Justice is suing Apple and five of the largest publishers (though three have already settled) for collusion to keep e-book prices high. The publishers didn't like that Amazon was charging only $9.99 for the e-book version of new hardcovers (and losing money when they did so); it made the hardcover price of $25 or more seem especially high to the customers. And it gave Amazon a near monopoly in the market because with almost $50 billion in sales—about seven times that of Barnes & Noble—and huge cash reserves, they could afford to sell the e-books so cheaply and their competitors couldn't. So when the Apple iPad came out, the publishers and Apple instituted a new business model, called Agency, where the publisher set the price for the books and just gave the retailer 30 percent. Amazon was not allowed to discount the books any further. The DOJ called this price fixing collusion; most people in publishing disagree.

The other interesting suit is between traditional publisher Harper-Collins and e-publisher Open Road. Harper published a young adult novel in the early 1970s called *Julie of the Wolves*. The original contract gave Harper a variety of rights (hardcover, paperback, etc.) including electronic storage and retrieval "in book form." Harper has interpreted that to include e-books, even though they didn't exist at the time. The author licensed e-book rights to Open Road, and Harper has sued. The basic question is whether or not a contract written before e-books existed still gives the original publisher electronic rights. Publishers tend to think so; agents and authors disagree.

JL: **What should authors expect to be paid now and in the future as a royalty for their e-book rights?**

SK: Right now, most traditional publishers offer authors 25 percent of the publisher's net revenue from e-book sales. Most agents think that is totally unfair and unacceptable since the publisher's costs are much lower with e-books than with print. Most electronic publishers, like Open Road, RosettaBooks, or Diversion Books offer 50 percent, which is more fair to the author. I believe this will eventually become the standard, but it could take a few more years.

JL: **Does an author have to grant these rights to publishers? Are there any other options?**

SK: There are options, so an author does not have to give up his rights. If an author wants to use a publisher, either traditional or electronic, he will have to grant that publisher exclusive rights for a period of time, generally between three and seven years, in order to give the publisher time to recoup the costs of covers, conversions, marketing, etc.

If the author simply uses a distributor, like Argo Navis or INscribe Digital, then the author retains all rights. These companies are not publishers—books are not curated or accepted; in other words, they take all books—and they charge a percentage of the sales for distribution to retailers as well as a variety of services, primarily cover design and marketing. The percentage they charge will depend on the services the author requires, and they'll ask for a year of exclusive distribution. These companies generally do not deal with authors directly, but rather with literary agencies who can bring them a significant number of titles.

Finally, if the author chooses to go directly to a retailer like Amazon or Barnes & Noble, he or she will retain all rights, but he or she will also be responsible for providing the retailer with clean digital files and covers.

JL: **When a license is made for an e-book, is it made in perpetuity or for a term of license?**

SK: Everything is so new now, there are really not that many rules. Very little is now in perpetuity, and the length of term is always negotiable. In fact, today pretty much everything is negotiable.

JL: **What percent of the market is currently e-books, and how do you see that growing over the next five years?**

SK: What kind of books are we talking about? In order to answer that question, it wouldn't be fair to lump a Harlequin romance with an Ansel Adams art book. That said, most immersive reading books—fiction and narrative nonfiction—are selling between 20 and 40 percent in e-books right now, depending on the author and genre. Many bestselling thriller and romance authors are already selling over 50 percent in e-books. My prediction is that immersive reading books will plateau at about 70 percent by about 2015. There's always going to be that 30 percent who prefer print books, but as device prices continue to drop, e-books will be just too easy and convenient for most people.

JL: **What do you make of authors self-publishing an e-book? Can you tell us of any good examples where self-publishing has been successful? And what do you make of publishing an e-book simultaneously with a print book?**

SK: Anything that gives an author more options is a good thing. There are many great self-publishing success stories: Amanda Hocking, John Locke, J. A. Konrath, Boyd Morrison, and many others. But their stories are different, and whether to self-publish or not will depend on the individual author's ultimate goals. Morrison and Hocking began by publishing their own works on Kindle and Nook, and parlayed their success into lucrative contracts with traditional publishers. Konrath, on the other hand, had been traditionally published but decided he could make more money going it alone.

The author must decide what's important. Does he or she just want the most money? Going direct on Kindle, the royalty is 70 percent, but the author must do all of the work, including making people aware of the book—i.e., marketing. There are literally hundreds of thousands of self-published titles on Amazon alone right now—how will customers hear about them? How can any of them stand out? And, if the author wants the "legitimacy" of a traditional publisher, right now the royalty is only 25 percent of the publisher's net.

E-books and their print editions *must* be published simultaneously; audio and any other formats as well, if possible. The key to success is not to focus on e-book vs. print. It is to give the customer the choice; let the author decide what format he or she wants.

JL: **What are the top companies that specialize in e-books, and do you see that number growing?**

SK: RosettaBooks, Diversion, and Open Road are all e-publishers; they acquire rights and "publish" e-books, but they have to accept the books like any publisher. Argo Navis and INscribe Digital are distributors; they'll accept any book (though only through an agent) and distribute it for a percentage. And, of course, there are the retailers: Amazon, Kobo, and Barnes & Noble. There are smaller companies in all of these categories; some will grow and others won't. I see a moderate expansion, but the field is starting to get crowded already.

JL: **Do you see e-books getting to the point where they actually compete with the conventional book, or do you see them coexisting?**

SK: Again, it's not about electronic vs. print vs. audio. They must and will coexist for the purpose of giving the customer a choice. The smart publisher, smart author, smart retailer must be format-agnostic. They must say to the reader: "Here's a great book. How do you want it?"

Steve Kasdin is a publishing consultant and director of Digital Strategy at Curtis Brown, Ltd., a literary agency. Previously he was in the Kindle group at Amazon.com. He has been an agent; a marketing director at St. Martin's Press, Scholastic, and Harcourt; and began his career twenty years ago as a buyer at Barnes & Noble.

Poets may have the hardest path in terms of a literary career, and getting a collection published is not easy. The finances are tough, too, unless you win a Nobel Prize. Even then it may, of course, help sell some books, but you most likely will not be able to retire. Poets have remarkable passion and stamina. Here are words from a poet who has been widely published and has taught poetry at Columbia University. She has had a distinguished career.

Seeking Visibility in a Mist of Rising Choices

by Colette Inez, Poet

You've studied T. S. Eliot, W. B. Yeats, Adrienne Rich, Mary Oliver, or John Ashbery, majored or minored in creative writing, read the hot new anthologies, attended reading series at your school, and want to go on to publishing your work. You've been bitten by that bug. So what's next?

My experience as a *wannabe* poet harks back to the days of carbon paper and Underwood typewriters. Working in offices by day and enrolled at Hunter College at night, I published my first poem in the early sixties, which appeared in the school's literary magazine. It had been entered in a contest, scarce in those days, and I won first prize, a hundred dollars—enough to cover a month's rent for my walk-up plus dinner at the Chelsea Hotel, where one could also sniff the pheromones of the great poet from Wales, Dylan Thomas. I had heard him read at the 92nd Street Y, his voice a burnished mahogany, rousing in its way, not unlike first hearing Elvis croon "Love Me Tender" on an old 78.

Nobody said "pobiz" then. On her horse farm in New Hampshire, Maxine Kumin posted a sign over her barn using that now coined word, despite her urgings that poets make a "commitment to the language." And in that mixed spirit of seriousness and play, here are some pobiz tips and tricks to be shared.

As a poet hungry to be in print, I stayed close to home and chose to hang out in the Gotham Book Mart, now famous for its group photo of Bishop, Lowell, Auden, E. E. Cummings, Jose Garcia Villa, etc., and the Eighth Street Bookshop. All offered samples of small literary magazines on their rear bookshelves.

The Beat poets'—Ginsberg, Kerouac, Corso—surrealist influences, their focus on the absurdity of existence, were beginning to be the talk of the literary quarterlies. I read the *Evergreen Review* but knew enough not to send them my largely rhymed verses. I copied addresses, typed submissions with SASE enclosed, and wrote to those at *Poetry* who called the shots and had published Hart Crane and Wallace Stevens, two of my favorite poets. I sent work to Howard Moss at *The New Yorker* and saved his "sorry" notes, excited to be noticed. Getting a comment with a rejection slip softened the blow of having my work dismissed. "Diction too ornate for the poem's needs" was a useful critique.

I was eager to develop an audience. And, yes, after I forget how many "send more" rejection slips received and taken seriously, an acceptance letter came from Nick King, then the poetry editor of the *Herald Tribune*. Winning the lottery couldn't have made me happier. I was in print and would be visible, a state of being my unwed parents, an American scholar-priest and his paramour, a historian in Paris, did not wish for me, having hustled me off as an infant to the care of Catholic nuns in Belgium.

With the facility of the Internet, you might locate an off-campus group of stimulating or offbeat poets to engage you. In my case, I signed up for a poetry course at The New School and shared the silvery and elegant poet Jean Untermeyer with a small class of her devotees—savoring the art whose power was felt by Emily Dickinson, "as if the top of [her] head were taken off." We were assigned roundelays and clerihews, free verse and translations. I also cultivated the friendship of Elizabeth Culbert, who had studied with the brilliant but eccentric Jose Garcia Villa and was a translator of Spanish poetry into English. She introduced me to the work of Lorca,

Machado, and Guillén. I ventured to share my poems with her, and they were always met with respect and encouragement.

In the mid-sixties, I studied with the consummate poet Denise Levertov at the 92nd Street Y and still have her class notes on the craft of poetry. In her general precepts she wrote, "Engagement with art makes you live more intensely. The manhole cover is suddenly seen as the entrance to the underworld. Keep your eyes open to the physical world—look at the sky every day." Her notes still pulse on the page.

Before my marriage to Saul, I had joined the Poetry Society of America and was inspired by their monthly meetings and famous guest poets; May Swenson read from her first book, *A Cage of Spines*. I met Robert Graves, poet of the complex *The White Goddess*. He insisted I was Spanish, "Oh, Inez?" he said and invited me to Mallorca. I judged a villanelle contest with Louis Ginsberg, a respected poet of light verse, but it was the fame of his son Allen that drew me to Paterson, New Jersey, where Ginsberg-père and I decided on the villanelle winners. Years later at the Naropa Institute, I was cast under Allen's spell as he talked about the seventeenth-century poet John Skelton's resemblance to our current rap artists. Allen had invited me to participate in the conference.

Check out conferences and link up to poets—most are smart, witty, and good talkers. Take notes, enrich your consciousness, that great gift from the universe. Lists of places provided can be gleaned from *The Writer's Chronicle, AWP,* or *Poets & Writers* on the web. You will also want to check out The Academy of American Poets and The Poetry Society of America. Make yourself visible in the increasingly competitive and numerous markets for poetry. Plenitude can only strengthen our art in the world.

Keep your hand in. There is something to be said for writing every day, for keeping a journal and a list of words you love. Dante's "hairy" and "buttery" words: scabrous and emerald. Take your thesaurus out to lunch and click away. Yes, I still like to dandle my *Roget*'s on my lap and take comfort in knowing Sylvia Plath also had the same habit.

Be productive. More magazines now allow multiple submissions. Be prepared to wait as long as six months for a response. Most magazines will announce their reporting times. To be a poet, you must have a tough snout for punishment. You need a thin skin and a tough hide. Check the directories and follow the rules. Publishing a large body of poems gets your name out there. Read and support poetry journals, subscribe to one or more, and rotate your subscriptions. If your budget allows, combine a little magazine with an establishment publication. Consider the elegantly edited *Parnassus Poetry in Review, Hudson Review, Bomb, Pembroke, Ploughshares, Hanging Loose,* or the feisty *Rattle* out on the West Coast.

A subscription to *Poets & Writers* magazine should keep you riddled with information about contests. Winning one or more might well also win you a head shot in *Poets & Writers* or in the *AWP Journal,* and in the onrush of excitement, you'll forget postage and Xerox costs plus those "sorry, try again" notes.

Even in these days of Facebook, blogs, Twitter, and tweets, you are still eligible for the Discovery Award at the 92nd Street Y and for the prestigious and still thriving Yale Series of Younger Poets (for poets under forty) at Yale University Press in New Haven.

Flaubert described talent as "a long patience." I persisted, and after five years, my first book, *The Woman Who Loved Worms,* was published by Doubleday & Co. in 1972. I had passed my fortieth year to heaven by a year. The book won a Great Lakes College Association Prize, and I found myself reviewed in *The New York Times* by Thomas Lask. He called the collection "a substantial achievement." I was off and running. Soon after, I received a letter from Hayes Jacobs of The New School asking me to teach a poetry workshop. I remembered his polite turndown of the year before when I had applied for a job, and his yes tasted sweet.

I organized tours in the Midwest, and checked with editors who had been friendly to my work. Philip Dacey, a poet and longtime friend, had interviewed me for *Crazyhorse* and offered a reading at Southwest Minnesota College. In Wisconsin, I touched base with the poet Peter Cooley, who later honored me with a Florie Gale Arons Award at Tulane University.

After the MFA, as postgraduate students you will need to think about juggling your full-time or part-time job with teaching private students, writing reviews, and writing book introductions. None of this will make you rich, but writing makes for a rich life. Be inspired by your fellow students. As a teacher, I learned a great deal from my students. A Kashmiri introduced me to the classic Arabic ghazal—I only knew Adrienne Rich's looser versions of the form from her translations of Ghalib—and an Irishman helped me explore Gaelic poetry.

Learn a second language, such as Swedish to read Tranströmer in his native tongue, even though we may be grateful to Robert Bly's translation of *The Half-Finished Heaven*. Try Chinese to hear the great T'ang Dynasty poets: Li Bo, Du Fu as they may have sounded in the capital city of Chang'an in the eighth century.

Delve into translations, yes, and while you're at it, why not step into other realms? How about scuba diving? Note the high voltage blues and yellows of tropical fish. Call your local astronomer and learn the names of asteroids that orbit between Jupiter and Mars. Or hike with a group, spotting spring warblers, which are surprisingly numerous even in urban centers. So much comes to your door. You need to escape the uproar, and poetry is a kind of meditation, a freedom from the onslaught of images in our twenty-first–century lives.

But being a poet is a privileged life. When Richard Wilbur (*Conversations with Richard Wilbur*, ed. William Butts) was asked: would you recommend poetry as a profession?" he answered, "Oh, yes . . . there's nothing so wonderful as having constructed something perfectly arbitrary . . . out of pure delight and self-delight, and then to find that it turns out to be useful to a few others." That says it for me, too, and likely says it for you, too.

Colette Inez has published ten books of poetry and received Guggenheim, Rockefeller, and two NEA fellowships, as well as two Pushcart prizes. She is widely anthologized and taught in Columbia University's Undergraduate Writing Program for many years. Her memoir The Secret of M. Dulong *was published by The University of Wisconsin Press in 2005. A recent collection of her poetry, titled* Horseplay, *was released by Word Press in late 2011.*

Many authors today are self-publishing. They may be frustrated with traditional publishing. Publishers at large houses today hope to see first print runs of 20,000 or so. This is such a high bar that it is not surprising that things have shifted, and authors may seek a small publisher or self-publish. Of course, if your book is a big success this way, larger publishers will become interested.

We are now guided by a woman who decided to self-publish her book.

Self-Publishing: How It Works, Who It's Right For

by Irene Gunther, Author of *Kibbutz: A Novel*

D elivering a manuscript to a traditional publisher is usually the occasion for a sigh of relief. Finally, someone else is about to take charge of the work you've been sweating over for months, even years, and guide it along the winding road from a manuscript to a bound book. The journey would include side trips to the designer, the illustrator, the proofreader, and others, but your editor would be comfortingly in charge.

Self-publishing is a different experience. I know because I've been down that road. Not once, but twice. The first time was in 2001, when print-on-demand (POD) was in its infancy. I had already had two books published in the traditional way—the first, a young adult biography called *A Spy for Freedom: The Story of Sarah Aaronsohn*, by E. P. Dutton, and the second, *Editing Fact and Fiction,* by Cambridge University Press. But when I wrote a memoir entitled *Only A Girl: Remembering My Syrian-Jewish World*, my agent could not find a home for it. While she reported nice comments—"affecting, beautifully written"—the bottom line was "not enough commercial potential."

Around then, I saw an ad in *The New York Times* for a company called Xlibris, offering to publish a book—almost any book, as long as it wasn't pornographic or libelous—for as little as $200. The price has gone up since; the base cost starts at around $500 and rises to as much as five figures depending on the services you choose, which include marketing evaluation and editorial services. Authors would receive a 25 percent royalty on books sold through their website and hold on to their rights forever. And the POD technology meant there was no minimum print run—authors could order as few or as many copies of their book as they required. Moreover, the book would be stored as a digital file, which meant it would never go out of print. Sounded good.

Still, when I signed on in August 2001, I was filled with apprehension. The company was in its infancy and had hardly any track record. And neither did I when it came to self-publishing. I had stepped into the unknown.

I was given a list of rather daunting things to do: supply a manuscript in digital form (at that time most manuscripts were delivered to the publisher as hard copy); write the cover copy, author bio, and summary; and get my photos scanned and sized (I ended up hiring someone to prepare the photos, which added about $200 to my costs). I would also be expected to proofread and correct galleys and, perhaps, finally, to promote and sell my own book.

Soon after sending in my manuscript, I was assigned a number. I was to identify myself as 12230, not Irene Gunther, author of *Only A Girl*. I'd stopped being a person and become anonymous. I was also assigned an author representative, a go-to person who would work with me, answer my questions, and keep me up to date on the progress of my manuscript—an editor who didn't edit, you might say. He tried hard to be helpful, but he was learning on the job himself and was not always able to supply satisfactory answers.

My galleys arrived on schedule a few weeks later, together with a correction sheet, both in electronic form—and with them came my first real problem. At my level of service, which cost $500, I was only allowed twenty-five free changes. For additional ones, I had to buy a "corrections service," which at that time cost $50 plus $2 for each correction. As I started to read the galleys, I regretted that I hadn't proofread my manuscript more carefully. I knew the material so well that my eye had skipped over many small errors.

Another problem: Xlibris corrected its own errors free of charge, which is standard in publishing—but you had to catch them the first time around. No one catches everything the first time around. On the plus side, when my photos came out blurry in the first batch of books I ordered, Xlibris immediately agreed to replace all fifty free of charge.

Five months after submitting my manuscript, a sample copy of my book arrived in the mail. I was pleased to see that it looked like a regular hardcover trade book, not a cheaply put together version. The paper was good and the type was very readable. And the cover, with the photograph I'd submitted, was beautiful.

My second experience with self-publishing came in 2009 with a novel called *Kibbutz*. I had started research on this project in the 1980s, spending months on a kibbutz doing personal interviews, traveling the country, and searching through archives. I wrote the first version when I came back to the States but then let the manuscript sit around for more than twenty-five years. The simple explanation: life—and other projects—had gotten in the way. A pity because in the intervening years getting a novel—any novel from a nonfamous writer— published had become increasingly difficult.

Once again I found myself having to make a choice between iUniverse and Xlibris, still the two leaders in the field. I ended up selecting iUniverse, partly to try something different and partly because the people I spoke to on the phone impressed me as being more professional.

This experience was quite different from the first. In the intervening years, things had changed a lot. Eight years earlier, the concept of print-on-demand was unfamiliar to most writers and would-be writers. Few knew exactly how the process worked—how the books were produced, printed, and distributed; what kind of quality to expect; and what the roles of the authors and the publishers were. Now enough has been written about the subject—and enough books have been published in that medium—to make it easy to get answers to those questions and to give writers the confidence to try it. In other words, self-publishing has become a profession.

Still, after I emailed my manuscript to iUniverse, I worried almost as much as the first time about how my book would come out. Would I be happy with the format? Would I hate the cover? (Many people have complained about poor-quality cover design and cheap paper, but I haven't personally come across such problems.) Would the book actually come out in the time that had been promised—about three months—or would it take longer? But, as with my first experience, this one went well, and I came away holding a book I could be proud of.

Thinking back, the weirdest thing about publishing those two books was that in the course of the months-long process, no one at either house had read a word I had written. Oh, maybe the cover designer had skimmed a page or two to get a sense of what the subject was, but that was it.

Of course, I wasn't necessarily the typical customer. I had ample experience as both an editor and a writer and was also lucky enough to have writer friends—some of them in my family—who had read and commented on the manuscript along the way. I chose one of the lower-priced packages, which did not include editing or proofreading. Still, it seemed to go against the whole concept of what books were about.

Publishing the books was just the beginning. Selling them was another story. My first book, *Only A Girl,* was set to sell on the Xlibris website for close to $19, way above the equivalent price for a small trade paperback at that time. POD, I was told, cost more than regular printing, which was the main reason for this discrepancy. My second book, from iUniverse, was equally high-priced on the iUniverse and Amazon sites, where it stayed for a few months, only to disappear after selling virtually no copies. The POD companies do offer packages to promote and sell their books. Skeptical though

I was, I once bought a marketing package for $500 from Xlibris. It sold just two books.

Still, by giving some well-attended readings and with help from friends and family—and considerable discounts!—I sold about three hundred copies. A tiny number by commercial standards, but in both cases it felt good to hold a new book in my hand, one I'd helped shape as well as write. And it beat leaving a manuscript to gather dust in a bottom drawer.

In the three short years since my second book came out, things have changed a lot in the publishing world—and in the self-publishing world. The biggest change is electronic publishing. With the arrival of the Kindle and the Nook, the iPad, the iPhone, and other electronic devices, readers now have many choices in addition to the printed word as to how they want to "consume" their news, literature, textbooks, how-tos, or whatever.

Self-publishing has, of course, changed, too. For one thing, it is no longer a dirty word as it once was in some eyes. The lines have blurred among other types of publishing, and no one really knows—or cares—anymore by what method a book has come to life. What matters is that it is worthwhile reading.

And there are other publishing options. A writer with a very short book might try to sell it as an Amazon Kindle Single. Another option is to create one's own website, where you can publish whatever you choose. I created one myself about a year ago titled "Essays And Poems And Such." It has given me the pleasure of sharing my writing and developing a modest following.

Recently, I met a woman in my yoga class who wrote a memoir about her experiences in World War II. It tells how, at the age of six, she had to leave her home in Poland in 1939 to escape the Nazis. It is a touching and dramatic story of her long journey to safety, which took her and her family through Siberia, displaced persons camps, and endless poverty and deprivation, until she arrived ten years later in the United States. Since this woman had never written before and intended her memoir for family and friends, she decided to skip looking for an agent or a traditional publisher and go with a self-publishing house. It seemed, in her case, a good choice.

Irene Gunther graduated from Manchester University in England, and studied at the Sorbonne in Paris before moving to the United States. She is the author of Kibbutz: A Novel *and of* Only A Girl: Remembering My Syrian-Jewish World, *and co-author of a young adult biography,* A Spy For Freedom *(Lodestar), and of* Editing Fact and Fiction: A Concise Guide to Book Editing *(Cambridge University Press, 1994).*

Translators are an undervalued and supertalented lot. They often bring us new voices, which we can only access because of their hard, hard work and passion for an author. Two star translators tell us how they have made a career. Many of the other writers we know originally wrote in other languages. Translators bring us the best from around the world. Think about it: Franz Kafka, Umberto Ecco, Gabriel García Márquez, Isaac Babel, and so many others are with us because of the translators' hard work. They deserve to be treated well and to have proper contracts and credit. They have literally brought us the "world."

Getting Started as a Literary Translator

by Jason Grunebaum, Translator of *The Walls of Delhi*

When you're ready to begin your life as a professional literary translator, you should first be sure that you're ready to translate. Read widely and deeply in your source language. If you translate poetry, read more prose. If your affections are drawn to nineteenth-century specimens of your language, pick up a contemporary comic book. Try to find reasonably analogous voices in English for the kind of work you'd initially like to bring over—this will help situate the work.

The next step is finding the right work to translate. An ideal starting point is to fall in love with a work unavailable in English. And, to paraphrase the translator Michael Henry Heim, you should feel that it's a crime that this work hasn't been translated.

Begin by spending time in the stacks of the library, browsing books for voices that resonate with you as a writer. Contemporary writing may be a bit more salable, but since so little has been translated from any period in any language, a worthy work translated well is bound to sound "new." Identify and read both print and on-line literary magazines in your source language, as well as literary or translation blogs both in your language and in English. Make note of what kinds of works and which writers are being translated from your language to get a feel for what others are doing and noticing. If you translate from a less commonly translated language, you will have many more works to choose from. But whether you are translating from Spanish or Indonesian, you should dig as deeply as possible. A reasonable goal would be to begin with a list of half a dozen potential projects.

If you intend on your translation project, large or small, ever seeing the light of day, make sure as soon as possible that the English-language rights are available before you invest any substantial time in the project—and ensure that you can secure those rights. Securing the rights may include one of several possible paths: Is there a literary agent involved, or are you free to take the work to publishers directly? Check if you need permission from the publisher or proprietor, or if you need to secure permission directly from the author.

Literary journals that publish few translations might not bother asking about rights, but it's still your responsibility. Journals like *Words Without Borders* and *Two Lines* that exclusively publish translations will always ask for proof of rights. There are too many woeful tales of enthusiastic translators working on projects for years, only to find out that a grouchy executor of a literary estate is unwilling to grant the necessary permissions. It may seem burdensome, but there's no cutting corners here—and you owe it to yourself and to your author to be diligent. You don't want to begin your career as the translator who tried to sneak a few Borges poems into an unsuspecting literary magazine.

As you get ready to submit to your translations, revise your work again and again. Let your friends who are writers and translators read it and make suggestions. If you translate from a less commonly translated language, chances are that literary magazines won't have a reader for the source language. They may not even check against the original even if it's in French or Spanish. If you feel shaky about any questions of meaning, ask your linguistically gifted or native-speaker friends very nicely if they wouldn't mind comparing the two versions. You obviously want to make sure your translation is as accurate as possible; at the same time, be cautious of readers who may have a greater emotional bond with the original language than with your English prose. Someone may, for example, insist that you simply can't use the English word "table" for word X, because in the original language, word X has five legs instead of four. In other words, while acknowledging that you may need guidance from a native speaker or language expert from time to time, you should also learn to trust your own English ear. Beginning translators sometimes suffer from "permission anxiety" and feel they may not have earned the license to "deviate," as they see it, more than a certain degree from the original. But if you're confident about meaning and have formulated an elegant solution in English, feel free to ignore the "language police" and stand by your work.

Now you're ready to send out your translations—but where? The website no-mans-land.org maintains the most comprehensive list currently online of literary magazines that publish translations either exclusively or occasionally.[3] Spend considerable time reading the magazines you think would be most appropriate for your work before you start dashing off cover letters. When you do begin to write them, articulate why you think a particular magazine is a good fit for your translation and demonstrate that you've done your homework. Perhaps most important, share your passion for the author. Since editors are not likely to be familiar with your author or the work, situate him or her in the literary tradition of that language, and make a case for why this author and this work are important and relevant. Try, however, to be succinct: make a quick case so the editor will come to your translation eager to read it, and give just enough background for it to make sense. Once your work is accepted, you can always fill in more of the blanks.

If your work isn't accepted (it's been known to happen), do what a translator friend of mine does every time she gets a rejection slip: She gives herself twenty-four hours to send it out somewhere else. If you're not getting rejection slips, you're not trying to get your work

[3] http://www.no-mans-land.org/links_translation_magazines.htm#1

published. Once you do begin to get published, begin submitting translations of other genres of writing to show what a versatile translator you can be.

Join the American Literary Translators Association[4] and attend their annual conference. Apply for their travel fellowship, available annually to promising beginner translators.[5] You will meet other literary translators, attend panels dedicated to the craft of translation, and have a very fun time indeed since literary translators are, as a friend nicely put it, "writers with humility."

Finally, if your author is alive and well and you two have been in touch, keep him or her apprised. You don't have to write an email about every up and down of submission and rejection. But when good news happens—"We're getting published!"—share it soon, and be sure to secure a permission agreement with the journal or publisher. A book or even a single translation published in a literary magazine not only enlarges the conversation of literature, but it can also make a big difference in the life of a writer somewhere far away.

Jason Grunebaum is the translator of Uday Prakash's The Girl with the Golden Parasol *and* The Walls of Delhi, *both from the Hindi. He has been awarded an NEA Literature Fellowship and a PEN Translation Fund grant for his work, and his own fiction has been recognized in Best American Short Stories. He teaches Hindi at the University of Chicago, where he is also a member of the Committee on Creative Writing.*

---

[4] http://www.utdallas.edu/alta/
[5] http://www.utdallas.edu/alta/conference/travel-fellowships

Your First Book-Length Translation Project

by Peter Constantine, Translator of
The Essential Writings of Machiavelli

Once you have published translations of poems, short stories, and essays in various literary magazines, your CV will make you more eligible from a publisher's standpoint to undertake a book-length project.

As you become better known, editors or literary agents might approach you with a translation project involving a book for which they have acquired the English-language rights. This has the great advantage that you can begin the translation project right away (on signing a contract[6]) without having to set out on the lengthy and uncertain path of finding a project and preparing and sending out a proposal and sample translation to various publishers. The disadvantage, however, is that the publishers will often propose a contract less advantageous to you, as they consider the book their acquisition that they have brought to you; this can give you less flexibility in negotiating your fee.[7]

Both beginning and seasoned translators, however, will also search for book projects that they can propose to publishers. American publishers have few (if any) editors who can read

---

[6] Pen American Center has published its Handbook for Literary Translators available online at http://www.pen.org/printpage.php/prmID/271 It has useful chapters such as "Negotiating a Contract" and also provides a model contract.

[7] Though no official rates for literary translation have been published by any American institution, the British Society of Authors offers guidelines that can be useful to American translators as well: http://www.societyofauthors.org/rates-and-guidelines

foreign languages and, consequently, rely to a large extent on translators they know to introduce them to foreign literary projects. One thing that translators often forget, however, is that it is a major investment for a publisher to commission a book. Besides the money that must be paid to the translator and to the author's publisher for the rights, there are the considerable costs for editing, production, marketing, distribution, and advertising; the result being that acquisition editors are cautious and reticent in acquiring a translation. Even if a book has done very well in its country of origin, the American and British markets are quite different from any other market in the world—and, as the acquisitions editor usually cannot read the book you are proposing in the original, the purchase has to be made almost entirely on speculation. The editor has to be convinced by your proposal and sample.[8] So how extensive should the sample be? One of my editors at Random House said:

> *I always wanted as many pages as I could get, but twenty to thirty pages is more or less standard. Ideally, along with the sample pages, there would be a description of the whole book and some reviews/testimonials from the foreign press. When I was seriously interested in a book that I couldn't read (because of the language), I would hunt around for one or two readers (ideally at the publishing house) who could read in that language and also considered paying $100–$300 for an outside reader's report from a translator unconnected to the project, who could offer an objective opinion and was familiar with books in the genre or category I was considering.*

---

[8]ALTA, the American Literary Translators Association, offers guidelines and ideas on how to write a proposal for a book-length translation on its website: http://www.utdallas.edu/alta/pdf/ProposalForABookLengthTranslation.pdf. See also Chapter X on writing proposals.

It is important never to rush into translating beyond the initial sample you are providing and not to embark on a project until you have a signed contract with a publisher.

In proposing a book for translation to an American publisher, it is important to be as familiar as possible with the kinds of books they publish—their list—and to develop a keen understanding of current literary tastes and trends in America. Many translators are so immersed in the literature and culture of the language they are translating that they neglect their medium— English. Reading extensively in English is more important than reading exclusively in the language in which you are specializing. Working on your English is indispensible to producing successful translations.

Ross Benjamin, who has extensively translated German fiction and poetry from the nineteenth and twentieth centuries, has pointed out that finding interesting books to translate and sending out proposals to publishers is also a useful way of networking with publishers, which can often bring you more than just the book project you are proposing. Benjamin says:

In my experience, you never know where actively proposing projects of genuine interest to you is going to lead. Even when a submission does not ultimately turn into a contract, it is a way of reaching out, expressing your enthusiasm, demonstrating your abilities, letting the translation and publishing world know that you are eager and ready, and conveying a sense of what sort of work speaks to you and suits you. A publisher who does not accept one proposal might come back to you sometime later—maybe weeks, maybe a year or more—with something that makes them think of you, that strikes them as perhaps being right for you...and this can only happen if they have gotten to know your interests and strengths by the submissions and overtures you've made previously. Each proposal is not only an attempt to realize a particular project—which may or may not come to fruition, depending on many factors beyond your control—but a way of making yourself and your individual sensibility, talent, and professional ethos known. Some of my most exciting work has come to me by a circuitous route but could always be traced back to the intense effort I had put into continuously contacting and meeting with publishers, writing summaries, and preparing samples of work I found appealing, important, and worthy of translation.

We often hear that the translator is invisible, but a recent generation of translators is striving to achieve a new visibility and position of importance within a project. This means that the translator's name must be on the title page and should be on the dust jacket or cover. The translation must be copyrighted by the publisher in the name of the translator, and translators now also try to negotiate better advances and some percentage of the royalties. Those wishing to familiarize themselves further with these procedures and with the field of literary translation can turn to the following publications:

- PEN Translation Committee. *Handbook for Literary Translators*, 4th ed. New York: PEN American Center, 1999. http://www.pen.org/printpage.php/prmID/271.

- Biguenet, John, and Rainer Schulte, eds. *The Craft of Translation (Chicago Guides to Writing, Editing, and Publishing)*. Chicago: University of Chicago Press, 1989.

- Rabassa, Gregory. *If This Be Treason: Translation and Its Dyscontents, A Memoir*. New York: New Directions, 2005.

- Grossman, Edith. *Why Translation Matters*. New Haven: Yale University Press, 2011.

- Bellos, David. *Is That a Fish in Your Ear?: Translation and the Meaning of Everything.* New York: Faber & Faber, 2011.

Peter Constantine is a literary translator and editor. His recent transla-tions include Sophocles's Theban trilogy, The Essential Writings of Machiavelli, *and works by Gogol, Tolstoy, Dostoevsky, and Voltaire. He co-edited the anthologies* A Century of Greek Poetry: 1900–2000 *and* The Greek Poets: Homer to the Present, *and was awarded the PEN Translation Prize for* Six Early Stories by Thomas Mann, *and a National Translation Award for* The Undiscovered Chekhov. *He has just completed his first novel.*

It has never been easy for anyone to get published, but if you are black or Latino or Asian, for example, you may want some specific direction about ways to be published. Our contributor has spent her adult life making sure many voices are heard by anthologizing diverse authors and often helping them be published for the first time. She has also recommended international authors to publishers and agents, and recently discovered an Armenian princess whose book is now forthcoming in America. She also does consulting on Latino authors for a major publishing house.

She has perhaps made the largest lifetime commitment to making sure many voices have been heard. I wish I could bestow a medal. She's also a brilliant novelist.

The New American Page

by Lori Marie Carlson, Editor, Translator, and Novelist

Every spring, I teach two seminars in literature at Duke University. I'm always thrilled by the diversity of my classrooms, for in addition to having students who are the children of first-, second-, third-, and fourth-generation Americans, I also instruct kids who are immigrants themselves. My young scholars represent every ethnic heritage and racial combination imaginable. While most of them are of Asian, African, Indian, European, and Middle Eastern backgrounds, a large number are also multiethnic and multiracial. The thrust of my writing and creative work has been concerned with issues of identity and cultural legacy, so I find working with these students particularly inspiring.

I am the child of a Swedish American father and an Italian American mother. When I was growing up in Jamestown, New York, I was acutely aware of how important my ancestral history was to my understanding of self. My grandparents—both sets were first-generation immigrants—took care to teach me songs, poems, and aphorisms in their native tongues. They enthusiastically taught me their customs, values, and traditions. My grandmothers shared their understanding of cuisine. Giovanna rolled and cut exquisite pasta; Alida fashioned heaven-scented cardamom braids. Two distinct frameworks and nationalities informed my view of the United

States and the world. Remarkably, I am still best known for writings unrelated to my own heritage.

I have devoted my career to the study of Latin American/Latino cultures. My efforts to reach out to youth, in particular, have resulted in publications such as *Cool Salsa*, *Red Hot Salsa*, *Voices in First Person: Reflections on Latino Identity*, and *The Sunday Tertulia*. And I have also composed anthologies that explore American Indian and Asian American sensibilities.

Some readers may wonder, why? Why have I devoted so much time and energy to addressing the underserved communities in our land? The answer is, I suppose, rather straightforward: I saw a need. I detected a vacuum in publishing that upset me, and I decided to do something about it.

In the 1980s, just out of graduate school with an MA in Hispanic literature, I began writing for the Latino community. I was surprised and saddened by the lack of awareness among commercial publishers in New York City; there were hardly any books that dealt with the problems of Latino adolescents. And when I began to ask executives the reason for this paucity, they simply looked dumbfounded. They didn't know what I was talking about, because they didn't understand how America was changing and growing. Perhaps this is because the percentage of so-called "minorities" in publishing is small. Many of our editors, if not most, come from privileged backgrounds with insular schooling. In the 1980s, publishing professionals hadn't been exposed to the marginalized groups I had come to understand vis-à-vis my studies and work environment.

In those years, creating and then publishing my books was especially difficult because I had to first convince editors that my concepts were commercial enough for their investment. It was as simple as that. They needed to be persuaded that there were "buyers in large numbers" for the kinds of books I wanted to produce. Now, in the twenty-first century, it seems impossible to believe that this was ever so, because the Latino population has made itself heard and seen in every arena of American life, from Hollywood to Capitol Hill. But in those years, the scenario was very different, indeed.

One has to be a dreamer to be a writer. In order to make one's vision a reality, faith comes in handy. I could not have accomplished so much in my career without believing in myself and my ideas. And, likewise, I urge anyone with an insistent message or story to persist on their path. It can be extraordinarily hard to believe in your vision when few want to validate it. But believe me: If your desire is powerful enough, your goals will be achieved. And today's technological advancements allow for myriad possibilities to be heard, even if a publishing house is out of reach. Not only can writers avail themselves of traditional avenues for showcasing their work via print—journals, magazines (*Latina, California Magazine, Chicago Review, Slice,* and *Bamboo Ridge* are just a few examples), newspapers, newsletters, and pamphlets—but they can also find endless and exciting opportunities to publish online. Just think of all the blogs, forums, and new publishing ventures, such as New America Media, which are being created by visionaries every day.

As I tell my students, "Your imagination is probably your greatest asset. Without creative sight, there is no progress, evolution, or victory."

Lori Marie Carlson is an editor, translator, and novelist. She divides her time between New York, Connecticut, and North Carolina.

Look at the enormous sales of books for children that are graphic. Works such as Big Nate *or the* Wimpy Kid *diaries and also graphic books for adults have been huge sellers. Meet two guys who have both had cartoons published by* The New Yorker *and books published by the major publishers Clarkson Potter at Random House, St. Martin's Press, and Norton. Our second contributor also had an exhibit of his paintings and a mystery published. Neither have MFAs and are self-made with original visions.*

Getting from There to Here

by Ken Krimstein, Cartoonist, *The New Yorker*

I was a horror to English teachers growing up. "A" for content, "F" for mechanics. As for the five-paragraph structure—and the process known as outlining, Roman numerals and all—I'd see it and freeze up. I couldn't type.

And I read comic books. But not just superheroes, no. I preferred this stack of yellowing comics I inherited from my dad's cousin, something from the '50s called *Classics Illustrated*. I got my *Moby Dick* and *Great Expectations*, but I got them with pictures in boxes, and with speech balloons full of prose that crossed well into the purple.

If my English teachers knew what I was reading instead of what they were assigning, I'm sure it would have been thrombosis city.

But I loved every word. And picture.

Add to that my friend's dad's collection of creepy Charles Addams cartoons, sprinkle in a drop of my dad's *Mad Men*-era copywriter partners, and it was the recipe for . . . me.

The stew just kept thickening. Rock 'n' roll and marching band music equaled jazz. Chicago gospel TV shows and a steel-string guitar made me a blues player. And then strange books like *One Hundred Years of Solitude* rescued me from teen-vetted, school-prescribed classics. (Thinking back, I must admit there are times when I wish I'd paid more attention when I was reading *To Kill a Mockingbird*, or *Sounder*, or whatever they were forcing us to read.)

Thank goodness some naughty Boy Scouts smuggled an R. Crumb X-rated underground "comix"—a slang term for a kind of underground comic—up to Camp Makajawan. That and the root beer machine kept me sane that summer. Mr. Natural also proved remarkably effective in swatting North Woods mosquitos!

So I wrote and drew and played instruments and waited for something to happen. Along the way, I moved to New York, though I didn't know why at the time. (Some years later, my friend and mentor, cartoonist extraordinaire S. Gross, growled out to me in his distinctive Bronx meets Broadway accent, "not a lot of gag cartoonists in Chicago.")

I began submitting cartoons every week to *The New Yorker* magazine for what would be nine years. And back in the days when you got paper rejections, small ones, not more than 3 x 5-inch slips of yellow paper, I could have decorated the walls of a medium-sized suburban bathroom with them.

But I persisted. I kept thinking of those Charles Addams books. I kept looking at the old, tattered volumes I'd buy for fifty cents at Salvation Army thrift stores. I couldn't stop.

And then, while working at an ad agency—as a copywriter—I took a short story writing course at NYU to research an ad.

It felt good.

It was just about this time I had scaled Everest barefoot with no oxygen and finally sold my first cartoon to *The New Yorker*. Just a quick nine-year journey. And in what must have been the most epically bad career move since the commander of Troy said, "Oh, let the horse in. What harm can it be?"—I decided to give up cartooning to become Saul Bellow.

Dumb?

I wanted to be a writer.

So, I stopped cartooning and started writing. I got an agent based on some of the stories I had been placing on the web. How? She was a friend of a friend and we struck up a conversation at a picnic and she seemed amenable to my ideas, and I, well, pounced. I put together a package of all my pieces and got them to her. We started pitching book ideas and publishing humor in places like *The New York Observer.* But I couldn't quite figure out my graphic novel/humorous memoir/satire young adult book. And despite more articles and humor pieces, I decided another agent might be a good thing.

I felt bad about this.

I felt terrible.

But then I dipped my toe in the waters and found another agent who not only got me, but got the whole package. At least as much as I did. Cartoons *and* writings were dusted off, and before I could say "oy!" my first solo collection of cartoons was bought by a major publisher, Clarkson Potter, which bought *Kvetch as Kvetch Can—Jewish Cartoons.*

I had cartoons on parenting and Nietzsche and dogs, but my agent and I realized we needed a theme, and based on a gag I had sold to *National Lampoon* of two pigs sitting in a realtor's office saying to the rather shocked agent, "Actually, we'd prefer a Jewish neighborhood," I had my theme.

Those crazy Jews!

I walked through the halls of Random House and couldn't believe it was real. *There must be a mistake,* I thought. But I didn't act it. And when I told my prior agent, she wished me well. Really.

Once again, I felt great.

Then I had to make the book. And make it good. I had a vision of how I wanted it to be. I wanted it to be like one of those Charles Addams collections.

Easier said than done. But at least I had a goal. And in one of my first conversations with my editor, I said, "I want it to be funny first, Jewish second."

And she nodded in agreement.

And then, I had to make the book.

Which was an absolute delight. The harder I worked, the happier I felt. And when I held the finished product, cardboard, paper, glue, ink, my drawings—well, again, I thought there must be a mistake. Except that I had by then put in almost two years of work, and I knew there wasn't.

I vowed before I got published to never be one of those authors you read about who moan about their problems once they got published. And I'm not going to be. But, as a possibly informative aside, here's a funny little snapshot from the world of publishing and what happens.

———

So there's this huge conference where all the people who book authors for tours to Jewish book festivals and JCC's and events around the country convene, and all authors with as much as a mention of the word 'bagel' in their manuscripts get TWO ENTIRE MINUTES to stand on a stage and pitch themselves as the next Sholom Aleichem. (Think of it as *American Idol* meets *Revenge of the Nerds.*) Well, anyhow, I was all set to present my book, nicely entitled *Jew-toons*, to the group. It was printed in the program, etc., etc., etc. And the night before the event I got a call from my editor (not always a good thing…usually means "trouble right here in River City…").

I picked up the phone.

"We have a problem," my editor said.

"How big of a problem?" I asked.

"How big does it have to be?" my editor said.

"Try me," I said.

"The guy who is in charge of buying all the Jewish books for bookstores across New York City has a problem with the title "Jew-toons.""

"Did you say New York City?" I asked.

"And the greater Tri-State area," she said.

"I always hated that title," I responded and furiously began scribbling. I couldn't present a book without a title.

And out popped *Kvetch as Kvetch Can—Jewish Cartoons.*

I'm not complaining. Just telling you that stuff like that happens. Anyhow, the book did come out.

And then I had to start promoting it. Which I'm still doing. Twitter, Facebook, and whatever else they come up with—I'm in. I can make a projector work in any kind of room, with any kind of power, on any kind of screen. I can do a presentation of the book in three minutes or three hours.

But again, I'm loving it. Because as long as I'm promoting it, it's still out there.

But another wonderful thing happened as a by-product of doing the book. No, I didn't become Saul Bellow. But I did get up the gumption to contact *The New Yorker* again—this on my own since it's not an "agented" thing—and after much work, they've started buying again! In fact, in just a year and half since I've been back, they've bought five, and I've had four published. I'm back on my regimen of submitting ten new ideas every week. (If only I could get back on my running regimen, but that's another story...)

And I'm working on a bunch of new books and proposals. And my agent and I have a professional relationship that I believe says something like "I'll be your milk cow if you be mine." In other words, we can each help each other make money—and books.

And it feels good.

Ken Krimstein is a cartoonist for The New Yorker *magazine, the author of the book* Kvetch as Kvetch Can—Jewish Cartoons, *published by Clarkson Potter, and has written humor for McSweeney's,* The New York Observer, Forbes, *and sometimes, albeit inadvertently, for his college English professor. He's also an award-winning advertising creative director and teaches in the Communications School of DePaul University as well as the writing department of the School of the Art Institute of Chicago. Bats, left. Throws, left.*

$\iff$

The Accidental Writer

by Peter Steiner, *New Yorker* cartoonist and author of *The Resistance*

I didn't set out to be a novelist. I didn't study writing; I never belonged to writers' groups. In fact, no one was more surprised when I became a novelist than I was. I still do not know some of the things you learn by studying writing at a university. I don't have the support group that other writers enjoy, or the connections and friendships one makes in a writing program.

The amateur—which is how I think of myself—is free from many of the practicalities and demands that confront the professional and can thus exercise his passion in an uninhibited and unconstrained way. I have finished earning my living—I was a professional artist—and so can pursue novel writing like a lover pursues the object of his affection.

This does not mean that I am uneducated as a writer. It's just that my training followed a singular and idiosyncratic route. It began long before I gave the slightest thought to writing novels, when I was a college professor teaching German language and literature. I read Thomas Mann and Goethe and Kleist as carefully as I could and helped my students to read them in the same way. This meant, for instance, figuring out how Mann could create such a myriad of characters in *The Magic Mountain* and keep them all alive in the reader's mind.

He borrowed a technique from Richard Wagner, assigning each character a leitmotif, that is, a phrase or action that is shorthand for that character. When the door in the dining hall slams, it means

Clawdia Chauchat has arrived in all her interesting complexity and erotic allure. I learned how Thomas Mann used language with complexity and humor to build a solid edifice whose reality was fantastical but indisputable. I learned how he built suspense into situations where, in real life, suspense and tension are hard to imagine. I was teaching my students, of course, but I was also teaching myself, like a child taking apart an alarm clock.

I left teaching eventually to become a visual artist, something to which I had aspired since childhood. I began painting, which was new for me, and cartooning, which I had done all my life. The cartooning eventually paid off, but not until after a long and excruciating apprenticeship. I submitted a dozen or so cartoons to *The New Yorker* every week for about two years, over a thousand cartoons I would guess, until they finally bought one. Each week I would mail a fresh batch of cartoons to the magazine. Each week the last week's batch came back. I wonder now how I managed to keep my spirits and hopes alive.

Cartooning professionally consisted of conjuring up cartoon ideas and making weekly submissions to a selection of publications, starting with *The New Yorker* and working my way down the list of magazines that used cartoons. The conjuring consisted of finding the otherwise unnoticed, absurd, and ludicrous aspects of ordinary life and presenting them in a funny way. In addition to a decidedly contrary and eccentric temperament, it required a disciplined and yet loose and playful frame of mind.

Cartoons are drawings, but they come about mostly through writing and then editing. The cartoon's idea is the fulcrum on which the whole thing is balanced; it must be clear and concise. The drawing has to communicate the idea but not get in its way. It must not be overexplicit to avoid getting in the way of the reader's imagination and playfulness. It must be well drawn to fulfill its purpose, but not overdrawn—or too broad—so that it steps on its own humor.

Part of the cartoonist's discipline has to do with meeting deadlines. For the thirty-five years I have been a cartoonist, the deadlines—

from others or self-imposed—have been constant. In the process of meeting deadlines, I learned to work through every hiccup, block, and other difficulty. I developed the technique of not stopping work when I was having trouble, but rather stopping just at that moment when things were going well and I *wanted* to continue.

The lessons learned in all these various endeavors accumulated and organized themselves in my brain where they waited for the right moment.

In the nineties, my father developed the cancer that would eventually kill him. In an effort to try to sort through our relationship and the general upheaval in my soul, I began writing down my thoughts in a sort of journal. I was writing mostly about emotions and tensions and other family business, which, after a while, simply did not hold my interest. Still, something in the exercise made me want to go on. I enjoyed the writing, the sorting out of things by putting the difficult and the vague into words. I liked the sense of myself it offered me, the thoughtfulness and reflectivity I found inside myself. I liked appearing smarter than I knew I was.

I no longer know how the idea first came to me, but I thought one day, *what if I gave person to the business I was writing about, created characters who carried the thoughts and emotions, and wove them into a story?* And that is how my first novel began. I invented a father and son, much more extreme in their differences than my own father and I were, but sharing some of our qualities. I set the story in Austria in 1938—which infused my fictional characters' tensions with the tensions of that historical moment.

I felt freed from both the abstraction of my earlier ruminations and from my own story. Now I was writing about someone else somewhere else, dealing with a far graver business than I had ever dealt with. I was writing about other people, and whatever problems I had were being subconsciously transformed, by my writing, into their problems. My own personal happiness and unhappiness became theirs.

My invented father and son were Jews who were enemies, and who ended up fleeing the Third Reich together. They had far more to sort out than I did, and a far more dangerous arena in which to do it. I enjoyed the writing from start to finish—first draft, subsequent drafts, editing, all of it. And, without my realizing it at the time, all my earlier training—my understanding of the writers I had taught and studied, my recollection of their methods and devices, but also the editorial precision of working a cartoon into shape, the tenacity, the discipline that came with deadlines, the images and scraps of this and that which I had stored up—all of it came into play.

When the novel was finished, I showed it to some family members and to friends. They all liked it (or said they did) and suggested I try to publish it. I knew very little about how to do that, but a colleague at *The New Yorker* steered me in the direction of his agent. I wrote to her, she looked at the work and decided to take it on. She got several encouraging rejections but did not succeed in getting it published. But just having gotten this far felt like a triumph, and so I began the next novel.

I began it in a similar fashion. I had just returned from a vacation in France and had so enjoyed being there that I began writing about that experience—the landscape, the food, the culture. Once again I found that my writing needed focus, and once again I invented characters and a situation.

My agent and I parted ways when she eventually ran out of publishing ideas for the first novel. I found my next agent through a childhood friend who was friends with an entertainment lawyer who contacted an agent he worked with. The agent agreed to read forty pages of my writing, and he then asked to see the entire manuscript. That was *A French Country Murder*, my first published novel. It was rejected by many publishers before it was eventually bought by St. Martin's Press. With this agent I published two more novels.

All three books were part of a series of mystery-thrillers. In the meantime, I had written three other novels that were not part of the series. They were neither mystery nor thriller and, despite my agent's efforts, they remain unpublished. The three published books were critically successful, but not commercially.

After I finished my last book, I went looking for a new agent. This time I finally studied a bit about agents and agenting, read about inquiry letters and approaches, looked at many Internet sites, and then sent inquiry letters to a number of agents. Having three books under my belt, I got positive responses from a few agents. I met a number of them and then made my choice (she is the editor of this book). It was lovely being sought after, but the most useful thing about the search was having a better sense of the variety of agents working. Each has his own modus operandi, personality, interests.

When I had first started writing fifteen years ago, I imagined I would stay with the same agent my entire life. The first breakup felt like a failure. It wasn't, of course. I soon realized the writer-agent relationship is extremely tricky. It is made difficult by the fact that you and your agent agree to work together without knowing very much at all about one another. No matter how thoroughly you study everything available about an agent—who her clients are, her successes, her reputation to the extent you can discover it—she remains almost entirely opaque until the actual work begins. It turns out, agents can be moody or slow or ponderous; they don't return calls; or they are thoughtful or solicitous or timid or wonderful. Some agents are looking for potential stars, others for a kindred spirit, and others may have a particular slot they want to fill. You just don't know. And so it is neither unusual nor wrong when the relationship ends. It is a normal part of the process.

The way I write has grown out of who I am and what I want to gain by writing. Who I am is a seventy-plus-year-old man; what I want from writing is amusement and joy. I don't want to take on any ambitious or grandiose projects. I'm not interested in doing something startling or new. I don't want fame or celebrity. I don't want to shock or surprise or impress anyone with my writing brilliance or intellectual bona fides. Excuse me, but those are youthful games. I have already earned my living, and so I can ignore the fact that I'm not making my money from my writing.

I'm mainly interested in imagining and telling diverting and amusing stories, with interesting thoughts and ideas buried behind them. I'm interested in researching my own mind, but not in other sorts of research. I did plenty of heavy research when I was in academe, and I don't want to do any more. I like making stuff up and then convincing my readers that it is true.

For me, the writer's art is to some degree a conjurer's art. And the conjuring comes in the language, the careful formulation of a story that carries the reader along in exactly the direction and at exactly the speed you want him to go. For me, the speed should be a comfortable to slow one, even as the story moves briskly along. The tone should be ironic and slightly detached. Every sentence should be clear and to the point, and every sentence should transport the reader into the world I am building.

Nothing I or anyone else writes can be as powerful as what the reader's intelligence and imagination bring to a story; I always try to leave plenty of room for that. Having that room is also useful when it comes to suggesting that I know things I do not actually know. The hero of my three published novels, Louis Morgon, is a long-retired CIA operative whose past keeps intruding into his life. It was incumbent on me to either know something about the CIA or to convince the reader that I did. I chose the latter strategy.

One method I employed was having a character who is supposed to be part of the CIA casually use a word or phrase that is part of the jargon we read in the papers or see in movies—"wet operations," "tradecraft," etc.—that suggests more about the character than it actually should. The reader then adds his own conviction to my implications about that character.

I also avoid all but the sketchiest physical description of places and people for the same reason. Given just the faintest suggestion, the reader will imagine him or it fully. That has allowed me to write well enough about places I have never been to and things I have never done so that people familiar with the place or thing are convinced that I know what I'm writing about. An acquaintance who was in fact in intelligence work long ago came to believe, from reading my book, that I had been also. Of course, the more I denied it, the more convinced he was that he was right.

Still to this day, I do not plan out a novel. I do not make outlines or draw maps or post plot points on cards tacked to bulletin boards, as I know some fine writers do. I have an idea that I want to explore and enlarge upon. It is not unlike a cartoon idea in that it will involve a configuration of characters in a particular place and time. I do not know the characters in the novel until I need them, at which point I invent them. If I have ideas about where it might end up, I resist thinking about these ideas so as to keep the end as vague as possible until I'm nearly there.

No part of the novel should have any but the most ephemeral form until I arrive at that particular point. Then the writing should discover, pick out, and define the moment. In my first draft, I am closing in on the moment; subsequent drafts draw me still closer, until I am there. In essence, I am reading the novel for the first time as I write it. The process always feels magical to me, and that is what makes the experience entirely pleasurable.

Peter Steiner left a college teaching career to become an artist. His cartoons have appeared in The New Yorker *for more than twenty-five years. He has had three novels published. A fourth,* The Resistance, *comes out this summer from St Martin's Press.*

There are two final contributors who have vast experiences in the field. They have both taught, edited, and been published broadly. They round out our book with some broader insights about teaching and having a life in the world of letters. Leslie Sharpe is an extraordinary author, professor of writing, and former editor at Farrar, Straus & Giroux, and Melvin Bukiet is a writing teacher as well as author of numerous reviews, stories, anthologies, novels, and recently, books for young readers.

On Writing Smart: Tips and Tidbits

by Leslie T. Sharpe, Author, Editor, and Educator

WHY WE WRITE

We write to be read; it's as simple as that.

Whether you are writing poetry, novels, or memoir—whether you are writing the most commercial fiction or nonfiction, genre or how-to—you are writing to be read. And that means, of course, that you are writing to be published.

That word "published," which is such a Holy Grail for writers—that magical phrase that seems to vet us as successful, "I am a *published* writer"—actually has rather modest etymological roots. "To publish" just means to make public. And to "make public," of course, means to get your work out there.

So how do you "get your work out there" so that it can be read by that eager, awaiting public? First things first: How do you even get started in the writing process? How do you start translating that great idea in your head onto the page? And perhaps even more crucial, how do you keep going? How do you keep the writing faith, in yourself and in your project, so that you can reach that true Holy Grail of writing—the finish line?

This essay will answer these questions in the same honest-as-I can-make-it, commonsense terms that I discuss them with my writing students. My answers will try to address what you have on your writing mind, why you have bought this handy tome, with the purpose of helping you become the writer that you want to be—and the published writer that you dream of being.

GETTING STARTED AND KEEPING GOING!

To make your own work public and to be published, the first thing you must do is write your words down on the page.

Obvious, you say? It's more complicated than that. I can tell you, the hardest thing to do is to start. To pick up that pen, to stop staring at that screen, to take that first step, and start writing. Once you do that, you are already making your words public because someone else can read them. When you take that first bold (and bravest) step, when you finally see your own words on the page, then you have overcome the single biggest obstacle in writing.

Procrastination is all too often our affliction as writers. Most of the time, we don't invent strategies to write, but *not* to write. Anything will do, from cleaning the house to fiddling with the margins of the page...and why not? Writing is hard. There is *nothing* harder. Be assured that any and all of us who aspire to write and who have written (and yes, who are published!) have been there.

I have known so many "writers"—smart, talented people with something to say—who can't do it, who are forever asking me for advice, strategies, even "tricks" to get them to commit their thoughts to the page. Sometimes they can write in fits and starts. Sometimes they have written something previously but can't find it in themselves to write again. Whatever we call this, usually "writer's block," there really is only one solution. And that is just to start.

Tip: Set yourself a writing routine and stick to it.

Writing is work, so treat it as such. Decide on the same time, every day, to write. And commit to writing for a certain amount of time. Also decide on a place that gives you the privacy and peace that you need to write. Sometimes life will intervene, it's true. But you can always manage a few sentences. The point is to make writing part of your everyday routine—to make it the habit you *don't* want to break.

Now, to you true shamans out there who are working in that manifest unconscious state of creativity and who have *no* such trouble starting and continuing, congratulations. (And, of course writing can be fun. All of us, if we keep at it, experience those joyful moments when everything just clicks—when our writing flows, our style sparkles, and it all seems so effortless.) But, for the rest of us, who more often than not struggle in our solitude to create something magical on the page, realize that you are in good company. To repeat, writing well is hard work. (In the words of the great writing teacher William Zinsser—whose classic *On Writing Well* I recommend to writers in all forms—"I hate writing. I love having written.") When people read your work and marvel at the fluidity of your language, the clarity and crispness of your style, the cogency of your ideas...what they are *not* seeing is the art that hides the art. That effortless prose has taken, well, a lot of effort—a lot of wordsmithery and a lot of thought, for starters. That "art that hides the art" is our secret. But people who don't write don't know that; they don't even have an inkling about how hard writing well is. This brings me to my next tip:

Tip: *Beware that reader to whom you show your writing!*

So, you have finally "published" your work on the page and are dying to show it to someone. Usually, your first choice is family members or close friends. My advice: is *don't*! The problem is this: When you ask people for their opinion, they will give it. And when it comes to writing, the average person is clueless. Everyone thinks they can write because in the course of the day, everyone does. And, after all, good writing appears effortless, right? Well, as we have just said, *wrong*! And, as you are learning your craft (and this goes for all of us who write, for however long we have been doing it—we are *all* continually learning our craft, striving to improve it, no matter what our success), as you feel that elation of getting your words down, of seeing them come together in a thematic puzzle, spelling out your story, you do *not* need anyone saying, "Well, yes but…"

For example, when writing novels or those creative non-fiction forms—especially memoir and personal essay, which so often draw on our own experiences and family life—our relatives can have something personal at stake, to say the least. Forget it! Better to start your own writing group among (hopefully) objective friends who are also writing, or to find a creditable writing community at a local university or some other writing program, including, increasingly, online. (And *please!* do your due diligence here. Check all credentials, of all programs and any instructors, and get recommendations, preferably from people you know, but you also should be able to find such on the web. Your writing is your baby and you are entrusting it to strangers, so carefully vet them.)

Even those who are not personally invested can get their own ego involved. I was horrified recently when a poet I know showed me "feedback" a friend had given her on a poem—which was to re-write it! That is *not* editing—that person, as I told my friend, should write her own damn poem and leave *her* work alone. You never know what feelings can be provoked by being shown one's writing—everything from protectiveness, to a sincere desire to help, to yes, jealousy. I have seen, on more than one occasion, writers stopped in their tracks by such "feedback." Sometimes for a long time. Just consider the source and find the best person possible to read your work, hopefully a writing or editing professional who will have one goal and one goal only, that is, to help make your writing its best possible self. Criticism is one thing; just make sure that it's intelligent and that you trust the critic. And that it makes your work better.

Look, criticism and rejection are the name of our writing game, it's true. You gotta be tough. And that brings me to my next tip:

Tip: Hang in there! Don't take no for an answer, and never say no to yourself.

This is not an essay meant to give individual writing lessons. That said, I would mention here just a few writing tidbits, which have been wrung from my own experience.

First, if you get stuck once you have started, you should always go back to your subject (what you are writing about) and your theme (what you are saying about that subject). This really works for fiction as well as nonfiction, and for poetry, too. An easy example is biography—biographies aren't a time line of their subject's life. Take Lincoln, for instance. The reason there are so many biographies of arguably our greatest president is because different writers have different takes on the same subject, and they reinterpret the events in that subject's life and times to construct their own POV (point of view), which is essentially the theme that makes their work uniquely their own. I am convinced that most cases of writer's block are about losing those threads that, when pulled together, comprise our theme, and when pulled apart, can make us feel lost in our writing. So, if that happens to you, if you get "stuck," take a minute to remember what you are writing about, and then remind yourself what it is that you want to say about your subject. In order to write clearly, you have to think clearly.

My next writing tidbit is this: Don't try to write when you are tired. It's amazing what a good night's sleep can do, how those words that eluded you the night before can magically appear on the page the next morning. I also like so much Hemingway's advice in *A Moveable Feast*, his incandescent memoir of his early years in Paris, when he said he never stopped writing until he had the first line of his next day's work down on the page (and once he had it, he went to sleep). Knowing when to stop writing, as well as when to start, can be crucial.

My final tidbit (my "mantra," according to my grad students) is that everything you write must do work. And what this means is that everything you write has to go back to that subject and theme of yours. Everything, even the smallest detail, has to help build the narrative arc, move the plot forward, develop characters, or give the reader promised information.

But even if you do all this, and do it well, chances are, your work will be rejected on the way to acceptance. (A wonderful little volume, *Rotten Rejections,* gives writers instant perspective and a few laughs—including one of my favorites to Herman Melville, rejecting *Moby-Dick* "because we do not think it would be at all suitable for the juvenile market.") And, when you are published, your work will certainly be criticized as well as praised. It's a rough racket, in a word or two. And in order to be successful, you have to hang in there. So take any knock as a boost. Use it to fuel you to "show them." (Success is indeed the best revenge.) You just need one agent, one editor, one writing teacher, one friend to believe in you. Don't be daunted by the "no" word. And whatever you do, don't get so discouraged that you don't try—which is what I mean by don't say no to yourself. (One of my graduate students spent four years having her narrative nonfiction book rejected by editors. But she had an agent who believed in her, and together, they made some modifications to her work for the market that did not compromise the book's integrity. It was finally published and went on to receive a prestigious regional award. *All because she didn't give up!*)

So just keep going. Be tough, be determined, be stubborn. (And, if you can't hang in there, you probably should be doing something else, to be frank.) The literary world is full of publishing pros who were wrong about writing. John Kennedy Toole's *A Confederacy of Dunces,* rejected by esteemed editor Robert Gottlieb and famed literary agent Candida Donadio, eventually published after Toole's tragic death (thanks to his mother, who dragged that manuscript around to publishers for years—again, you just need that one person to believe in you!), won the Pulitzer Prize for Fiction in 1981. They don't always know everything, these guys. Believe in yourself; believe in your book.

What Makes a Writer?

This brings us to graduate writing programs, which can be transformative in a writer's experience, but with which I also do have an issue. My concern is that they can cultivate the idea of creative writing as professionalized through the awarding of an MFA or MA degree in writing. That somehow, with that degree in hand, you are automatically anointed as a "writer." Well, it ain't necessarily so. What it signifies, at best, is the end of the first phase of one's writing apprenticeship. (I remember being stunned by a letter I received from novelist and essayist Susan Sontag, whom I had the privilege of working with, when she wrote that after writing numerous books, she now finally considered herself at the end of her "apprenticeship." Now *that's* perspective.)

What an advanced writing degree will do for you, in practical terms, is give you your entry-level union card in this way: with an MFA, chances are that agents, and even editors, will be more likely to read your work. (Indeed, one of my graduate students in fiction reported how agents, who had snubbed him before, were suddenly eager to read his manuscript once he could say he was an MFA candidate.) But that's still *not* a guarantee of representation. Similarly, most academic writing jobs stipulate that a candidate must have a "terminal degree," such as the MFA, to be considered for a teaching position. But again, very often, without publications, that MFA isn't enough.

So, what's an aspiring writer to do? Do you really need an advanced degree in order to write? Do you even have to go to school in order to learn *how* to write?

People ask me that all the time. The answer is simple:

Tip: The best way to learn how to write is to read, read, and read!

Read everything you can get your hands on, fiction and nonfiction, and don't neglect poetry. Writers who aren't poets can't forget to read poetry. It should be the first thing on your reading list—to learn economy of language, for starters, the crystallization of the perfect word. Everything that you read is doing the work of preparing you to write. And the other advice I offer is simply to live your life. To live to write, if you will. But beware of writing to live—that usually ends up putting too much pressure on one's soul. The one thing about writing you can be sure of is that the more you chase it, the more it will elude you, the more it will flee, like some infernal cat. Let your writing come to *you*. Live to write, yes. There's a joy in that. But to write to live—that can be a trap.

Graduate writing programs, redux: If you have the time and means, if you can give a couple years of your life to your writing and to immersing yourself in the cloister of an academic writing community, then go for it. For me, a good graduate writing program is like a Renaissance workshop where talented young painters and sculptors are apprenticed with the leading masters of their day to learn artistry and craft as they were starting to create their own works. What I would only suggest is that you choose a program that also features not just writing workshops but also seminars and lectures—yes, classes in which you *read*, in which you can develop your ability to think critically. You have to be able to be objective about your own work (and it takes practice, believe me), to be dispassionate when you hear criticism and to make calls, in what you add and cut and change in your writing, that depend on your own judgment. So find a writing program that allows you to stretch your intellect, one that feeds your mind, stimulates your thinking, and stirs your imagination as you are polishing your style. One that puts a premium on reading and thinking critically about writing in order to understand why it works or doesn't—lessons you will be able to adapt and apply to your own work.

But whether you are writing on your own, or in a vaunted writing program, remember:

Tip: Your "voice" is you on the page.

Your greatest asset as a writer is having your own voice. Your own style. That is your signature. It is a voice that will change and grow as you change and grow as a writer. But that voice, what makes you uniquely you as a writer, is *you* on the page. Helping you to find your own voice and perfect it is a priority of any true writing teacher. If anyone ever tells you to write like somebody else (other than as a classroom exercise, of course)—or insists you write like them (or according to the "style" of some writing "school")—run! I am reminded of the American artist Georgia O'Keeffe, who left a graduate program in painting after two weeks because "they wanted me to paint like them. I wanted to paint like me." Which doesn't mean you shouldn't listen and try to separate your ego from the sting of criticism—even, perhaps especially, tough criticism, which can be the most productive—as long as you trust the source; that that person has the best interest of *your* writing at heart to help you find *your* voice and to help you say what *you* want to say.

TAKING YOUR WORK PUBLIC

Here's a bold statement: This is the best time to be writing if you want to take your work public. Is there a catch, since I said "to take your work public" rather than "to publish your work"? Let me explain. When we think of getting published, what comes to mind are the big houses that are household names, such as Random House and Simon & Schuster. It can be a daunting prospect, getting past these gatekeepers that so often consider the bottom line first and, as a result, have become increasingly cautious about taking on new writers. But that said, editors everywhere get into this business because they want to publish good writing on important subjects, whether nonfiction or fiction. The rub is that editors are pressured to buy writing that will hopefully sell enough copies to justify the costs of publishing even one book—this includes everything from the author's advance to printing and publicizing it. For these commercial publishers, a literary agent is deemed a must. (And remember that they are useful to you, as well—as a matter of fact, your agent works for *you!*) Publishers would rather deal with an agent, on a business level, and you, the writer, need someone to steer you through all the complexities of this brave new publishing world, including electronic rights. And these days, it is the agent who often has the primary relationship with a writer—who "holds the writer's hand"—not necessarily the editor, many of whom come and go, often leaving behind orphaned books in their wake. Find an agent who gets you and your writing, who believes in your work, and especially, who will stick with you. There can be no greater asset for a writer.

Now here's the good news: There has been a proliferation of small presses with the advent of new technologies, such as print-on-demand, which allows writing to be stored digitally and, as a result, allows publishers to print one book at a time. Paper, printing, storage—these have been the traditional big ticket items for publishers. Print-on-demand—as well as desktop publishing software and the availability of laser printers—has not only allowed small houses to bloom (and many of these *don't* require an author to have an agent) but also has allowed for the reissue of midlist books, literary fiction especially, which had gone OP (out of print). Do the small presses pay like the big houses? No. But getting your work in print with a smaller press will often get you noticed by reviewers as well as editors, and sometimes get you even *more* attention as that unexpected literary "treasure" that has been "discovered," which can make you a lead author as opposed to one of hundreds. And let's not forget all the innovations wrought by the web—blogging, Twitter, to name just a couple—*all of which you can use to take your work public!* Many new writers have been awarded book contracts on the basis of their blog (which also allows you to start building a "platform" for your work—a way to reach a demonstrable audience, which publishers love). Self-publishing through print-on-demand, and also original e-book publishing, is an increasingly acceptable option (and is a time-honored tradition of writers who haven't been able to break into the commercial publishing world—Beatrix Potter is my favorite example). There are also so many new opportunities to be published via websites and new electronic as well as print literary magazines. (Or start your own! Most literary magazines have their origin in a group of "young Turks" who couldn't break into the hallowed halls of *The New Yorker*—why not you and your fellow writers?)

This is what you have to know: that without *you*, the writer, there is *no* publishing industry. You are *not* a disposable part; you are the heart and soul and guts of this industry.

And finally, keep this in mind:

Tip: The means of production is now in the writer's hands.

I love that sentiment, expressed to me by a writer friend who started his own publishing house. It conjures up, for me, writers committing radical acts on behalf of their own writing, to make it public, to publish it, to see it in print. And doesn't our writing deserve that? Writing is, after all, the *most* radical act—a radical act of courage and commitment, and above all, of belief in oneself.

Leslie T. Sharpe is an author, editor, and educator. She received an MA from Columbia University, where she was a Woodrow Wilson Fellow, in Ancient Greek Language and Literature. She is co-author of Editing Fact and Fiction: A Concise Guide to Book Editing *(Cambridge University Press, 1994), and her essays and articles have appeared in a wide array of national publications. As an editor, she has worked with many notable authors and illustrators and has edited literary, as well as commercial, fiction and nonfiction, children's books, and poetry. She has taught nonfiction writing in Columbia University's School of the Arts Writing Program for sixteen years, as well as writing, editing, and publishing courses at New York University, The City College of New York, and online at mediabistro.com.*

To MFA or Not to MFA?

by Melvin Jules Bukiet, Novelist and Professor at Sarah Lawrence College

Before there are published writers, there are unpublished writers. Before there are unpublished writers, there are writers. Before there are writers, there are would-be writers. And often enough in the culture that's evolved in America over the last half century, before there are would-be writers, there are students.

Sometimes students take a writing class because they believe they have a story to tell. Maybe they're correct. Sometimes they take a writing class because they think that anything they have to say is worthwhile simply because they're saying it. They're wrong. And sometimes they take a writing class because they've loved books since they were old enough to read.

For that last group, the idea of sitting on the other side of the typewriter is scary as hell. Of course, I've aged myself here by using one particular word in that last sentence, but it sounds better than "the other side of the computer" because that includes everyone from Bill Gates to the E★Trade baby, and sometimes I can't tell which is which. Okay, that was gratuitous, but I also think it's funny. The point is that for those students whose reading lives are more powerful than their day-to-day existences, the idea of creating an imaginative world of their own is nothing short of revelatory. The vision is magnificent; it's also incendiary, just as likely to immolate as to inspire the recipient of the vision.

For those students who contemplate putting their own names on a title page with fear and trembling, the pen or the keyboard is not merely a tool for necessary communication or self-indulgent expression. It's Excalibur, and although they yearn to extract it from the stone more passionately than they ever craved romantic love or dreamed of fabulous wealth, they know that they may not be up to the task.

Many people believe that because they can tell stories, they can write. On the other hand, everyone (well, almost) hears music, but only an idiot would dare to assume he could pick up a violin and step onto the stage of Carnegie Hall. In fact, there are five-year-old musical prodigies so miraculously in tune with an instrument that they can perform brilliantly at the first touch of bow to string. Yet there's no such thing as a literary prodigy. A twenty-eight-year-old with a fine first novel is remarkable. At forty, when baseball players and ballet dancers are retired, novelists are still, in the parlance of the trade, "emerging."

Preemergence, everyone tells stories: at the breakfast table with family, at lunch with friends, over the water cooler in an office. Since narrative comes naturally to us—in cups, I'd argue that narrative defines us as a species more so than opposable thumbs—many believe that we can simply put those stories that enthralled our buddies over a few beers onto a page and have the same effect. Ain't necessarily so.

Consider the question: Who does the writer write for? Most answers will be the reader or the writer. Yes, you hope for an audience, but if you write for it, you're a panderer. And, yes, you wish to express yourself, but if that's all you're doing, you're a solipsist. It'll sound odd, but I believe that you write the novel for the novel. The ultimate aim is to make the thing what it must be. Finally, yes, the obvious analogy is appropriate. Novels are like children. You want them to be smart and brave and good, but they will inevitably become themselves. Nature can be nurtured. It can be stunted. It cannot be changed. Any writing class that aims to change the soul of a manuscript should be shunned.

It's not a matter of having a story to tell. Of course, there are big subjects of predetermined value: war and prejudice and peace and crime and pride and punishment. But there's also the splendid nineteenth century Russian novel *Oblomov*, in which the plot pivots over whether the laziest hero in literature will rise from his couch. Take my word for it; the thing is thrilling. It keeps you on the edge of your own couch with anticipation. It's how you tell the story that matters.

Years ago, when I was the fiction editor of a national magazine, we held a conference at Columbia University. There were multiple readings and sessions in various rooms, and there was one panel for anyone who was interested in writing for us. Frankly, I dreaded the event because I thought it was a sop for people who'd paid to attend the conference with the single goal of thrusting a manuscript into an editor's hands. Anyway, the book review editor spoke and so did the general nonfiction editor. The former mentioned the kind of books we were interested in and the tone a review ought to take and the general length reviews ought to be. The latter explained that potential contributors should send her clips of previous work and tell her what they hoped to write about. Say that a young writer named Gustave wanted to write about red shoes: The editor could answer that we were not a fashion magazine, and Gustave was a dolt. Or she could say that we ran an article about red shoes last year and felt that we'd covered the subject. Or that we ran a great piece about blue shoes and would love Gustave to do a parallel one about red shoes. In any case, she could answer. But when it came my turn to speak, I couldn't offer such clear advice. Imagine I received a letter that read, "I'd like to write about a boring, suburban housewife. Yours, Gustave Flaubert." It's how you tell the story that matters.

Unfortunately, most young writers think the opposite, especially if the story they have to tell is a faintly disguised version of their own life. Of course, their toilet training and adolescent heartbreak are compelling to them, but it takes more than that to make such glamorous episodes compel a reader. It's a matter of turning sentences around. Or turning around sentences. It's not a matter of around sentences turning. Granted, most young writers accept grammatical norms that allow us to understand each other. A real writer, however, is someone who will spend hours in torment deciding whether to turn around sentences or to turn sentences around. A real writer may be arrogant in the face of the world but is always humble before his or her own syntax.

If I had to sum up, while standing on one foot, what I tell my students every week from September until May, I'd say, "Words matter," and then put my foot down. Prior to that great day when a novel appears in a bookstore window (and probably leaves a day later, but let's not get depressing), prior to the great day when an editor says that she wants to turn your manuscript into a book headed for that window, prior to the great day when an agent says that she wants to take your manuscript to an editor who will...there are thousands of days in which a writer lives alone with his or her imagination and language.

In lieu of the glory of the hardcover, there are scores of lesser but still wonderful things a young writer may do to keep off the streets. First, there are stories—maybe excerpts from the novel in progress—that ought to be sent out. Of course, you send to *The New Yorker* and *Harper's* and the few remaining "general interest" magazines first. They probably won't take your work, but some editor may see talent and encourage future submissions. Believe that because editors are tough and won't open their door if they don't want the writer to eventually come in. And if you receive a rejection slip rather than an "I like it, but..." letter, don't sweat. Send out work again, and again, and again. After all, you have nothing to lose but your pride and self-respect. There are legions of stories about subsequently well-known writers who once papered their walls with rejection slips.

Still, the novel is the Grail. For me, a novel can start anywhere. One began with an object, another with a setting, another with several lines of dialogue, another with a title. After those initial sparks, I had to fan the flames. This consisted of two jobs undertaken simultaneously. The first was to find out who was looking at the object, or living in the place, or speaking the dialogue, or what on earth that two-word title that I thought was so striking meant. In each case, I typed the initial words and knew that I'd be lost to the world until I spent however much time was necessary (generally between one and three years) to arrive at the last words. My second job was to rewrite every single sentence on every single one of several hundred pages until they were as beautiful as I could make them.

Approaching the end of both endeavors, I tend to feel the ecstatic delirium of a pregnant woman with just one more centimeter to push and also the terrifying dread of an ancient seafarer who is sure he's about to fall off the edge of the world. There couldn't possibly be another fortuitous phrase or image or title in my head to justify the next era of my life. Then, about forty-eight hours of despair later, it happens, because for me the need is less so to write a particular book than to keep writing books. And if all else failed, I always kept a secret card up my sleeve: I could write some Oblomovian novel about how impossible it was to write. At least, I thought that card was my secret until I saw that the critic and occasional fiction writer George Steiner recently published *My Unwritten Books*. In it, he describes seven books he contemplated but did not produce. They range from one about sex in different languages to one about exile to another on cosmic emptiness. Together they provide a complex intellectual portrait of the writer himself.

Back to writing classes. Many share a common mantra: "Write what you know." This is bunk because what I—and you—know is small and insignificant. What we don't know is vast and fascinating. Encouraged by this dubious dictum, many student writers will, understandably, play to strength. This is just about the worst thing for a student to do. Sure, it may lead to workshop applause and the student will feel like he's taken a bath in a tub filled with warm milk. That's heavenly…for about five minutes because, when the cold wind comes down from the north, milky white icicles will hang from his nose. To protect against that wind, the student should risk—or better yet, seek—failure. The word "edgy" is popular these days. I don't want my students teetering precariously on the edge, windmilling to keep from losing their balance. I want them running and screaming over the precipice and splashing onto the rocks below. Then I want them to get up and do it again. That's how they grow strong.

Indeed, I'd have to describe my own pedagogy as perverse. No, not kinky—counterintuitive. If a student writes vigorous dialogue, I'll suggest a story that's entirely narrative. And the reverse. If a student sets everything on a farm, I'll urge her to explore a city. And the reverse. Most likely, the student is on an appropriate path, but the aim is to weed whack a new path. Maybe that newly turned earth will prove fertile. At the very least, the student will learn some healthy technical know-how and return to her original path with a greater sense that it's the right one for her to travel.

The structure of a writing class is the opposite of what happens out in the world. There, a review (another sideline young writers ought to explore because papers are in regular need of intelligent commentary) may fairly declare that a novel is well-written but entirely misconceived, and the reviewer may doubt that any reader who isn't paid to do so will be interested in a tale told from the point of view of a cheese grater. In class, we don't pass such judgments. Instead, we aim to revise the atrocity into the best chronicle of a cheese grater ever written. Having struggled to accomplish this task, the writer ought to be able to use his skills to produce a more persuasive character and more compelling narrative next time around.

And if writing classes are weird, writing programs are exponentially weirder. I do not categorically disdain them because two years away from the world figuring out how to write by yourself in the company of people who care about the same things is a gift to be treasured. If you happen to meet someone who can help—even become a mentor—that's spectacular, but it cannot be expected. Thinking that such a program will provide the key to bestsellerdom or the National Book Award is bound to lead to disappointment.

Consider the difference between an MD and an MFA. Someone who receives the former is a doctor. Maybe a good one, maybe a bad one, probably successful, maybe not, but a doctor nonetheless. Yet someone who graduates from a writing program is…a graduate of a writing program. Furthermore, if, say, one out of ten graduates from a particular medical school kills his patients, that school is going to be out of business. All right, I don't know squat about accrediting procedures, but I damn well hope the state would nail shut that incompetent institution's doors. But if one out of ten of my students publishes a novel, I'm a superstar of a teacher. Emendation: I'm a superstar if one out of ten of my students publishes a novel within ten years of graduation. Because the norm is failure (not moral, emotional, intellectual, or even literary—but purely, pathetically professional failure), schools have virtually no accountability. This means that administrations establish such programs as cash cows with greater or lesser levels of hypocrisy, sucking tuition out of aspiring novelists or poets who might be better served by applying to an MD program.

There has certainly been an increasing preprofessionalism in the arts over the last quarter century, and I suppose that I'm an example of it because I did receive an MFA and do teach in such a program now. Yet, back in the Pleistocene Era, my fellow students and I looked rather suspiciously at ourselves, thinking that if we had any integrity we'd have joined the Foreign Legion instead of registering for class. Back then, we would have been right.

Things are, however, different now. My guess is that if you plucked every first novel of that season when I was in school off the shelf of a local bookstore—ye Gods, there were local bookstores then—perhaps 15 percent of the author bios would have included the words "and received an MFA from XYZ University." Today, it would be closer to 50 percent. Maybe more. But no novel is published because of the academic gown the writer wore one balmy spring afternoon. Maybe that gown got the writer a slightly more considered read at an agency or publishing house. Maybe the agent would have scanned the first five pages of manuscript if it hadn't come with a shiny new degree but instead gave the writer the benefit of ten pages because of the degree. Maybe the writer started doing something wonderful on page nine. But unless that happens, the degree won't get the writer on the subway. There's no magic; there's only work.

Is this meandering? Is this helpful? There is a real world out there to navigate, but the first thing that you have to do is to build a boat.

Melvin Jules Bukiet is the author of eight novels and the editor of three anthologies. He teaches at Sarah Lawrence College.

Acknowledgments

I could not have edited this book without the fine work of all the contributors. Thank you all for sharing your ideas.

A special thanks to Oscar Hijuelos for the foreword (you are a national treasure) and to Lori Carlson for your contribution and constant support. What a great eye for new voices you have!

Also thanks to the ever-encouraging Leslie Sharpe and Liza Monroy, who not only contributed pieces, but are also already busy being ambassadors for the book.

And thanks to Jed Perl for constant encouragement.

Thanks to Michael Cader of Publisher's Market Place/Lunch.

And thanks to Daniella Gitlin for sharing a good query letter.

The editorial work was aided by Ruth Mirsky and Audrey Peterson, both talented minds and artists. You kept us all coordinated and on task. Audrey, we will see your book in print soon.

The next generation of writers' opinions were helpful to this book. Thanks to Elissa Hutson and Genevive Delion.

Thanks to Allworth Press and especially Tad Crawford and Delia Casa.

My thanks to the Lyons family: my talented painter mother and my three brothers Tony, Paul, and Charles. Tony, you especially supported this!

And to my family, the Brennans: my husband, Steve, and my children, Lara and Finn. Thank you for your unwavering support.

Afterword

Now that you have heard from so many contributors, we hope you will feel empowered to start or continue your career.

The world of publishing is hard to understand. I remember my first agenting meeting when terms like "advances," "publicity," "royalties," "subsidiary rights," etc. were bandied about. It takes time to understand but you will and we hope this helps you.

And the publishing landscape is likely to continue to change rapidly. For instance, in a recent interview on the site Digital Book World, the publisher of Hyperion, Ellen Archer, mentioned that she thinks that by 2015 the company will derive 50 to 60 percent of their revenues from e-books!

Our intention was to share our experiences with you and to help you achieve your goals. Also to say there are many paths to take. You have a personal path. We hope your work gets published.

Resources

We asked our contributors to suggest some resources that could be useful to readers of this book. This is by no means an exhaustive list, but it may help those of you who could benefit from some pointing in the right direction.

Recommended by Ken Krimstein

National Cartoonists Society   reuben.org

Recommended by Colette Inez

ABC of Reading by Ezra Pound (New Directions)

Poetry Handbook by Mary Oliver (Harcourt Brace & Co.)

The Directory of Poetry Publishers, Len Fulton, editor (Dustbooks)
    Available at dustbooks.com.

The Writer's Chronicle

Poets & Writers magazine

Recommended by Marcela Landres

Submit: The Unofficial All-Genre Multimedia Guide to Submitting Short Prose (DVD)

Recommended by Leslie Sharpe

InReads   *inreads.com*

> A resource for young writers sponsored by WETA, the Washington, D.C., PBS affiliate.

Mediabistro.com

> Offers events, blogs, courses (online and in person) covering a wide range of media—general, but particularly writing related—as well as job opportunities. It is a terrific resource with an excellent faculty.

Writer's BloQ   *writersbloq.com*

> Founded by 22-year-old Columbia MFA Nayia Moysidis, who was deeply dissatisfied with the undisputed fact that it often takes years to break into the industry. Moysidis's goal is to reduce barriers and establish a writing community. Writer's BloQ is aimed at MFA/Undergrad Writing Program students in particular, offering them a place to post their work, discuss, and find a way to get published.

The Authors Guild   *authorsguild.org*
31 East 32nd Street, 7th Floor, New York, NY 10016
212-563-5904

> Established in 1912 as the Authors League of America, the Authors Guild is a national organization that advocates and provides legal assistance for writers' interests, including fair contracts, copyright protection, and free expression.

National Writers Union   *nwu.org*

> The only labor union that represents freelance writers, "NWU works to advance the economic and working conditions of all writers," states the website. "Our members also directly benefit from the many valuable services the Union offers—including

grievance assistance, contract advice, and much more—while actively contributing to a growing movement of professional freelancers who have banded together to assert their collective power."

PEN International   *pen.org*

The worldwide association of writers founded in London in 1921 to foster fellowship and mutual intellectual pursuit among writers globally. Offers Associate/Student Associate memberships open to "everyone who supports PEN's mission."

New York Center for Independent Publishing   *nycip.wordpress.com*

Formerly the Small Press Center. Offers lectures, seminars, talks, workshops, and abundant information about the small, literary, and university press markets in which it is more and more crucial for serious writers to be published. The NYCIP hosts annual programs including the Independent and Small Press Book Fair and National Small Press Month.

Poet's House   *poetshouse.org*
10 River Terrace, New York, NY 10282
212-431-7920

Poet's House is a literary center and 50,000-volume poetry archive in New York City. It is an invaluable resource, with workshops and events as well as internships and volunteer opportunities.

Poets and Writers   *pw.org*

Established in 1970, *Poets & Writers* (both the print magazine and online) offers support, and guidance for creative writers, including poets, fiction writers, and creative nonfiction writers. The national office is located in New York City, with a branch in Los Angeles. *P&W*'s website has a comprehensive Conferences and Residencies database.

The Writers Room   *writersroom.org*
740 Broadway, New York, NY 10003
212-254-6995

> Called a "a nonprofit urban writers' colony in New York
> City," the Writers Room was created for those authors who
> need an affordable, distraction-free workspace. Offers 24-hour,
> 365-days-a-year access, free WiFi, and Lexis/Nexis, a phone
> room, and a kitchen/lounge. In 2011, members wrote thirty
> fiction and nonfiction books, as well as magazine articles,
> screenplays, and plays.

Association of Authors' Representatives   *aaronline.org*

> The AAR arose from the merger in 1991 of the Society of
> Authors' Representatives, founded in 1928, and the Indepen-
> dent Literary Agents Association, established in 1977, to keep
> agents up to date on the changing landscape of the publish-
> ing, theater, film, and television industries. Specifically geared
> toward aiding agents in representing authors' and clients' best
> interests, it's a good place for writers to begin their search for
> an agent because all agents must meet standards outlined in the
> AAR bylaws and agree to the organization's Canon of Ethics.

Writer's Residencies Recommended by Leslie Sharpe

The MacDowell Colony   *macdowellcolony.org*
100 High Street, Peterborough, NH 03458
603-924-3886

> The only criterion for acceptance to The MacDowell Colony
> is "artistic excellence." Artists "representing the widest possible
> range of perspectives and demographics" are encouraged to
> apply.

Bread Loaf Writer's Conference   *middlebury.edu/blwc*
Middlebury College, Middlebury, Vermont
802-443-5000

> Each summer writers, faculty agents, and editors convene in
> Middlebury, Vermont, for the Bread Loaf Writer's Conference.
> The 87-year-old conference, held against the backdrop of the
> Green Mountains, features workshops, lectures, and classes
> designed to engage participants in the "rigorous practical and
> theoretical approaches to the craft of writing." The website
> emphasizes that Bread Loaf is not a retreat but "provides a
> stimulating community of diverse voices in which we test our
> own assumptions regarding literature and seek advice about
> our progress as writers."

Ragdale   *ragdale.org/residency*
1260 North Green Bay Road, Lake Forest, IL 60045
847-234-1063

> Ragdale offers two- to six-week residencies for a small
> group of writers in the middle of a prairie, where artists
> come "to create, write, experiment, research, plan, com-
> pose, rejuvenate, brainstorm, and work." Participants enjoy
> solo time as well as the opportunity to connect with other
> artists.

Norman Mailer Center and Writers Colony Educational Center
nmcenter.org
627 Commercial Street, Provincetown, MA 02657
646-374-3939, extension 5

> Provincetown, Massachusetts, was a residence for Mailer for
> 30 years and has been a retreat for artists and writers since the
> turn of the last century. Artists live in the Mailer home or in
> nearby condos. Retreats are one to two months long and are
> offered during the fall, winter, and spring.

The Studios of Key West   *tskw.org/category/residencies*
Historic Armory, 600 White Street, Key West, FL 33040
305-296-0458

> Established in 2006 and based at the Historic Key West
> Armory, the Studios of Key West is a nonprofit charitable
> organization whose purpose is to support local artists,
> celebrate the island's unique history, and spur new col-
> laborative artistic works. TSKW offers up to forty juried
> residencies per year to working artists and writers from
> around the world. Up to four residents at any given time
> can be hosted at TSKW's cottages.

Ox-Bow   *ox-bow.org*
3435 Rupprecht Way, P.O. Box 216, Saugatuck, MI 49453
269-857-5811

> In operation for more than one hundred years, Ox-Bow's
> 155-acre campus comprises natural forests, dunes, a
> lagoon, and historic buildings and has been a haven for
> artists to explore traditional techniques while pushing
> the boundaries of new genres and formats. Two- to five-
> week residencies are available in the fall of each year.

Jennifer Lyons Literary Agency recommends

The article "The Amazon Effect" by Steve Wasserman
> Published in the *Nation*, June 18, 2012. View online at: *www.
> thenation.com/article/168125/amazon-effect*.

Latinidad   *www.marcelalandres.com/E-zine.html*

Words Without Borders   *wordswithoutborders.org*

Publishers Weekly   *publishersweekly.com*

A weekly trade magazine for publishers, librarians, book-sellers, and literary agents. Published continuously since 1872, PW mainly features book reviews.

Publishers Marketplace/Publishers Lunch   *publishersmarketplace.com*

This is where publishing professionals go to find the kind of critical information they need to do business better. Along with Publisher's Lunch, an online news-letter known as "publishing's essential daily read," Publishers Marketplace allows professionals to track deals, sales, reviews, agents, and editors.

Society of Authors   *societyofauthors.org*

As soon as you sign a contract—whether you are a novelist, textbook writer, academic, translator, ghost-writer, or illustrator—you are eligible to join the Society of Authors. For more than a century, the Society has been looking after the rights of writing profession-als. Benefits of membership include contract review, aid with professional disputes, meetings and seminars, the Society's quarterly journal, *The Author*, and ac-cess to a database of members' specializations.

The Center for Fiction   *centerforfiction.org*
17 East 47th Street, New York, NY 10017
212-755-6710

The only nonprofit organization in the United States dedicated solely to celebrating fiction, the Center for Fiction's continuing mission is to connect readers and writers, offering panels, lectures, and conversations at its building in midtown Manhattan. The Center also fea-tures workspaces, grants, and classes for emerging talents,

as well as reading groups and programs to encourage
children to read.

Society of Children's Book Writers and Illustrators   *scbwi.org*
Founded in 1971, the SCBWI is the only professional organization for children and young adult "writers, illustrators, editors, publishers, agents, librarians, educators, booksellers, and
others involved with literature for young people." The SCBWI
sponsors two international conferences annually and publishes
a bimonthly magazine, which includes awards and grants for
writers and illustrators.

The Children's Book Council *cbcbooks.org*
A national nonprofit trade association for children's trade book
publishers The CBC gathers members—from large international houses to smaller independent presses—to work together
on industry-wide issues, such as educational programming and
literacy advocacy as well as collaborations with other national
organizations.

Books: Print and Online

Jeff Herman's Guide to Book Publishers, Editors and Literary Agents:
   Who They Are! What They Want! How to Win Them Over!
   A must-have for writers, this book offers one thousand
   advice-filled pages that include a description of the inner
   workings of hundreds of U.S. and Canadian publishers,
   priceless tips from nearly 200 of the most powerful literary
   agents, and writer dos and don'ts to be wary of on your
   way to getting your book published.

Literary Market Place 2012: The Directory of the American Book Publishing Industry with Industry Yellow Pages. Edited by Karen Hallard, Mary-Anne Lutter, and Vivian Sposobiec

LiteraryMarketPlace.com

LiteraryMarketPlace.com brings the comprehensive directory that has been a mainstay of the book publishing industry to the Internet. Find publishers speacializing in a specific subject or type of publication. Search by city, state, ZIP code, or by first and last name if you're looking for a particular person.

2013 Children's Writer's & Illustrator's Market, Chuck Sambuchino, Editor

The Lion and the Unicorn   muse.jhu.edu/journals/lion_and_the_unicorn/

Published by Johns Hopkins University Press, The Lion and the Unicorn is a journal of international scope that promotes an ongoing review and discussion of children's literature, including "the state of the publishing industry, regional authors, comparative studies of significant books and genres, new developments in theory, the art of illustration, the mass media, and popular culture."

The Horn Book   hbook.com

Since 1924, The Horn Book has published a magazine devoted solely to the best in children's literature. It is supplemented by semi-annual print issues of The Horn Book Guide, which rates and reviews over 2,000 titles—practically every children's and young adult book published in the United States in a six-month period—and an online guide with a searchable database.

Associations and Conferences

Association of Writers and Writing Programs (AWP) Annual
Conference & Bookfair   *awpwriter.org/conference*
The Annual Conference & Bookfair appears in a different city in North America every year to highlight the
outstanding authors, writing programs, teachers, literary
organizations, and small presses in that neck of the woods.
The conference attracts nearly 600 publishers and more
than 10,000 attendees and features some 450 readings,
panel discussions, forums, and lectures as well as recep-
tions, book signings, and informal gatherings.

Useful Blogs

*I will be setting up a blog on the business of writing, so check our agency
website (www.jenniferlyonslitagency.com) for further information about that,
and a new site that will be just related to the book. In the meantime, here
are some helpful blogs. —Jennifer Lyons.*

Ron Hogan's Beatrice   *beatrice.com/wordpress*
Combining his experience as the founder of Beatrice.com,
which he launched in 1995 to open up the Internet literary
world, his several years writing about the business side of
publishing as a senior editor for *GalleyCat*, and his work at
Houghton Mifflin Harcourt as their director of e-marketing
strategy, Ron Hogan helps publishing companies and authors
create stronger connections to readers. Speaking frequently
at publishing conferences and book festivals, Hogan teaches
how to best use social networking tools and informs writers
and other industry professionals about industry advances and
trends. He also offers individual consulting services to those
who want to enhance and widen their online presence.

GalleyCat   *mediabistro.com/galleycat*

Calling itself "the first word on the book publishing industry," GalleyCat provides news on deals, bookselling, writer's resources, and jobs.

Publishing Perspectives *publishingperspectives.com*
An online journal of international book publishing news and opinion.

Goodreads *goodreads.com*
With more than 8.5 million members, Goodreads is the largest site for readers and book recommendations in the world. Users discuss all aspects of the books that they add to their virtual library shelves (more than 300 million and counting), reviewing and discussing everything from classics to works that are hot off the presses, which may be favorite books or future reads. Launched in January 2007, Goodreads' mission "is to help people find and share books they love. Along the way, we plan to improve the process of reading and learning through the world."

Bookslut *bookslut.com*
Beyond the racy name is a monthly web magazine and daily blog for those who love the written word. News, interviews, reviews, commentary, and opinion and underneath it all, insight.

Index

 **Books
from
Allworth
Press**

*Allworth Press is an imprint
of Skyhorse Publishing, Inc.
Selected titles are listed below.*

Publish Your Book: Proven Strategies and Resources for the Enterprising Author
by *Patricia Fry* (6 × 9, 256 pages, paperback, $19.95)

Talk Up Your Book: How to Sell Your Book Through Public Speaking, Interviews, Signings, Festivals, Conferences, and More
by *Patricia Fry* (6 × 9, 320 pages, paperback, $24.95)

Promote Your Book: Over 250 Proven, Low-Cost Tips and Techniques for the Enterprising Author
by *Patricia Fry* (5 ½ × 8 ¼, 224 pages, paperback, $19.95)

The Author's Toolkit: A Step-by-Step Guide to Writing and Publishing Your Own Book, Third Edition
by *Mary Embree* (5 ½ × 8 ½, 224 pages, paperback, $19.95)

The Writer's Guide to Queries, Pitches and Proposals, Second Edition
by *Moira Anderson Allen* (6 × 9, 288 pages, paperback, $19.95)

Starting Your Career as a Freelance Writer, Second Edition
by *Moira Anderson Allen* (6 × 9, 304 pages, paperback, $24.95)

Starting Your Career as a Freelance Editor: A Guide to Working with Authors, Books, Newsletters, Magazines, Websites, and More
by *Mary Embree* (6 × 9, 256 pages, paperback, $19.95)

The Profitable Artist: A Handbook for All Artists in the Performing, Literary, and Visual Arts
by *Artspire; copublished with the New York Foundation for the Arts*

Business and Legal Forms for Authors and Self-Publishers, Third Edition
by *Tad Crawford* (8 ⅜ × 10 ⅞, 160 pages, paperback, $29.95)

The Writer's Legal Guide: An Author's Guild Desk Reference
by *Tad Crawford and Kay Murray* (6 × 9, 320 pages, paperback, $19.95)

Writing the Great American Romance Novel
by *Catherine Lanigan* (6 × 9, 224 pages, paperback, $19.95)

The Complete Guide to Book Marketing, Revised Edition
by *David Cole* (6 × 9, 256 pages, paperback, $19.95)

The Complete Guide to Book Publicity, Second Edition
by *Jodee Blanco* (6 × 9, 304 pages, paperback, $19.95)

Marketing Strategies for Writers
by *Michael Sedge* (6 × 9, 224 pages, paperback, $24.95)

The Journalist's Craft
edited by *D. Jackson and J. Sweeney* (6 × 9, 192 pages, paperback, $19.95)

To see our complete catalog or to order online, please visit *www.allworth.com.*